Developing Reading Skills

Developing Reading Skills

A practical guide to reading comprehension exercises

Françoise Grellet

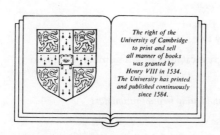

The right of the
University of Cambridge
to print and sell
all manner of books
was granted by
Henry VIII in 1534.
The University has printed
and published continuously
since 1584.

Cambridge University Press
Cambridge
New York   Port Chester
Melbourne   Sydney

To Alan

I am very much indebted to Guy Capelle whose works and ideas first made me conscious of how interesting the study of a written text could be made for the students. I hope he will find here a proof of my thanks and gratitude.

I also wish to thank J. D. Shepherd and R. Bowers who read the manuscript and made valuable suggestions.

Most of all, I am grateful to Alan Maley without whose help, constant encouragement and inspiring ideas, this book would never have been written. I am especially indebted to him for his help in writing the Introduction.

F. G.

Published by the Press Syndicate of the University of Cambridge
The Pitt Building, Trumpington Street, Cambridge CB2 1RP
40 West 20th Street, New York, NY 10011, USA
10 Stamford Road, Oakleigh, Melbourne 3166, Australia

© Cambridge University Press 1981

First published 1981
Tenth printing 1990

Printed in Great Britain
at the University Press, Cambridge

Library of Congress catalogue card number: 80–42040

British Library cataloguing in publication data

Grellet, Françoise

Developing reading skills.
1. English language – Text-books for foreigners
I. Title
428.2'4   PE1128   80–42040

ISBN 0 521 28364 7

Contents

To the reader

Who the book is for

This book was written with teachers and material developers in mind. It should be useful to teachers who do not use a reading course and who wish to produce their own material, as well as to people who are developing material for tailor-made courses. It may also be useful to teachers using a course which they wish to enrich.

What the book is about

The book attempts to describe and classify various types of reading comprehension exercises. It is not a textbook for students or a general handbook on reading. The exercises provided in the book are cited as examples and ought not to be used indiscriminately: they are illustrations of different exercise-types. It is the principle underlying each exercise which is of the greatest importance to the teacher and materials writer.

This explains why the book is not designed for any particular level. The level of difficulty of the texts is unimportant here: the exercise-types suggested can be adapted for elementary, intermediate or advanced levels. What is important is the degree of complexity of the *tasks* the students are asked to perform in relation to the text.

INTRODUCTION

Reading and reading comprehension

What is reading comprehension?

Understanding a written text means extracting the required information from it as efficiently as possible. For example, we apply different reading strategies when looking at a notice board to see if there is an advertisement for a particular type of flat and when carefully reading an article of special interest in a scientific journal. Yet locating the relevant advertisement on the board and understanding the new information contained in the article demonstrates that the reading purpose in each case has been successfully fulfilled. In the first case, a competent reader will quickly reject the irrelevant information and find what he is looking for. In the second case, it is not enough to understand the gist of the text; more detailed comprehension is necessary.

It is therefore essential to take the following elements into consideration.

What do we read?

Here are the main text-types one usually comes across:
- Novels, short stories, tales; other literary texts and passages (e.g. essays, diaries, anecdotes, biographies)
- Plays
- Poems, limericks, nursery rhymes
- Letters, postcards, telegrams, notes
- Newspapers and magazines (headlines, articles, editorials, letters to the editor, stop press, classified ads, weather forecast, radio / TV / theatre programmes)
- Specialized articles, reports, reviews, essays, business letters, summaries, précis, accounts, pamphlets (political and other)
- Handbooks, textbooks, guidebooks
- Recipes
- Advertisements, travel brochures, catalogues
- Puzzles, problems, rules for games
- Instructions (e.g. warnings), directions (e.g. How to use . . .), notices, rules and regulations, posters, signs (e.g. road signs), forms (e.g. application forms, landing cards), graffiti, menus, price lists, tickets

- Comic strips, cartoons and caricatures, legends (of maps, pictures)
- Statistics, diagrams, flow / pie charts, time-tables, maps
- Telephone directories, dictionaries, phrasebooks

Why do we read?

There are two main reasons for reading:
- Reading for pleasure.
- Reading for information (in order to find out something or in order to do something with the information you get).

How do we read?

The main ways of reading are as follows:
- Skimming: quickly running one's eyes over a text to get the gist of it.
- Scanning: quickly going through a text to find a particular piece of information.
- Extensive reading: reading longer texts, usually for one's own pleasure. This is a fluency activity, mainly involving global understanding.
- Intensive reading: reading shorter texts, to extract specific information. This is more an accuracy activity involving reading for detail.

These different ways of reading are not mutually exclusive. For instance, one often skims through a passage to see what it is about before deciding whether it is worth scanning a particular paragraph for the information one is looking for.

In real life, our reading purposes constantly vary and therefore, when devising exercises, we should vary the questions and the activities according to the type of text studied and the purpose in reading it. When working on a page of classified ads, for instance, it would be highly artificial to propose exercises requiring the detailed comprehension of every single advertisement. This would only discourage the students and prevent them from developing reading strategies adapted to the true purpose of their reading.

Reading involves a variety of skills. The main ones are listed below. (This list is taken from John Munby's *Communicative Syllabus Design*.)

- Recognizing the script of a language
- Deducing the meaning and use of unfamiliar lexical items
- Understanding explicitly stated information
- Understanding information when not explicitly stated

4

- Understanding conceptual meaning
- Understanding the communicative value (function) of sentences and utterances
- Understanding relations within the sentence
- Understanding relations between the parts of a text through lexical cohesion devices
- Understanding cohesion between parts of a text through grammatical cohesion devices
- Interpreting text by going outside it
- Recognizing indicators in discourse
- Identifying the main point or important information in a piece of discourse
- Distinguishing the main idea from supporting details
- Extracting salient points to summarize (the text, an idea etc.)
- Selective extraction of relevant points from a text
- Basic reference skills
- Skimming
- Scanning to locate specifically required information
- Transcoding information to diagrammatic display

In order to develop these skills, several types of exercises can be used. These question-types can have two different functions.
1 To clarify the organization of the passage.
  The questions can be about:
  - the function of the passage
  - the general organization (e.g. argumentative)
  - the rhetorical organization (e.g. contrast, comparison)
  - the cohesive devices (e.g. link-words)
  - the intrasentential relations (e.g. derivation, morphology, hyponymy)
2 To clarify the contents of the passage.
  The questions can be about:
  - plain fact (direct reference)
  - implied fact (inference)
  - deduced meaning (supposition)
  - evaluation

The above skills, question-types and question-functions are constantly related since a given exercise uses a certain type of question, with a certain function, to develop a particular reading skill.

Some assumptions

There are a number of considerations to be borne in mind when producing or using reading comprehension exercises.

1 Until very recently materials have concentrated on the sentence and units smaller than the sentence. This is still very largely true. It was assumed that a text was a succession of separate sentences thematically related and that it was necessary merely to deal with the structure and meaning of the sentences.

But, if reading is to be efficient, the structure of longer units such as the paragraph or the whole text must be understood. It is no good studying a text as though it were a series of independent units. This would only lead the students (a) to become dependent on understanding every single sentence in a text, even when this is not necessary to fulfil their reading purpose, with the result that they would tend to read all texts at the same speed and (b) to be reluctant to infer the meaning of sentences or paragraphs from what comes before or after.

2 It is clear, as a consequence of (1), that one should start with global understanding and move towards detailed understanding rather than working the other way round. The tasks given to begin with should be of a more global kind – within the competence of the students. Gradually, as they read more fluently and get the gist of a text more easily, a deeper and more detailed understanding of the text can be worked toward. Similarly, when constructing reading comprehension exercises on a given text, it is always preferable to start with the overall meaning of the text, its function and aim, rather than working on vocabulary or more specific ideas.

This treatment is important because:

a) It is a very efficient way of building up the students' confidence when faced with authentic texts that often contain difficult vocabulary or structures. If the activity is global enough (e.g. choosing from a list what function a text fulfils) the students will not feel completely lost. They will feel that at least they understand what the text is about and will subsequently feel less diffident when tackling a new text.

b) It will develop an awareness of the way texts are organized (e.g. stating the main information and developing it, or giving the chronological sequence of events). It is this awareness of the general structure of a passage that will allow the students to read more efficiently later on.

c) By starting with longer units and by considering the layout of the text, the accompanying photographs or diagrams, the number of paragraphs, etc., the students can be encouraged to anticipate what they are to find in the text. This is essential in order to develop their skills of inference, anticipation and deduction.

Reading is a constant process of guessing, and what one brings to the text is often more important than what one finds in it. This is why, from the very beginning, the students should be taught to use what they know to understand unknown elements, whether these are ideas or simple words. This is best achieved through a global approach to the text.

One could sum up this kind of approach in the following way:

Study of the layout: title, length, pictures, typeface, of the text	→ Making hypotheses about the contents and function	+ anticipation of where to look for confirmation of these hypotheses according to what one knows of such text types

↓

Second reading for more detail	← Further prediction	← Confirmation or revision of one's guesses	← Skimming through the passage

3 It is important to use authentic texts whenever possible. There are several reasons for this.

a) Paradoxically, 'simplifying' a text often results in increased difficulty because the system of references, repetition and redundancy as well as the discourse indicators one relies on when reading are often removed or at least significantly altered. Simplifying a text may mean
   – replacing difficult words or structures by those already familiar to the students
   – rewriting the passage in order to make its rhetorical organization more explicit
   – giving a 'simplified account', that is to say conveying the information contained in the text in one's own words.
   If a text is to be simplified at all, then techniques such as rewriting and simplified account seem to be preferable although they usually imply a change of rhetorical organization.

b) Getting the students accustomed to reading authentic texts from the very beginning does not necessarily mean a much more difficult task on their part. The difficulty of a reading exercise depends on the activity which is required of the students rather than on the text itself, provided it remains within their general competence. In other words, one should grade exercises rather than texts.

c) Authenticity means that nothing of the original text is changed and also that its presentation and layout are retained. A newspaper article, for instance, should be presented as it first appeared in the paper: with the same typeface, the same space devoted to the headlines, the same accompanying picture. By standardizing the presentation of texts in a textbook, one not only reduces interest and motivation, but one actually increases the difficulty for the students. The picture, the size of the headline, the use of bold-face type, all contribute to conveying the message to the reader. It is obvious that a reprint will never be completely authentic, since a textbook consists of several texts taken out of context and juxtaposed. But one should at least try to keep them as authentic as possible in order to help the student anticipate meaning by using these non-linguistic clues.

4 Reading comprehension should not be separated from the other skills. There are few cases in real life when we do not talk or write about what we have read or when we do not relate what we have read to something we might have heard. It is therefore important, to link the different skills through the reading activities chosen:
 – reading and writing, e.g. summarizing, mentioning what you have read in a letter, note-making, etc.
 – reading and listening, e.g. comparing an article and a news-bulletin, using recorded information to solve a written problem, matching opinions and texts, etc.
 – reading and speaking, e.g. discussions, debates, appreciation, etc.

5 Reading is an active skill. As mentioned earlier, it constantly involves guessing, predicting, checking and asking oneself questions. This should therefore be taken into consideration when devising reading comprehension exercises. It is possible, for instance, to develop the students' powers of inference through systematic practice, or introduce questions which encourage students to anticipate the content of a text from its title and illustrations or the end of a story from the preceding paragraphs.

Similarly, one should introduce exercises in which there is no single straightforward answer. This type of exercise has too often required students to exercise only their powers of judgement and appreciation, but extending the range of these exercises to cover other reading skills will lead to greater discussion and reflection on the text.

A second aspect of reading as an active skill is its communicative function. Exercises must be meaningful and correspond as often as possible to what one is expected to do with the text. We rarely answer questions after reading a text, but we may have to
– write an answer to a letter
– use the text to do something (e.g. follow directions, make a choice, solve a problem)
– compare the information given to some previous knowledge.
The third section of this book 'Understanding Meaning' suggests a number of activities of this kind, to which should be added the use of written texts for simulations and the use of games (e.g. board games) based on the reading of short texts providing the necessary information for the moves of the players.

6 Another important point when devising reading comprehension exercises is that the activities should be flexible and varied. Few exercise-types are intrinsically good or bad. They only become so when used in relation to a given text. Reading comprehension activities should be suited to the texts and to one's reasons for reading them. It is essential to take into account the author's point of view, intention and tone for a full understanding of the text. This may be covered by open questions, multiple-choice questions, right or wrong questions, etc. In other cases, the text may naturally lend itself to a non-linguistic activity such as tracing a route on a map, or matching pictures and paragraphs.

7 The aim of the exercises must be clearly defined and a clear distinction made between teaching and testing. Testing will obviously involve more accuracy-type exercises whereas through teaching one should try to develop the skills listed on pages 4–5.

The students must be taught how to approach and consider the text in order to become independent and efficient readers. It is also important to remember that meaning is not inherent in the text, that each reader brings his own meaning to what he reads based on what he expects from the text and his previous knowledge. This shows how difficult it is to test competence in reading comprehension and how great the temptation is to impose one's own interpretation on the learners.

Reading comprehension in the classroom

Constructing exercises

There must be variety in the range of exercises. This is an important factor in motivation and it is necessary if different skills are to be covered.

An exercise should never be imposed on a text. It is better to allow the text to suggest what exercises are most appropriate to it. In other words, the text should always be the starting point for determining why one would normally read it, how it would be read, how it might relate to other information before thinking of a particular exercise.

But it is important to remember that many texts are meant to be read and enjoyed, that too many exercises might spoil the pleasure of reading. A balance should be struck between leaving the students without any help on the one hand and on the other hand 'squeezing the text dry'.

Classroom procedures

The first point to be noted when practising reading in the classroom is that it is a silent activity. Therefore silent reading should be encouraged in most cases, though the teacher may sometimes need to read part of the text aloud. The students themselves should not read aloud. It is an extremely difficult exercise, highly specialized (very few people need to read aloud in their profession) and it would tend to give the impression that all texts are to be read at the same speed. Besides, when we read, our eyes do not follow each word of the text one after the other – at least in the case of efficient readers. On the contrary, many words or expressions are simply skipped; we go back to check something, or forward to confirm some of our hypotheses. Such tactics become impossible when reading aloud, and this reading activity therefore tends to prevent the students from developing efficient reading strategies.

It is useful to give the class some help on how to approach a new text. The following procedure, for instance, is very helpful with most texts.

a) Consider the text as a whole, its title, accompanying picture(s) or diagram(s), the paragraphs, the typeface used, and make guesses about what the text is about, who wrote it, who it is for, where it appeared, etc.
b) Skim through the text a first time to see if your hypotheses were right.

Then ask yourself a number of questions about the contents of the text.
c) Read the text again, more slowly and carefully this time, trying to understand as much as you can and trying to answer the questions you asked yourself.

Another classroom procedure can consist of helping the student to time himself and increase his reading speed little by little. It is necessary to reach a certain reading speed in order to read efficiently. This can be done by showing the students how to record their reading speed systematically on a chart and to try to improve it each time they read a new text.

To say that reading is a silent and personal activity does not imply that it only lends itself to individual work. On the contrary, it is particularly interesting to encourage comparisons between several interpretations of a text which will lead to discussion and probably a need to refer back to the text to check. Here are possible steps:
a) Silent reading followed by an activity which each student does on his own.
b) The students now work in pairs, each one trying to justify his answer. The group should try to agree on one answer or interpretation.
c) The groups exchange partners and students compare their results.
d) A general discussion involving the whole class may follow.

When to use reading comprehension exercises

Reading can be done as a class activity (see above) but reading activities can also be devised to individualize students' work at home. Instead of choosing one activity for the whole class, two or three sets of exercises of varying difficulty can be prepared based on the same text so that each student can work at home at his own level. If the text is then to be discussed in the class, each group of students who have worked on the same exercises will be able to talk about what they have done. This will certainly be stimulating for the weaker students, while the better ones will not feel held back.

If there is little teacher-control of the reading activity, then self-correcting exercises are extremely useful. The students are able to evaluate their work and can try little by little to improve their reading ability. They feel reassured and guided and using this type of material is one of the best ways of building up the students' confidence. (See *Multiread II* (S.R.A. Paris, 1973) and *Multiread A* (S.R.A. London, 1977).)

Reading comprehension exercise-types

Reading techniques

I SENSITIZING

  1 Inference: through the context
    Inference: through
    word-formation
  2 Understanding relations within
    the sentence
  3 Linking sentences and ideas:
    reference
    Linking sentences and ideas:
    link-words

2 IMPROVING READING SPEED

3 FROM SKIMMING TO SCANNING

  1 Predicting
  2 Previewing
  3 Anticipation
  4 Skimming
  5 Scanning

How the aim is conveyed

I AIM AND FUNCTION OF THE TEXT

  1 Function of the text
  2 Functions within the text

2 ORGANIZATION OF THE TEXT:
  DIFFERENT THEMATIC PATTERNS

  1 Main idea and supporting details
  2 Chronological sequence
  3 Descriptions
  4 Analogy and contrast
  5 Classification
  6 Argumentative and logical
    organization

3 THEMATIZATION

Understanding meaning

1 NON-LINGUISTIC RESPONSE TO THE TEXT

1 Ordering a sequence of pictures
2 Comparing texts and pictures
3 Matching
4 Using illustrations
5 Completing a document
6 Mapping it out
7 Using the information in the text
8 Jigsaw reading

2 LINGUISTIC RESPONSE TO THE TEXT

1 Reorganizing the information:
reordering events
Reorganizing the information:
using grids
2 Comparing several texts
3 Completing a document
4 Question-types
5 Study skills: summarizing
Study skills: note-taking

Assessing the text

1 FACT VERSUS OPINION

2 WRITER'S INTENTION

The exercises suggested in this book have been divided into four sections. The first is devoted to those reading skills and strategies that are essential to acquiring a basic reading competence. The three parts that follow aim to illustrate different ways of helping the students reach a better understanding of a text, starting from overall comprehension (Function and organization of the passage), moving towards a more detailed one (Understanding meaning) and ending with some guidelines to help the students assess and evaluate what they have read.

There is obviously, however, a certain amount of overlapping between these four parts.

Reading techniques

Most of the techniques dealt with in this part are already familiar to the students in their native language. But it is necessary to re-train them, as some students have difficulty in applying them to a second language.

1 Sensitizing

The aim of this section is to provide exercises that will develop the strategies that students need to cope with unfamiliar words and complex or apparently obscure sentences. It should ensure that they do not stumble on every difficulty or get discouraged from the outset.

1.1 INFERENCE

Inferring means making use of syntactic, logical and cultural clues to discover the meaning of unknown elements. If these are words, then word-formation and derivation will also play an important part.

When dealing with a new text, it is better not to explain the difficult words to the learners beforehand. They would only get used to being given 'pre-processed' texts and would never make the effort to cope with a difficult passage on their own. On the contrary, students should be encouraged to make a guess at the meaning of the words they do not know rather than look them up in a dictionary. If they need to look at the dictionary to get a precise meaning – which is an important and necessary activity too – they should only do so after having tried to work out a solution on their own. This is why, from the very beginning, it is vital to develop the skill of inference. The exercises suggested in the book try to

develop inference along different lines:
- One exercise (exercise 10) is devised to train the students to infer as quickly as possible the meaning of previously learned but incomplete words.
- The other exercises aim at making the students work out a strategy of inference for dealing with unfamiliar words.

- In the first part of the section on inference the exercises are meant to practise inference through the context.
- In the second part, they practise inference through word-formation.

- Most of the exercises simply require of the students that they should guess the meaning of unfamiliar words.
- One exercise, however (exercise 9), leads them to analyse their process of inference more systematically.

1.2 UNDERSTANDING RELATIONS WITHIN THE SENTENCE

Inability to infer the meaning of unknown elements often causes discouragement and apprehension in students when they are faced with a new text. A similar problem arises when students are unable to get an immediate grasp of sentence structures. This will be a definite handicap in the case of texts with relatives, embedded clauses and complex structures. It is therefore important to train the students, as early as possible, to look first for the 'core' of the sentence (subject + verb). In order to do that, the learners can be asked to divide passages into sense groups and underline, box, or recognize in some other way the important elements of each sentence in a passage. (See exercises 1–2.)

1.3 LINKING SENTENCES AND IDEAS

Another area in which it is essential to prepare the students is in recognizing the various devices used to create textual cohesion and more particularly the use of reference and link-words.

Reference covers all the devices that permit lexical relationship within a text (e.g. reference to an element previously mentioned – anaphora – or to one to be mentioned below – cataphora, use of synonymy, hyponymy, comparison, nominalization, etc.) It is important for the students to realize that a text is not made up of independent sentences or clauses, but that it is a web of related ideas that are announced, introduced and taken up again later throughout the passage with the help of references. Exercises such as 1 and 2 can help the students recognize this use of reference more quickly.

If the reader does not understand some words of the passage, some of the facts and ideas will probably escape him. But if he does not understand inter- or intra-sentential connectors, he may also fail to recognize the communicative value of the passage since those words act as signals indicating the function of what follows (e.g. announcing a conclusion, an example, a supposition). From the very beginning, students should therefore be taught not only to understand them when they come across them, but also to look out for such markers. This will be useful to them when skimming, since the simple recognition of those link-words will help them to understand the development of the argument in the passage.

Some exercises are suggested along the following lines:
- Recognizing the function of the connectors and finding equivalents (exercises 1–2).
- Completing texts with the missing link-words (exercises 3–5).
- Transforming a series of statements and propositions into a coherent text by joining sentences and adding connectors.

This last kind of exercise is a difficult one but very interesting since it admits of several possible solutions and the comparison of the results obtained will show different ways of presenting the same information.

2 Improving reading speed

Students who read too slowly will easily get discouraged. They will also tend to stumble on unfamiliar words and fail to grasp the general meaning of the passage.

One of the most common ways of increasing reading speed is to give students passages to read and to ask them to time themselves. A conversion table, taking the length of the text and the reading time into account, will tell them what their reading speed is and this will make it easier for them to try and read a little faster every time. Reading should also be followed by comprehension questions or activities since reading speed should not be developed at the expense of comprehension.

Most of the exercises in this book can therefore be used with faster reading in mind. Below is an example of a conversion table for 500-word texts (from Gerald and Vivienne Mosback, *Practical Faster Reading*, Cambridge University Press, 1976).

When practising faster reading systematically, the students can be encouraged to keep a record of their results, showing their progress (e.g. in the form of a graph). This should encourage them to read more.

The few exercises on speed reading included in this book are of a different kind since they aim to develop speed in recognizing words and their meaning.

Reading time (min/secs)	Speed (w.p.m.)	Reading time (min/secs)	Speed (w.p.m.)
1.00	500	3.10	158
1.10	427	3.20	150
1.20	375	3.30	143
1.30	334	3.40	137
1.40	300	3.50	131
1.50	273	4.00	125
2.00	250	4.10	120
2.10	231	4.20	116
2.20	215	4.30	111
2.30	200	4.40	107
2.40	188	4.50	104
2.50	174	5.00	100
3.00	167		

3 From skimming to scanning

One of the most important points to keep in mind when teaching
reading comprehension is that there is not *one* type of reading but
several according to one's reasons for reading. Students will never
read efficiently unless they can adapt their reading speed and
technique to their aim when reading. By reading all texts in the
same way, students would waste time and fail to remember points
of importance to them because they would absorb too much
non-essential information. The exercises suggested in this section
should therefore make the students more confident and efficient
readers.

3.1 PREDICTING

This is not really a technique but a skill which is basic to all the
reading techniques practised in this part and to the process of
reading generally. It is the faculty of predicting or guessing what is
to come next, making use of grammatical, logical and cultural
clues. This skill is at the core of techniques such as 'anticipation' or
'skimming' and will therefore be practised in those sections, but it
may be worthwhile to devote some time to more systematic
training by giving the students unfinished passages to complete or
by going through a text little by little, stopping after each sentence
in order to predict what is likely to come next (see exercises 1–2).

3.2 PREVIEWING

Unlike predicting, previewing is a very specific reading technique
which involves using the table of contents, the appendix, the

preface, the chapter and paragraph headings in order to find out where the required information is likely to be. It is particularly useful when skimming and scanning and as a study skill.

The exercises suggested in this part attempt to put the students into the sort of situation where they would quite naturally apply this technique (e.g. quickly locating an article in a newspaper or having a few minutes to get an idea of a book through the text on the back cover and the table of contents).

3.3 ANTICIPATION

Motivation is of great importance when reading. Partly because most of what we usually read is what we want to read (books, magazines, advertisements, etc.), but also because being motivated means that we start reading the text prepared to find a number of things in it, expecting to find answers to a number of questions and specific information or ideas we are interested in. This 'expectation' is inherent in the process of reading which is a permanent interrelationship between the reader and the text. What we already know about the subject and what we are looking for are probably just as important as what we actually draw from the text. When reading, we keep making predictions which, in their turn, will be confirmed or corrected.

This underlines the artificiality of the classroom situation in which students are often confronted with passages they know nothing about, do not and cannot situate in a more general cultural context and – what is even more important – have no particular desire to read. It is very difficult, in such conditions, to expect the students to learn to read better.

The practise of letting the students choose the topics they wish to read about should therefore be encouraged. However, when dealing with larger groups, it may not always be easy to agree on definite subjects and the teacher may also wish to introduce a new topic which he believes might be of interest. When this is the case it is often worthwhile to spend some time getting the students ready to read a given text. Before the students start reading a text, they can always be asked to look for the answers to specific questions. This will give an incentive to their reading activity. A few other possibilities are suggested in the exercises:

– Psychological sensitizing aimed at making the students think about the subject of the text and ask themselves questions (exercises 1–3).
– Using the title and pictures to talk about the various ways the text may develop (exercises 4–5).
– Using the key-words of the text (exercise 6).

3.4–5   SKIMMING AND SCANNING

Both skimming and scanning are specific reading techniques necessary for quick and efficient reading.

When skimming, we go through the reading material quickly in order to get the gist of it, to know how it is organized, or to get an idea of the tone or the intention of the writer.

When scanning, we only try to locate specific information and often we do not even follow the linearity of the passage to do so. We simply let our eyes wander over the text until we find what we are looking for, whether it be a name, a date, or a less specific piece of information.

Skimming is therefore a more thorough activity which requires an overall view of the text and implies a definite reading competence. Scanning, on the contrary, is far more limited since it only means retrieving what information is relevant to our purpose. Yet it is usual to make use of these two activities together when reading a given text. For instance, we may well skim through an article first just to know whether it is worth reading, then read it through more carefully because we have decided that it is of interest. It is also possible afterwards to scan the same article in order to note down a figure or a name which we particularly want to remember.

The first two exercises in the 'skimming' section are training and preliminary exercises. Those that follow (exercises 3–10) try to recreate authentic reading situations. They should contribute to building up the students' confidence by showing them how much they can learn simply by looking at some prominent parts of an article, by catching a few words only, by reading a few paragraphs here and there in a story. Their aim is certainly not to encourage the students to read all texts in such a superficial way (this would be in contradiction with the principle of flexibility mentioned earlier) but they should make the students better readers, that is, readers who can decide quickly what they want or need to read. So many students spend so much time carefully and thoroughly reading a newspaper (for instance) that by the time they find something of real interest, they no longer have time or energy left to read it in detail.

The exercises suggested to practise scanning also try to put the students in an authentic situation where they would naturally scan the text rather than read it. The students are therefore asked to solve a specific problem as quickly as possible – which is only possible by means of scanning.

How the aim is conveyed

In this second part the emphasis is on the function and organization of the passage.

1 Function of the text

It is obvious that being aware of the function of a passage is vital to its comprehension. Therefore, one of the very first things students should be led to do is to find out whether the text aims at convincing the reader, giving him information, asking him for something, etc. In many cases, the very form of the passage, the way it is printed, laid out, or the place where it was found, are sufficient to give us clues as to its function, and students should always be encouraged to make use of these non-linguistic elements. But it may sometimes be more difficult to determine the exact function of the passage and for this reason it is worth devoting some time to activities such as the ones in exercises 1 and 2.

2 Organization of the text

Given a specific function (e.g. convincing the reader) and certain information that has to be conveyed (e.g. some characteristics of a new car), there are many different ways in which this information may be presented and organized. One could compare the new car to other lesser cars for instance, thus using contrast to make the point. Or try to convince the reader by some kind of logical reasoning of the superiority of the car. Another possibility might be to use a chronological sequence of events (for instance listing the major events in the history of the manufacturer), revealing the main characteristics of the car little by little.

This shows that the organization of a passage is not always determined by its contents and by the nature of the information to be conveyed. The thematic pattern used is often a choice on the part of the writer and this choice, in its turn, alters the message.

Another reason why it is essential for the students to grasp the method used to present the information is that once they have recognized the pattern that is being used, they can apply their reading strategies to the text and predict what is likely to follow. If, for instance, we recognize the text as an argumentative one, we will look for arguments and counter-arguments, then for some kind of conclusion drawn from these arguments.

The first kind of organization dealt with is that built around a main idea, which is then developed throughout the text. It is often found in newspaper articles where the first paragraph usually sums

up the main point, the rest of the text consisting of expansions of various kinds. But one often finds this organization within the paragraph in all kinds of texts. Different types of exercises can be used to train the students to recognize this organization:
- Rejecting irrelevant information (exercise 2).
- Finding the topic sentences and what kind of relation they have to the rest of the text (exercises 3–5).
- Discriminating between generalizations and specific statements (exercises 6–7).
- Completing skeleton outlines of the structure of the text (exercises 8–10).

The sections that follow are devoted to other kinds of organization (chronological sequence, description, analogy and contrast, classification, argumentative and logical organization). In each of these sections, the exercises suggested try to involve the students actively, leading them to study the way the ideas are organized through activities or problems (e.g. filling in tables, or reordering passages) that should motivate them and oblige them to *think* about the text. They also use visual representations such as tables, tree diagrams and other diagrams as often as possible since they help the students to draw out only what is essential and to see the development of the text more clearly. It should also encourage them to use such devices when taking notes on what they read.

3 Thematization

It may be interesting to draw the students' attention to the way in which the order of the elements in a sentence can alter the message. A few exercises have therefore been included to illustrate the process of thematization.

Understanding meaning

Besides understanding the way a text is organized, it is of course essential to understand its contents. This part attempts to suggest different ways of doing this. It is usual to help – or check – comprehension through the use of various types of question (e.g. open questions, right or wrong, multiple-choice questions). It is not my intention to dwell on the value of these question-types (see Widdowson, *Teaching Language as Communication*, pp. 94ff). However, it should be pointed out that they can have the advantage of involving the students actively, i.e. if they need to think and reason in order to give an answer or make a choice (see Munby, *Read and Think*). It is therefore important to devise exercises in which there is no simple, obvious answer but which will force the students to examine the text and the different possibilities carefully in order to make up their minds. Some possibilities are suggested in 2.4 'Question-types'.

The other exercises suggested in this part are inspired by two different aims.

1 To make the students active in the reading process by presenting them with decision-making activities (e.g. drawing a diagram with the information given in the text, solving the problem, completing a table which reorganizes the information).

2 To devise activities which are as natural as possible, i.e. as close as possible to what one would naturally do with the text (e.g. answering a letter using the information given in that letter, completing a document, comparing several texts, etc.)

The activities suggested have been divided into two categories.

1 Non-linguistic response to the text

There is a whole range of comprehension activities that do not require any complex verbal response on the part of the learners. In these exercises, something is added to the text (a document, a diagram, a picture) and the students are asked to relate the text to that document. This can mean:

– a comparison (e.g. comparing texts and pictures, matching passages of the text and diagrams)
– a transposition of the information (transcoding the information into the form of a diagram, completing or labelling a document)
– using the information in the passage to find a solution, make a decision or solve a problem.

Although no actual questions need accompany this kind of exercise, it is one of the most useful ones since this is the way we often use what we read and the very fact of being able to make a proper decision will be proof that the student has thought about the text and understood it.

2 Linguistic response to the text

The exercises suggested enter the following categories:

2.1 REORGANIZING THE INFORMATION

In these exercises, the students are asked to present the information in a different way; to reorganize it according to a different pattern (e.g. completing a table, drawing up a chronological list of the events mentioned in the passage). These exercises emphasize the fact that there are many different ways of presenting the same information.

2.2 COMPARING SEVERAL TEXTS

This is a very natural activity since we often mentally compare different versions of the same event or incident, for instance what someone wrote in a letter and what we read in a paper, what a friend tells us about a country and what a guide-book or a travel brochure says. It is through the comparison between the different texts that the students' attention is drawn to what is specific to the passage they are studying. The passages offered for comparison may differ
- in their contents (e.g. one can study the development of an item of news over a period of time)
- in their point of view (e.g. several articles on the same subject taken from different newspapers).

2.3 COMPLETING A DOCUMENT

This is basically the same type of activity as the one mentioned under the same heading in the preceding section ('Non-linguistic response to the text') but this time the students are required to do more than simply provide labels or figures, they must, for example, use the contents of the text to answer a letter, fill in an evaluation card, an application form, leave a note, etc.

To these different categories, must be added the possibility of using the text for simulations or role-play. One can, for example, ask the students to study the information in the text and identify with one of the characters who will then have to react in different situations.

2.5 STUDY SKILLS

Study skills in fact cover many different tasks such as the use of a dictionary, a table of contents (see 'Reading techniques'), or underlining and boxing (see 'How the aim is conveyed') but only two major skills have been selected in this section: note-taking and summarizing.

Taking notes is essential in order to remember what one reads or listens to but it has a further use: when taking notes, it is necessary to establish the structure of the text and its key ideas and to learn to leave out unessential information. It is a difficult activity which sums up most of the strategies developed in the first three parts. (In fact, many of the tasks proposed in 'Understanding meaning', in the section called 'Linguistic response to the text', require the ability to take notes correctly.)

In summary writing, too, minor details must be rejected but
- a summary is usually written in one's own words.
- it does not necessarily imply outlining the structure of the passage, as note-taking usually does.
- it should be an accurate and objective account of the text, leaving out our reactions to it (whereas note-taking can be supplemented by note-making, i.e. briefly jotting down one's reactions and ideas about the passage).

Assessing the text

One vital aspect of reading comprehension has so far been left out: the ability to assess and evaluate the text. This means, first of all, that one should be fully aware of the writer's intention, of his point of view and possible bias.

1 Fact versus opinion

In this section the exercises aim at training the students to be able to discriminate facts from opinions. It is an important part of reading competence since any good reader should be aware of the way his judgement is influenced one way or another.

2 Writer's intention

In the second section the activities suggested are focused on the attitude of the writer, the particular kind of bias that can be felt through his writing. This is of particular interest, for instance, in advertising passages (exercises 6–7).

In order to be comprehensive this part should also deal with several other aspects which – to no lesser degree – contribute to conveying the message.
a) Tone is often one of the most difficult aspects of a text to grasp. But, it is essential, for what would we think of a student who reads Swift's *A Modest Proposal* and fails to recognize the irony in it? And yet, this same student might very well have understood all the facts in the passage. Teachers should therefore make sure that the students are familiar with the whole range of tone (e.g. irony, anger, persuasion, etc.)
b) The language used by the writer, the kind of sentences he chooses and the way he arranges them also contribute to conveying his meaning. This study of language should not be

left to specialists of literature only, since it is of vital importance, whatever the kind of text studied. This covers aspects such as the kind of vocabulary and sentence structure used, the different forms of speech highlighted, the use of images, the possible imitation of a certain genre, to give only a few examples.

c) Finally, it is obvious that the ideas expressed in the passage should be discussed and judged at some point. Whatever way these opinions were expressed one cannot help reacting to them and questions leading the students to compare their own views to those of the writer are a necessary component of any reading comprehension syllabus.

No exercises have been suggested to illustrate these last points, partly because many reading books have made use of them and most teachers are therefore familiar with them, partly because it would be extremely difficult to cover the main points in this section; there would in fact be enough material for another book. However, the exercise-types used to practise recognition of the writer's tone, technique and ideas do not differ from those seen in the preceding parts of the book. It is only the contents that are different and this is another reason why no examples have been given.

The fact that for the purposes of this book the exercises are divided up into several categories does not mean these four parts should be used consecutively when teaching reading skills. On the contrary it is necessary with most texts to draw examples from all four parts since one cannot dissociate form and contents.

The exercises

I · READING TECHNIQUES

1 Sensitizing

1.1 Inference: Deducing the meaning and use of unfamiliar lexical items through contextual clues

Exercise 1

Specific aim: To train the students to recognize synonyms and antonyms.

Skills involved: Deducing the meaning and use of unfamiliar lexical items.

Understanding relations between parts of a text through lexical cohesion devices of synonymy and antonymy.

Why? Many texts make use of synonyms and antonyms to convey their message more clearly. It is important for the students to be aware of these lexical relations as they often help to infer the meaning of unfamiliar words.

Programming people

Programming people means getting others to act consistently as you want them to act. Stern parents or employers often are pretty good at this, at least while the subjects are under observation. Hypnotists can obtain excellent results in achieving desired behavior from suggestible subjects for short periods.

What interests us here are precise techniques for altering long-term behavior patterns in predictable ways. These new patterns may be desirable by the subject or by the programmer or by the organization employing him.

For achieving certain kinds of long-term programmed behavior the programmer need not be a scientifically trained technologist. Consider how the intense and unattractive Charles Manson horrified and fascinated millions of people a few years ago by his control methods. He had an ability to induce sustained zombie-like behavior in his followers, mostly girls. They committed random murders in the Los Angeles area. When a number of his 'slaves' faced trial they vigorously asserted that the murders were their own idea. They wanted to protect Charlie, who was always somewhere else when the butcheries occurred.

In order to prove his theory that Manson had master-minded the killings the prosecutor, Vincent Bugliosi, had to spend months uncovering and

analyzing the sources of Manson's control over the presumably free and footloose young people. His most important findings were these:
– Manson was gifted at perceiving the psychological needs of others. He assured runaway girls needing a father that he would be their father. He assured plain-looking girls that they were beautiful.
– He was careful to destroy preexisting identities. All the members of his clan had to take on new names.
– He systematically destroyed inhibitions as part of his obedience training.
– He offered these insecure youngsters a bizarre religion, in which he was the Infinite Being who would lead them to a world of milk and honey.
– He was careful to identify and probe what each recruit was most afraid of, and to play on it.
– Finally, Manson apparently had some hypnotic powers.
Bugliosi succeeded in convincing the jury that Manson was, indeed, responsible for the murders.
(From Vance Packard: *The People Shapers* (Macdonald, 1978))

a) In paragraph 3, find two nouns meaning more or less the same as 'killings': ....
....

b) In paragraphs 2 and 3, find the equivalents of the following words:
changing: ....
take place: ....
declare: ....

c) In paragraph 3
– find an adjective which means the opposite of 'for short periods':
....
– find a noun which means the opposite of 'free and footloose young people' (para. 4): ....

d) In paragraph 4, find the words which mean the opposite of:
hiding: ....
fail: ....

The students could also be asked to match two lists of words (words and their synonyms or antonyms).

Exercise 2

Specific aim:	To train the students to recognize related words in a text.
Skills involved:	Understanding relations between parts of a text through lexical cohesion devices: lexical sets and collocation.
Why?	In a text about a given subject, there will usually be a number of related words that may not be synonyms but that help to create an atmosphere or convey an idea. Being aware that such relations exist and looking for them in a text is important in developing a strategy of inference.

In the text 'Programming People', one of the recurring ideas is the loss of one's independence and personality. Read the text again to find all the words related to that idea and fill in the following table.

	nouns	*adjectives*	*verbs*
dependence	e.g. slaves		
independence			

Can you think of other words to complete the table?

Exercise 3

Specific aim: To train the students to recognize equivalence and the use of general words to cover more specific ones (hyponymy).

Skills involved: Understanding relations between parts of a text through the lexical cohesion devices of equivalence and hyponymy.

Why?   It is extremely helpful to recognize devices such as equivalence and hyponymy when reading a text since both of them give clues to the meaning of words that may not be familiar to the students.

The throw-away spirit or the spirit of wastefulness has become part of American life and consumption only keeps rising. Besides, according to the economists, we depend so much on this wasting and buying that people will probably be encouraged to consume even more in the years to come if the US economy is to prosper. In other words, these marketing experts say that 'the average citizen will have to step up his buying by nearly fifty per cent in the next dozen years, or the economy will sicken.' This means that the producer of household commodities, i.e. a television manufacturer, will have to find some new means of making further sales since nine out of ten American homes nowadays have one television set. He could, for instance, launch a campaign to induce people to have a second TV set – or one for each member of the family – or he could produce a TV set so sophisticated that people would wish to replace their old set. (From Vance Packard: *The Waste Makers* (Pelican, 1961))

a) Find at least one instance of synonymy: ....
....

b) Find at least one instance of antonymy: ....
....

c) Find at least three markers of equivalence: ....
....
....

Which of these words introduce(s)
- an example: ....
- a rephrasing of what has been said before: ....
- an equivalent expression: ....
d) Using general words to cover more specific ones:
   i) As an instance of 'producer of household commodities', the writer mentions ....
   ii) In the text, the word 'marketing expert' is one instance (i.e. it is less general) of what the writer meant when using the word 'economist' before. The relation between the two words can be shown as follows: economist → marketing expert

   Can you complete the following relationship?
   producer of household commodities →

Exercise 4

Specific aim: ⎫ Same as for exercise 3 but the students are asked
Skills involved: ⎬ to fill in a table in order to show the devices used
Why? ⎭ to express equivalence.

In each of the following sentences (from D. Hunter and P. Whitten: *The Study of Anthropology* (Harper and Row, 1976)) a different device is used to explain the meaning of a word or an expression. Read the sentences and complete the table.

	word which is explained	explanation (equivalence)	device used
e.g. These characteristics include the regulation of temperature, the capacity for prolonged physical labor, protection against ultraviolet radiation from the sun, immunological (defensive responses to infectious disease) and nutritional and metabolic flexibility.	immunological	defensive	parentheses
In addition, the concept has been criticized as being tautological – that is, circular in its reasoning – and we should examine that accusation.			
They [the Hanunoo] recognize four non-biological components of the environment: daga?, 'ground, soil, earth'; batu, 'rock, stone'; danum, 'water, liquid'; and lanit, 'sky'.			
Exchange marriage, in which two men marry each other's sister, is often found.			
The Greek marriage was monogamous – men and women were allowed only one spouse at a time.			
Many societies, however, practice different kinds of polygamy, or multiple marriages.			

A similar kind of exercise can be done at the level of the paragraph. In that case, the explanatory or redundant sentence is introduced by expressions such as 'that is to say', 'in other words', etc.

Exercise 5

Specific aim: To train the students to infer the meaning of unfamiliar words.
Skills involved: Deducing the meaning of unfamiliar lexical items through contextual clues.
Why? This kind of exercise (cloze exercise) will make the students realize how much the context can help them to find out the meaning of difficult or unfamiliar words.

Read the following paragraph and try to guess the meaning of the word 'zip'.

Zip was stopped during the war and only after the war did it become popular. What a difference it has made to our lives. It keeps people at home much more. It has made the remote parts of the world more real to us. Photographs show a country, but only *zip* makes us feel that a foreign country is real. Also we can see scenes in the street, big occasions are *zipped*, such as the Coronation in 1953 and the Opening of Parliament. Perhaps the sufferers from *zip* are the notable people, who, as they step out of an aeroplane, have to face the battery of *zip* cameras and know that every movement, every gesture will be seen by millions of people. Politicians not only have to speak well, they now have to have what is called a '*zip* personality'. Perhaps we can sympathize when Members of Parliament say that they do not want debates to be *zipped*.
(From *Britain in the Modern World* by E. N. Nash and A. M. Newth)

zip means □ cinema
□ photography
□ television
□ telephone

Exercise 6

Specific aim: ⎫
Skills involved: ⎬ Same as for exercise 5 but the students have to provide missing words that all derive from the
Why? ⎭ same root.

In the following text, several words have been taken out. But they are all derived from the same root (e.g. kind – kindly – kindness – unkind, etc.) Read the text carefully and try to supply the missing words.

Automation and computers

Ever since the beginning of time man has made tools. At first they were very primitive ones of stone; later bronze was used, and then men learned to work with iron. But however much tools were improved, man still had to use his hands. Nails had to be hammered in, wood carved, and stone chipped. Every table, every pair of shoes and every yard of cloth was made by [   ] and trained labour.

When, at the end of the eighteenth century, steam was used to drive machinery and it was found that, for instance, cotton could be spun by a machine, the need for so much [   ] labour declined. The labour force was divided into a small, [   ] section and the vast mass of [   ] and [   ].

In the present age we see machinery beginning to perform what used to be done by the [   ]. We can see how this works if we take a motor-car as an example. When they were first manufactured at the beginning of this century, each part was separately made and then assembled by [   ] engineers. The first step was made when the complicated process was broken up into separate parts, and each part done by a machine. If you had gone into a factory in Coventry forty years ago you would have seen men (and women) standing in front of a moving belt, and automatically dropping a nail in a hole as it came by. Or else, perhaps, a man would have to give a turn to a screw as it passed him. This work was deadly monotonous and required little [   ]. Now machines are undertaking this, dropping in the nail and turning the screw. There is much less need for the [   ] labour which used to make up about eighty per cent of the labour force of every factory.

Not only are machines undertaking the work of the [   ]. They are themselves being controlled by electronic computers. These are electric brains, which are so [   ] and intricately designed that they can start an operation, check it, correct an error, and register measurements. It is easy to see one effect of all this. What is to happen to the workers in a factory run by automation? For instance, in 1963 a factory was built in Kent which cost £2,000,000, but it is operated by exactly seven employees. In a motor-car factory, in 1965, 555 things are done to a cylinder block by a continuous automated process.

Automation does not only invade the factory it is also making a revolution in offices. Computers can do calculations in half an hour which it might take a mathematician or an accountant two years to work out. Many offices have installed computers to do work which was once done by clerks.

More highly trained scientists are needed to design the new devices, more engineers to make and service them, and fewer [   ] workers to do mechanical tasks.

(From *Britain in the Modern World*, by E. N. Nash and A. M. Newth)

Exercise 7

Specific aim:	Same as for exercise 5 but this time about one
Skills involved:	word out of eight has been taken out of the text
Why?	and must be deduced by the students.

Read the following text and complete the blanks with the words which seem most appropriate to you.

What is apartheid?

It is the policy of .... Africans inferior, and separate from Europeans.

.... are to be kept separate by not being .... to live as citizens with rights in .... towns. They may go to European towns to ...., but they may not have their families ....; they must live in 'Bantustans', the .... areas. They are not to .... with Europeans by .... in the same cafés, waiting-rooms, ... of trains, seats in parks. They are not to .... from the same beaches, go to the .... cinemas, play on the same game-........................... or in the same teams.

Twelve per cent of the .... is left for the Africans to live and .... on, and this is mostly dry, ..., mountainous land. .... the Africans are three-quarters of the people. They are .... to go and work for the Europeans, not .... because their lands do not .... enough food to keep them, but also .... they must .... money to pay their taxes. Each adult .... man has to pay £1 a year poll tax, and ten shillings a year .... for his hut. When they .... into European areas to work .... are not allowed to do .... work; they are hewers of wood and drawers of water, and their .... is about one-seventh of what a European .... earn for the same .... of work.

If a European .... and African to do skilled work of the kind .... for Europeans, ... as carpentry, both the European and his .... employee may be fined £100. Any African who takes part in a strike may be .... £500, and/or sent to .... for three years.
(From *Britain in the Modern World*, by E. N. Nash and A. M. Newth)

Here are the answers as an indication:
keeping – they – allowed – European – work – there – native – mix – sitting – compartments – bathe – same – fields – land – farm – poor – yet – forced – only – grow – because – earn – African – tax – go – they – skilled – wage – would – kind – employs – reserved – such – African – fined – prison

An easier version of this exercise, which can be useful in preliminary training exercises, involves taking out a few words

from the text and proposing a choice between three or four
possibilities for each of these words.

e.g.
It is the policy of keeping Africans ....1.........., and separate from
Europeans.
    They are to be kept separate by not being ....2.......... to live as citizens
with rights in ....3.......... towns. They ....4.......... go to European
towns to ....5.........., but they may not have their families
..........6..........; they must live in 'Bantustans', the ....7.......... areas.
They are ....8.......... to ....9.......... with Europeans by sitting in
..........10.......... cafés, waiting-rooms, compartments of trains, seats in
parks.

1 a) superior b) inferior c) equal	5 a) work b) live c) drink	9 a) play b) mix c) talk
2 a) obliged b) encouraged c) allowed	6 a) working b) there c) at home	10 a) the same b) other c) the black
3 a) British b) African c) European	7 a) European b) native c) white	
4 a) cannot b) may c) should	8 a) sometimes b) often c) not	

Exercise 8

Specific aim: To train the students to infer the meaning of
unfamiliar words by asking them to do a cloze
exercise in their native language before doing one in
English.

Skills involved: Deducing the meaning of unfamiliar lexical items
through contextual clues.

Why? Most students could infer the meaning of
unfamiliar words much more quickly if they only
realized this is something they already do all the
time in their native language.
    One way of making them conscious of this is to
give them first a short cloze test in their native
language. Most students will have no difficulty in
guessing the meaning of the missing words and in
understanding the gist of the passage.

After this has been done, the students can be given a short text in English, in which the same proportion of words as in the first text has been taken out. But this time, the words have been replaced by imaginary words, or very difficult ones, which they obviously do not know. In many cases, the students will stumble on these unfamiliar words which may even prevent them from understanding what the passage is about.

Comparing these two exercises may be useful to show the students that they *are* able to understand a lot if they do not allow themselves to be discouraged by a few difficulties.

(About one word out of eight has been taken out in each text.)

1   Read the following text and fill the blanks with the words which seem most appropriate to you.

Le 26 mai, pour peu que les conditions _____ s'y prêtent, dix-sept ballons représentant dix différents _____ de Long-Beach, en Californie, pour participer à _____ 1979 de la légendaire épreuve de ballons _____ la Coupe Gordon-Bennett. Après quarante années _____ d u e s d'abord à la guerre, puis à l'irrémédiable _____ des « plus légers que l'air », la Coupe Gordon-Bennett, _____ en 1906 par le fondateur de l' « International Herald Tribune », _____ en effet de ses cendres. Un _____ qui, à l'époque des long - courriers supersoniques et de la _____ en place de stations orbitales, _____ bien quelques commentaires.

(*Le Monde*)

2   The following text contains a number of imaginary words. Can you guess their meaning?

TRAIN DERAILED

Plicks are believed to have caused the dolling of a two-car diesel passenger train yesterday. The train, with 24 biners on board, hit a metal object and ratteol 100 yards of track before stopping four pars from Middlesbrough. Three people were taken to hospital, one slightly rapped, the others finding from shock.

(*The Daily Telegraph*)

Exercise 9

Specific aim:	To train the students to infer the meaning of unfamiliar words and to help them to analyse their process of inference.
Skills involved:	Deducing the meaning and use of unfamiliar lexical items through contextual clues. Understanding relations between parts of a text through lexical cohesion devices.
Why?	The main purpose of this exercise is to develop in the students the ability to analyse their own process of inference. Such an analysis should make them conscious of how they can deal with an unfamiliar word and make them ready to use the different techniques of inference more quickly and efficiently.

Nobody's watching me

I am a foot taller than Napoleon and twice the weight of Twiggy; on my only visit to a beautician, the woman said she found my face a *challenge*. Yet despite these social disadvantages I feel cheerful, happy, confident and secure.

I work for a daily newspaper and so get to a lot of places I would otherwise never see. This year I went to Ascot to write about the people there. I saw something there that made me realize the stupidity of trying to conform – of trying to be better than anyone else. There was a small, *plump* woman, all *dressed up* – huge hat, dress with pink butterflies, long white gloves. She also had a *shooting-stick*. But because she was so plump, when she sat on the stick it went deep into the ground and she couldn't pull it out. She *tugged* and *tugged*, tears of rage in her eyes. When the final *tug* brought it out, she crashed with it to the ground.

I saw her walk away. Her day had been ruined. She had made a fool of herself in public – she had impressed nobody. In her own sad, red eyes she was a *failure*.

I remember well when I was like that, in the days before I learned that nobody really cared what you do . . .

I remember the pain of my first dance, something that is always meant to be a wonderful occasion for a girl . . . There was a fashion then for diamanté ear-rings, and I wore them so often practising for the big night that I got two great *sores* on my ears and had to put sticking-plaster on them. Perhaps it was this that made nobody want to dance with me. Whatever it was, there I sat for four hours and 43 minutes. When I came home, I told my parents that I had a marvellous time and that my feet were *sore* from dancing. They were pleased at my success and they went to bed happy, but I went to my room and tore the bits of sticking-plaster off my ears and felt *forlorn* and *disconsolate*.

(Adapted from an article in *The Listener* by Maeve Binchy)

Read the whole text first, then look at the words which are italicized and try to guess their meaning from the context. The following types of relation between the word and the context may help you:
- equivalence: a synonym is mentioned in the text.
- contrast: the word means the contrary of another word or expression given in the text.
- cause: the meaning of the word can be guessed because it is the cause of something described in the text.
- consequence: the word describes or appears in the description of the consequence of something. If the cause is known, it may be possible to guess what the consequence is.
- purpose: the word applies to an object whose purpose is described in the text.
- explanation/illustration: the meaning of the word is explained or an example is given.
- generalization/specification: the word is just one specific instance of a more general thing or idea mentioned in the text, or, on the contrary, after a number of specific examples have been given, a generalization is made.

When you have finished, complete the table opposite.

Exercise 10

Specific aim: To train the students to read faster and to recognize words more quickly.

Skills involved: Inferring the meaning of incomplete words. Predicting.

Why?   This is an activity that we are constantly led to practise, even in our native language: when we receive a letter which is difficult to read because of the handwriting, or when a document has been damaged and some of the words are not legible. In order to reconstruct the words, it is necessary to study what we can see of them in order to predict what letters are likely to be missing, and/or to study the context in order to infer the general meaning of the words. This is usually done very fast and almost unconsciously in our first language, and the aim of this exercise is to train the students to do the same thing in a foreign language. More generally, even when dealing with perfectly legible texts, it should also help the students to recognize words more quickly and therefore to read faster.

Here is a possible way of completing the table.

	Equivalence	Contrast	Cause	Consequence	Purpose	Explanation Illustration	Generalisation Specification
challenge		face = a challenge yet I feel happy ⇒ something negative					face = a challenge thus: social disadvantage → a disadvantage/something unpleasant
plump			plump → stick went deep into ground ⇒ heavy, fat				
dressed up						all dressed up — huge hat...dress coat...gloves with aerosol/or clothes one notices	
shooting stick					she sat on the stick → a stick you can sit on		
tugged/tug	pull → tug ⇒ pull		tug → brings stick out ⇒ pull				
failure				- fact of himself -impressed nobody → a failure ⇒ no good			
sores/sore				sore (+ sticking-plaster) → nobody wants to dance → something unpleasant	wearing ear-rings often damaging a lot → sore fact → instruction/prompt		
forlorn disconsolate		happy ≠ disconsolate ⇒ unhappy					

1 You live in Boston and you are in the train on the way to West Concord to visit a friend. It is dark outside and you want to know where you are. It is not easy to read the names of the stations as you cannot always see the whole name. When you see the following signs, can you tell what stations you are passing? (See Davies and Whitney, *Reasons for Reading*, p. 15).

I N	O L	: _____
R T	S	A R	: _____
A	R L E	: _____
U T	A	T O	: _____

Did you manage to get off in South Concord?
Here are the stations on the line:

Saturdays Only

Leave Boston North Station	ARRIVE: Porter Square	Bel- mont Center	Wav- erley	Wal- tham	Bran- deis/ Rob- erts	Ken- dal Green	Lin- coln	Con- cord	West Con- cord	South Acton

2 You are in a second-hand bookshop, looking at old books. Some of them are in a rather bad state and parts of the words on the covers have disappeared.
   Can you tell what the titles of the following books are?
   a) The   devent   es of Robinson Cr   oe.
   b) The m   tery o   the ol   cast   .
   c)   to bui   your own hou   .
   d) A   ew Engl   gram   .

3 You have just received this postcard. Unfortunately is is raining hard and some or parts of the words have disappeared. Can you guess what was written?

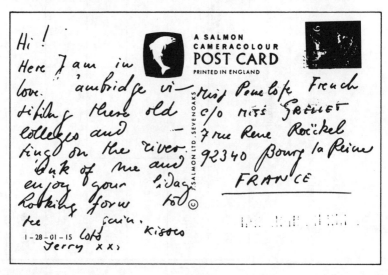

Inference: Deducing the meaning and use of unfamiliar lexical items through understanding word formation

Exercise

Specific aim: To train the students to recognize word formation and derivation.

Skills involved: Deducing the meaning and use of unfamiliar lexical items through understanding word formation.

Why?   Being aware of how words are formed and of the value of prefixes and suffixes will help the students to discover the meaning of a great number of unfamiliar words.

See text on pages 28–9.

a) Two words with the suffix '-ible' appear in the text. What are they? What effect does the suffix have on the meaning of the word? Can you think of other words formed in the same way?

b) Underline the suffixes in the following words:
   - hypnotist
   - predictable
   - beautiful
   - apparently
   - observation

   - Can you guess the meaning of each of the suffixes?
   - Can you think of other words formed with the same suffixes?

c) Find two words with a prefix in the text:
   - Define the value of each prefix.
   - One of them is used to make a word negative. What prefix would you add to each of these adjectives/nouns in order to make them negative?
   - predictable:.............................
   - trained:.............................
   - organization:.............................
   - ability:.............................

d) At the beginning of the text, you can find the word 'hypnotist'.
   - Can you find another word formed in the same way? ....
   - At the end of the text you can also find the corresponding adjective, 'hypnotic'. Can you complete the following table with the appropriate words, bearing in mind that these words do not all appear in the text, that the word-formation may not be the same for all of them and that some boxes may remain empty.

noun	adjective	person	verb	adverb
hypnosis hypnotism	hypnotic	hypnotist hypnotizer	hypnotize	hypnotizingly
		employer		

noun	adjective	person	verb	adverb
	psychological			
science				
	free			

e) Look at the following words and find what the root of each of them is.
   Then build as many words as you can from that root.
   - presumably
   - uncovering
   - followers
   - observation

Inference – further hints

One useful exercise involves giving the class a short passage to read
and asking them to underline all the words they do not understand.
Then the whole class can consider each of these words and see how
much they can guess about them. The following steps can be taken
to help the students during the exercise:
- look at what can be guessed from the word itself. (Is it a noun, a
  verb, an adjective? Can its form help?)
- look at the context. (Is the word repeated anywhere else? Is there
  any contrast or analogy that can help you derive the meaning of
  the word?)
- try to make a guess even if it is a vague one.

1.2   Understanding relations within the sentence

Exercise 1

Specific aim: To help the students to recognize the structure of
                   complex sentences.
Skills involved: Understanding relations within the sentence.
Why?   In order to read efficiently and not to stumble on
                   every word it will be essential for the students to
                   grasp the structure of the sentences they read at
                   once. They should therefore be taught to discrim-
                   inate quickly between what is essential (subject –
                   verb – object, i.e. the 'core' of the sentence) and the
                   padding (i.e. modifiers, relative clauses,
                   oppositions, etc.) which, in each sentence, only
                   introduces some further details or qualifies the idea.

Sensitizing

Read the following sentences and underline the subject and the main verb of each of them.

'One team that performed more than two hundred operations found that nearly half the patients underwent a change of personality. In one publicized case in England a young salesman with an apparent compulsion to gamble was arrested for larceny.'

Exercise 2

Specific aim:
Skills involved: } Same as for exercise 1.
Why?

The sentences that follow are all from *Time*. Read them and answer the questions that follow.

1 Mostly because of inflation, but also because taxes have been creeping upward, the actual buying power that people have been getting from the money in their paychecks has declined by nearly 4% over the past twelve months.
Match subjects and verbs.
taxes   have been creeping upward
buying power   have been getting
people   has declined

2 One index of how financially pressed Americans feel is the popularity of grocery coupons, those little pieces of paper snipped from product labels or newspaper ads that housewives have long used to save nickels and dimes at the check-out counter.
What is the subject of 'feel'?
What is the subject of 'is'?
What noun phrase does 'that' refer to?
a) newspaper ads
b) product labels
c) pieces of paper
d) popularity

3 Magazine writers, or the authors of books about current affairs, often find themselves gratefully surprised by how much remains unexplored and untold about major events that the day press and television once swarmed all over, then abandoned.
Find the subjects in the first column that match the verbs in the second column.
a) Magazine writers   A) find
b) books   B) remains
c) current affairs   C) swarmed
d) how much   D) abandoned
e) major events
f) the day press and television

.........A   ....B C   ....D

43

4 One of the major reasons photo collecting has flowered only recently was the realization that a photograph, unlike a painting or a drawing, can be reproduced forever, as long as the negative exists.
What is the subject of 'was'?
What is the subject of 'can'?
a) a photograph
b) the realization
c) a painting
d) a drawing

Exercise 3

Specific aim: Same as for exercise 1 but the students are asked
Skills involved: to divide the sentences of a text into sense groups
Why?   so as to grasp the structure of the sentences more
                     quickly.

Divide the following sentences into sense groups.

Here is a possible way of doing it.

You must excuse/a letter from somebody/you may this morning/not even remember./It is the lonely young man/with the black face/beside the door/to whom/you were so kind/last night./I have only just returned/from Cambridge,/to Calcutta,/and know no one here./It was a real ordeal/to find myself/at Government House,/at such a large party,/all alone in the world.
(From *Letters of an Indian Judge to an English Gentlewoman* (Futura, 1970))

1.3   Linking sentences and ideas

Exercise 1

Specific aim: To prepare the students to recognize the relations
                     within sentences or between sentences.
Skills involved: Understanding relations between parts of a text.
Why?   Although this exercise mainly deals with semantic
                     relations within the text, it can be useful to prepare
                     the students to look out for some of the relations
                     that can exist between different parts of a text.

The following text contains six mistakes. Can you find what they are and what words should appear instead?

American serviceman Andrew Nelson wanted to take his cat Felix home with her to San Francisco so he asked Trans World Airlines to quote him a price to carry Felix with him as hand luggage.

T. W. A. wanted to know Felix's height 'from tip of nose to base of tail, width across shoulders while in a standing position, and his length from base of paw to top of head (not ears) whilst standing and looking straight ahead.'

Mr Nelson loves Felix, but not that much, so he asked B.O.A.C. for a quotation. They told him he could calculate this cost by following these simple rules:

1. Measure the dog's crate in inches and divide the result by 427.
2. Weigh Felix in his crate.
3. The charge is the higher of (1) or (2) above at the appropriate rate, to the minimum charge of £10.40.
4. To this figure add the U.K. handling charge of £2.75, and the American handling charge, which is about the same.

It was all too much for Mr Nelson. He put Felix in a basket and carried him aboard the boat as hand luggage. Free.

(From C. Ward, *How to complain* (Secker and Warburg, 1974))

Linking sentences and ideas: Reference

Exercise 2

Specific aim: To train the students to recognize and understand reference.

Skills involved: Understanding relations between parts of a text through reference.

Why? One common way of linking structurally-independent sentences in order to get a meaningful text is to use words such as this, that, it, etc. which refer to something already mentioned (anaphora) or to something which is going to be mentioned (cataphora). Failure to understand such anaphoric links will probably lead to a serious misunderstanding of the text. This exercise will be useful to help the students perceive these links through a careful study of the text.

In the following passage all the italicized words refer to something mentioned before, or after, in the text. Read the passage carefully and complete the table underneath.

The idea of evolution (*which* is gradual change) was not a new *one*. The Greeks had thought of *it*, so had Erasmus Darwin, the grandfather of Charles, and also the Frenchman, Lamarck. *It* is one thing to have an idea; we can all of us guess and sometimes make a lucky guess. *It* is quite another thing to produce a proof of the correctness of that idea. Darwin thought he had *that* proof in *his* notebooks. *He* saw that all animals had a struggle to survive. *Those* which were best at surviving *their* environment passed on

the good qualities which had helped *them* to *their* descendants. *This* was
called 'the survival of the fittest'. For example, in a cold climate, *those* who
have the warmest fur will live. Darwin believed that *this* necessity for an
animal to deal with *its* environment explained the immense variety of
creatures.

(From A. M. Newth: *Britain and the World* (Penguin, 1966))

	refers to something		
	before	after	what it refers to:
which	x		*the idea of evolution*
one	x		*idea*
it	x		*the idea of evolution*
It		x	*to have an idea*
Now go on!			
It			
that			
his			
He			
Those			
their			
them			
their			
This			
those			
this			
its			

Exercise 3

Specific aim: Same as for exercise 1 but the students are now
Skills involved: asked to use underlining and circling to visualize
Why?   the relations in and between the sentences.

In the following paragraph, the use of reference has been made clear by
arrows.

The idea of evolution (which is gradual change) was not a new one. The
Greeks had thought of it, so had Erasmus Darwin, the grandfather of
Charles, and also the Frenchman, Lamarck. It is one thing to have an idea;
we can all of us guess and sometimes make a lucky guess.

Can you now do the same thing with the rest of the passage?

It is quite another thing to produce a proof of the correctness of that idea. Darwin thought he had that proof in his notebooks. He saw that all animals had a struggle to survive. Those which were best at surviving their environment passed on the good qualities which had helped them to their descendants. This was called 'the survival of the fittest'. For example, in a cold climate, those who have the warmest fur will live. Darwin believed that this necessity for an animal to deal with its environment explained the immense variety of creatures.

Reference – further hints

Similar types of exercises could be done using other cohesion devices such as nominalizations, verbal or clausal substitution or comparisons.

It is also important to remember that anaphora and cataphora can also work at the level of the paragraph, of the chapter, or even of the whole book (e.g. announcing the ending of a novel). Exercises could also be devised to deal with this aspect of reference.

Linking sentences and ideas: Link-words

Exercise 1

Specific aim: To train the students to understand the value of link-words.

Skills involved: Understanding relations between parts of a text through the use of logical connectors.

Why?   It is extremely important to be able to recognize connective words. Not only are they essential to the understanding of the ideas and facts mentioned in the passage, but they also indicate the rhetorical value (e.g. reinforcing, explaining) of what follows.

In the following text, a number of link-words have been italicized. Replace them by other link-words, or rewrite the sentences, making sure the meaning remains the same.

Botany Bay

'Australia became prosperous *because of* the wickedness of England,' someone said. What was meant by this?

Simply that in the beginning Australia was a place to which convicts were sent. It was expensive to keep them in prison *so* the government was anxious to be rid of them. Before 1783 we had shipped convicts to the American colonies. *But* the United States of America after 1783 did not want any more of these unruly immigrants. For a year or two they were kept in disused rotting ships on the Thames, *until* the suggestion was made that Australia, 12,000 miles away, would be an excellent country to harbour them. Captain Cook had sailed round the Coast and discovered a place he called Botany Bay *because* the flowers there were so wonderful, and this was chosen for a convict settlement.

A certain Captain Phillip was given charge of the first group to go there in 1788. *After* five months' sailing they arrived at Botany Bay, *but* Captain Phillip decided it was not suitable and went farther on and landed at what is now called Sydney Harbour. The term Botany Bay was *nevertheless* used for this colony.

The government had shown little imagination in beginning this venture. Captain Phillip begged for more supplies. He needed seeds, farm implements and food. *Instead* he was sent more convicts. *After* four years of unrewarding labour Captain Phillip retired because of ill-health. (Adapted from A. M. Newth: *Britain and the World* (Penguin, 1966))

Exercise 2

Specific aim:
Skills involved:
Why?
} Same as for exercise 1 but the students are asked to classify the link-words according to their function. This kind of exercise is useful to train the students to recognize the rhetorical value of the sentence by simply looking at the connector that is used.

Look at the text called *Botany Bay* and classify the italicized link-words according to their function:
Cause:..
Consequence:..
Time sequence:...
Concession:...
Opposition:..

The exercise would obviously be more difficult but also more interesting if one used a text offering a greater variety of link-words which would not have been indicated beforehand.

Exercise 3

Specific aim:
Skills involved:
Why?
} Same as for exercise 1 but this time the link-words have been taken out and the students are made to choose between four possibilities in order to complete each blank. This will lead them to look at the context carefully in order to find out the function of the missing link-word as well as what is grammatically correct.

Read the following text and select the most appropriate link-words from the list given below.

A colour consultant from Toronto explained to the Inter-Society Colour Council meeting in New York an ingenious scheme which a client company had conceived for increasing the sale of potato peelers. He began by pointing out a puzzling fact. .... 1 ....
potato peelers 'never wear out', enough are sold in two years in his country to put one in every home. What happens to them? He gave this answer. 'Investigation reveals that they get thrown away with the potato peelings.' One of his colleagues, he added, had then come up with a dazzling plan for helping along this throw-away process. He proposed that their company paint their peelers 'as much like a potato peeling as possible.'
.... 2 .... a potato-coloured peeler wouldn't have much eye-appeal on the sales counter. They decided to solve that by displaying the peeler on a colourful card. Once the housewife got the peeler home and removed the bright card, the chances that she would lose the peeler were excellent. . .
   In some cases the consumers have no choice but to be waste makers .... 3 .... the way products are sold to them. Many paste pots come with brushes built into the cover, and the brushes fail by a half-inch to reach the bottom. . . .. 4 .... millions of 'empty' paste jars are thrown away with a few spoonfuls of paste still in them. .... 5 ...., millions of 'used' tubes of lipstick are thrown away with a half-inch of lipstick remaining in the tube.
(From Vance Packard: *The Waste Makers* (Pelican, 1961))

1 a) because
  b) although
  c) for example
  d) since

2 a) in addition
  b) on the contrary
  c) in this way
  d) however

3 a) in spite of
  b) because of
  c) as
  d) in addition to

4 a) similarly
  b) for example
  c) however
  d) thus (= in this way)

5 a) likewise (= similarly)
  b) on the contrary
  c) yet
  d) for instance

Exercise 4

Specific aim: ⎫ Same as for exercise 3 but it is slightly more
Skills involved: ⎬ difficult since only a jumbled list of link-words is
Why? ⎭ provided.

Read the following passage and fill in the blanks with the appropriate words, from among the following: *therefore, thus, yet, first, but, then.* All these words have to be used but some of them may be used twice!

Numerical infinity had been causing trouble from the time of Zeno and his paradoxes. If we recall the race between Achilles and the tortoise, we might put one of the puzzling aspects of this contest as follows: for every place Achilles has been at, there is a place that the tortoise has occupied. The two runners have ☐ at any time assumed an equal number of stations. ☐ obviously Achilles covers more ground. This seems to run counter the common sense notion that the whole is greater than the part. ☐ when we deal with infinite collections this is no longer so. ☐ , to take a simple example, the series of positive numbers, which is an infinite collection, has in it odd and even numbers. Take away all the odd numbers, and you might think that what is left is half of what you begin with. ☐ there remain as many even numbers as there were numbers altogether at the start. This somewhat startling conclusion is quite easily demonstrated. ☐ , we write down the series of natural numbers, and ☐ , alongside it, a series resulting from it by doubling each member in turn. For every number in the first series there is a corresponding entry in the second. There is, as mathematicians put it, a one-one correspondence between them. The two series ☐ have the same number in terms. In the case of infinite collections, ☐ , a part contains as many terms as the whole. This is the property that Cantor used to define an infinite collection.
(From Bertrand Russell: *The Wisdom of the West* (Macdonald, 1959))

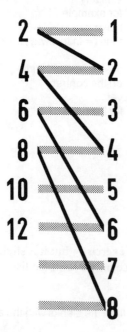

One of Cantor's paradoxes: there are as many even numbers as there are numbers

Exercise 5

Specific aim: ⎫ Same as for exercise 3 but now no link-words are
Skills involved: ⎬ suggested and the students must fill in the blanks
Why? ⎭ with the connectors they think most appropriate.

Read the following text and fill in the blanks with the link-words which seem most appropriate to you.

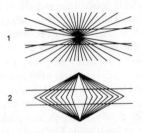

1

2

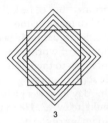

3

Optical illusions

.... the fact that the lines in figures 1 and 2 look discontinuous, they are parallel. As for the square in figure 3, it is perfectly straight .... it may look distorted. It is .... these optical designs are very rare that the eye is not used to them and that the brain is .... unable to evaluate these patterns properly.
Here is a further example. Which of these two horizontal bars is the longer?

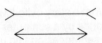

Most people think it is the top one. And ...., both are exactly the same length. ...., the illusion may be carried one step further: if you touch these bars with your fingers, you will still have the feeling that one bar is longer than the other, ... if you know what the reality is.

Exercise 6

Specific aim: ⎫ Same as for exercise 1 but the students are only
Skills involved: ⎬ given a succession of sentences which they must
Why? ⎭ connect and often rewrite in order to produce a
⎭ coherent text.

In the following passage, most of the connective words are missing. Rewrite the text, adding link-words where necessary. Be careful! Many

structures will have to be changed and you will probably not keep the same number of sentences. Here are some of the link-words you may find useful:

Then	However	The only result
And	But	Although
When	Yet	So
That's how	Instead	

Television was invented by John Logie Baird. When he was young he built an aeroplane. He tried to fly in it. It crashed down below. Baird was fortunate not to be killed. It did not discourage him. When he was older he tried to make diamonds from coal. There was an enormous explosion. He was not injured. He became a business man. His business failed. He thought of working at television. His family advised him not to. He did not listen to them. He rented an attic. He bought the apparatus he needed. He started working. He worked for a long time. He was not successful. One day he saw a picture on his screen. He rushed out to get someone he could 'televise'. He found an office boy. He took him back to his room. No image of the boy appeared on his screen. The boy, terrified, had put his head down. He put it up again. His picture appeared on the screen. Television had been discovered.

Exercise 7

Specific aim:
Skills involved: } Same as for exercise 6.
Why?

The following passage is an extract from a story called *Murder Mystery 1* which was produced in nineteen seconds by a computer in 1973. As you can see all the sentences are simple sentences and no use is made of link-words or reference between different sentences. Can you rewrite this short passage to make it look more natural? This will mean adding or removing words and putting some of the sentences together.

The butler announced tea.

Everyone went to the garden. The butler served tea. The day was cool. The sky was cloudy. The garden was nice. The flowers were pretty. Marion complimented Lady Buxley.

Ronald talked with Marion.

Tea time was over.

Everyone went to the parlor.

The cook went to the kitchen. Maggie prepared dinner.

Dr Hume asked Edward to play tennis. Edward agreed. Lord Edward went to the tennis court with Dr Hume. They played tennis. Dr Hume was the good player. Edward played tennis well.

The butler announced dinner.

Dr Bartholomew Hume stopped playing tennis. Edward stopped playing tennis.

Everyone went to the dining room. Everyone sat down. The butler served the food. Supper started.

Marion talked with Florence. Florence argued with Marion. Marion said that Florence was idiotic.

Florence talked with Lady Buxley.

Supper was over. The men went to the parlor. The men smoked fat smelly stogies. The men drank sherry. The women went to the drawing room. The women gossiping drank coffee.

Everyone went to the parlor.

Marion talked with Jane.

James went to the library. James read the good paperback. Edward asked Ronald to play tennis. Ronald agreed. Ronald went to the tennis court with Lord Edward. They played tennis.

John suggested the game of bridge. Lady Buxley agreed. Dr Bartholomew Hume agreed. Jane agreed. They played bridge.

The servants went to bed. Everyone went to bed.

(From *Murder Mystery 1* produced by Univac 1108, first presented at the International Conference on Computers in the Humanities, Minneapolis, July 1973)

2 Improving reading speed

Exercise

Specific aim: To develop word–recognition and word–comprehension speed.

Skills involved: Recognizing the meaning of words as quickly as possible.

Why? Besides the more common speed reading exercises that consist in timing one's reading of a text, some preliminary exercises (see Harris, *Reading Improvement Exercises*) can help the students to overcome some of their difficulties in recognizing words and their meaning.

The following exercise should be done as quickly as possible and timed. In order to be efficient, each question should contain far more items.

a) Underline the word which is the same as the first one given.

cat	cab	told	bold
	cut		told
	cap		hold
	cat		bolt

b) Here is a series of two expressions. They are sometimes the same and sometimes different. Go through the list and when the expressions are different, underline the word that differs in the second expression.

cat nap	cat nap
well paid	well said
old looking	cold looking
one-way	one day
happy few	happy few
self-taught	self-caught
he's bound to see the lamp	he's bound to see the lamb
Can you heat the tin?	Can you hit the tin?
they pricked my fingers	they pricked my fingers
you startled the party	you started the party

c) Decide whether the following words have similar or different meanings.

cry	weep
laugh	whisper

finish   stop
help   assist
avoid   warn
menace   threaten

d) Find the word which means the same thing as the first word mentioned.

wood   oak   grab   hold
       tree   snatch
       forest   leave
       land   give

e) Which of the following words should complete the sentence?
––––– in poor neighbourhoods usually charge high prices.
i) The police   ii) districts   iii) shops   iv) books

f) Some of the following sentences contain a mistake. When this is the case, underline the word which should be changed.
– If you want to sew this dress you'll need some soap and a needle.
– Developing countries often lack badly-trained teachers.
– If you get lost in the jungle, you should always try to follow a river: it will lead you back to the wilderness.

3 From skimming to scanning

3.1 Predicting

Exercise 1

Specific aim: To train the students to make predictions and guesses when reading a text.

Skills involved: Predicting.

Why? Reading is an activity involving constant guesses that are later rejected or confirmed. This means that one does not read all the sentences in the same way, but one relies on a number of words – or 'cues' – to get an idea of what kind of sentence (e.g. an example, an explanation) is likely to follow. The aim of this exercise is to help the students acquire this crucial ability. The idea comes from an article by K. W. Moody ('A Type of Exercise for developing Prediction Skills in Reading', *RELC Journal*, vol. 7, no. 1, 1976) and it consists of giving the students only the beginning of a text and asking them to predict what is likely to come next.

After reading each of the sentences in column 1, look at column 2 and choose the sentence which you think is most likely to follow (the first column could be covered by a strip of paper while you are considering the possibilities in the second column).
Go on in the same way until you reach the end of the text.

The average person in the world now uses approximately 43,000 calories per day.

a) However, there are few 'average' people in the world.
b) However, calories are essential to live.
c) Some people may use more.

However, there are few 'average' people in the world.

a) Most people should use far less calories.
b) The Egyptians, for instance, consume 9,200 calories a day.
c) Some people use far more energy than that, while most use far less.

Some people use far more energy than that, while most use far less.

a) An average citizen of the so-called 'developed' countries uses 136,000 calories each day.
b) The number should be much higher.
c) But on the whole, everyone consumes far too many calories.

An average citizen of the so-called 'developed' countries uses 136,000 calories each day.

a) In Japan, for instance, the average figure is 74,000 calories per day.
b) However, more than two-thirds of the world's people live in the 'developing' areas, where the average person uses only 8,200 calories of non-metabolic energy daily.

However, more than two-thirds of the world's people live in the 'developing' areas, where the average person uses only 8,200 calories of non-metabolic energy daily.

a) This is why it is so difficult to be an average person.
b) This explains why one part of the world is much poorer than the other.
c) Such vast differences are hard to comprehend.

Such vast differences are hard to comprehend.

Exercise 2

Specific aim: To train the students to make predictions and guesses when reading a text.

Skills involved: Predicting.

Why? When supplying the missing punctuation of a text, we try to predict where the sentences are likely to stop and look for certain words functioning as signals of a new sentence or paragraph.

In the following text, all punctuation has been removed. Can you put it back? Start a new paragraph when you think it is necessary and don't forget part of the text may be a dialogue and will have to be punctuated as such.

he emerged wearing black trousers and a brown-and-white shirt he put on black shoes and slicked his hair with oil from a bottle on the dresser Flora gave Gabi a clean pair of jeans a red-striped shirt and sneakers as they went

downstairs Flora said let's go to the A and P things are cheaper there all
right I don't care but those people don't sell on credit so what Flora
answered crossly we have to economize they passed a record shop Flora
give me a dollar Simplicio said I want to buy *La mano de Dios* are you crazy
Flora burst out we aren't going to have any money left over and you want
to buy a record besides you broke the arm of the record player and that's
expensive so don't think we can get it fixed right away I hope it's never
fixed because when it works all you do is play records so loud the whole
neighborhood can hear ah Flora give it to me Flora opened her purse and
threw a dollar bill at her husband.
(From Oscar Lewis: *Days with Simplicio in New York* (Random House,
1965))

Predicting – further hints

- The students can be given unfinished passages and asked to
  propose an ending.
- Widdowson ('The process and purpose of reading' in
  Explorations in Applied Linguistics) also suggests taking a written
  text, dividing it into utterances and asking the students to ask
  pertinent questions about what should follow at differing points
  in the passage. Thus they will see the various directions in which
  a text may naturally develop.

3.2 Previewing

Exercise 1

Specific aim: To train the students to use titles and tables of
contents to get an idea of what a passage is about.

Skills involved: Reference skill.
Anticipation.
Scanning.

Why? This exercise is one of many that can be used to
show the students how much they can guess about
a passage by simply looking at its title and at the
table of contents. This will be useful to most
students later in the course of their studies.

You have been given a page from a book to read.
It is entitled 'The New Famines'. What do you think the passage is about?
Think of at least three possibilities.
The title of the book is *The End of Affluence* (Paul R. Ehrlich (Ballantine,
1974)) and here is the beginning of the table of contents. Does this lead
you to reconsider your former opinion and make a more accurate guess
at the contents of the passage?

CONTENTS

INTRODUCTION: APPROACHING THE
FUTURE. *You learn the reasons for
reading this book—how it will help you
to understand and plan for the great dis-
locations that will occur in the coming
decades.*   1

1. THE EDGE OF THE CRISIS. *We describe
our first encounters with the age of
scarcity and outline the greatest threat in
the immediate future: the food crunch.*   15

2. THE WORST AND THE DULLEST. *The
value of depending on industry and government to save us is questioned by examining how they are managing America's
energy supplies.*   37

3. WE ARE NOT ALONE. *You discover the
sizable roles that foreign governments
and industries will play in your future as
the interdependent nations of the world
struggle over the division of a shrinking
resource "pie."*   89

4. MINERS' CANARIES. *Attention is focused
on Japan and Brazil as nations to watch
closely for developments that will have
grave repercussions for Americans.*   117

Exercise 2

Specific aim: To train the students to use a newspaper index.
Skills involved: Reference skill.
Why?   Being able to use an index is essential when
                    scanning to locate specific information.

You have just bought *The Daily Telegraph* in order to know the latest
news. Here is the index to the pages.
1 On what pages would you expect to find an answer to the following
   questions?

INDEX TO OTHER PAGES

	PAGE		PAGE
Home News ...	2, 3, 6 and 11	Leader Page	10
Foreign News	4	Obituary	8
Arts Notices	7	Personal	8
Births, Marriages and		Personal View	8
Deaths	18	Social Events	8
City News	13 and 14	Sport	14, 15 and 16
City Prices	12	TV and Radio	
Entertainments Guide	17	Programmes	17
Films	7	Woman's Page	9

TV and Radio Programmes
and Entertainment Guide
Inside Back Page

a) Have the U.S.A. decided anything about the Teheran hostages?
....

b) Is it true that Sir Norman Denning has died? ....

c) Are there any Letters or Opinions about the article on libraries that appeared a few days ago? ....

d) What's on TV tonight? ....

e) Is there a review of that new film with Anthony Quinn?
....

f) Is the new Education Bill likely to be passed? ....

2 On page 2 an article is entitled: QUAKE NUCLEAR WARNING
You can guess it is about an earthquake   in South America
                                          in England
                                          in the United States
On page 4 a headline says: RAIL CRASH KILLS 13
Some friends of yours have taken the train to go to Scotland. Would you get worried on their account?

Exercise 3

Specific aim: To train the students to use the text on the back cover of a book, the preface and the table of contents to get an idea of what the book is about.

Skills involved: Reference skill.

Why?   It is often important to be able to get a quick idea of what a book is about (e.g. when buying a book or choosing one in the library). Besides, glancing through the book, the text on the back cover, in the preface and in the table of contents gives the best idea of what is to be found in it.

You have a few minutes to skim through a book called *The Rise of The Novel* by Ian Watt and you first read the few lines written on the back cover of the book, the table of contents and the beginning of the preface. What can you tell about the book after reading them? Can you answer the questions that follow?

1 For what kind of public was the book written?
2 The book is about
☐ reading   ☐ eighteenth century
☐ novelists   in the   ☐ Middle Ages
☐ literature in general   ☐ nineteenth century
3 What major writers are considered in this book?
4 The main theory of the author is that the form of the first English novels resulted from:
☐ the position of women in society
☐ the social changes at that time
☐ the middle class

From skimming to scanning

published by Penguin Books

In these studies of Defoe, Richardson, and Fielding, Ian Watt investigates the reasons why the three main early eighteenth-century novelists wrote in the way they did — a way resulting ultimately in the modern novel of the present day. The rise of the middle class and of economic individualism, the philosophical innovations of the seventeenth century, complex changes in the social position of women: these are some of the factors he finds underlying an age which produced the authors of *Robinson Crusoe, Pamela*, and *Tom Jones*.

'An important, compendious work of inquiring scholarship . . . alive with ideas . . . an academic critic who in lively and suggestive detail is able to assemble round his novelists the ideas and facts among which they worked' — V. S. Pritchett in the *New Statesman*

'This book is altogether satisfying within the wide framework of its scheme, and certainly a major contribution to the subject, in some respects the most brilliant that has appeared. . . . Every page of Dr Watt's admirably written book repays study, as enlivening and enriching the works the purport of which we are too often inclined to take for granted' — *The Times Educational Supplement*

Cover design by Bruce Robertson

United Kingdom £1.50
Australia $4.95 (recommended)
Canada $3.95

Literature
ISBN 0 14
02.1480 1

Contents

Preface

IN 1938 I began a study of the relation between the growth of the reading public and the emergence of the novel in eighteenth-century England; and in 1947 it eventually took shape as a Fellowship Dissertation for St John's College, Cambridge. Two wider problems, however, remained unresolved. Defoe, Richardson, and Fielding were no doubt affected by the changes in the reading public of their time; but their works are surely more profoundly conditioned by the new climate of social and moral experience which they and their eighteenth-century readers shared. Nor could one say much about how this was connected with the emergence of the new literary form without deciding what the novel's distinctive literary features were and are.

---

5 The different chapters are arranged – chronologically
    – thematically
6 What kind of influence did the literature described in this book have?
7 Does the book have an index?
8 Does the book have a glossary?

3.3   Anticipation

Exercise 1

Specific aim: To encourage the students to think about the theme of the passage before reading it (psychological sensitizing).

Skills involved: Anticipation.
Why?   One of the most important factors that can help us
                   in the process of reading is the desire we have to
                   read about a given subject. The more we look
                   forward to reading and anticipate in our minds
                   what the text could hold in store for us, the easier it
                   will be to grasp the main points of the passage. In
                   this exercise, questions are asked before the text is
                   read to make the students aware of what they
                   know, what they don't know, what they wish to
                   learn about the topic.

Before studying a text about robots:

1 What is a robot?
2 Is there any difference between a robot and an automaton?
3 What can robots be used for?
4 Do you think they can ever completely replace human beings for some
  jobs? Which ones?

Exercise 2

Specific aim: ⎫
Skills involved: ⎬ Same as for exercise 1 but a quiz is used instead of
Why?   ⎭ questions.

Decide whether the following statements are true or false.

a) The first automatons date back to 1500.
b) The French philosopher Descartes invented an automaton.
c) The first speaking automatons were made around 1890.
d) In the film *Star Wars* the most important characters are two robots.
e) One miniature robot built in the United States can imitate most of the
   movements of an astronaut in a space capsule and is only twelve
   inches tall.
f) Some schools have been using robot teachers for the past few years.
g) One hospital uses a robot instead of a surgeon for minor operations.
h) Some domestic robots for the home only cost £600.
i) A robot is used in Ireland to detect and disarm bombs.
j) Some soldier-robots have already been used for war.

What's your score?

ꟻ(ꞁ ꓔ(ꜞ ꓔ(barısı4 ꟻ(6 ꓔ(ꞁ ꓔ(ə ꓔ(p ꟻ(ɔ ꓔ(q ꟻ(ɐ

You have probably discovered that there is quite a lot you don't know
about robots. The following will probably tell you some of the things you
wish to know about them.

The advantage of a quiz is that it allows students to think for themselves, to get involved, to commit themselves. This can often create the desire to learn and read more effectively than simple questions.

Starting with a quiz or with questions doesn't mean that the answers will be found in the text. It is not a 'pre-questioning' type of exercise in which students are asked to look for detailed information in the text.

Here, the aim is simply to create the need and wish to read as well as to familiarize the students with some of the ideas they will come across in the text.

Exercise 3

Specific aim: Same as for exercise 1 but this time a picture –
Skills involved: which lends itself to a variety of interpretations –
Why?   is used as the starting point of a discussion.

What do you know about robots and what do you think of them?

Edward Kienholz. *The Friendly Grey Computer — Star Gauge Model 54,* 1965; materials include fibreglass, paint, electronic components, doll parts, rocking chair; 40 x 39¼ x 24½ in. (101.6 x 99.4 x 62.2 cm). collection: Museum of Modern Art, New York

Directions for operation
Place master switch in *off* position. Plug computer into power supply. Print your problem on yellow index card provided, in rack. Word your question in such a way that it can be answered with a simple 'yes' or 'no'.
IMPORTANT: Next, program computer heads (C-20 and G-30) by setting dials in appropriate positions. You are now ready to start machine. Throw master switch to *on* setting. Red bulb on main housing and white tube on C-20 will light indicating computer is working. Remove phone from rack and speak your problem into the mouthpiece exactly as you have written it on your index card. Replace phone in rack and ding dinger once. Under NO circumstances should you turn computer off until answer has been returned. Flashing yellow bulb indicates positive answer. Flashing blue bulb indicates negative answer. Green jewel button doesn't light so it will not indicate anything. Computers sometimes get fatigued and have nervous breakdowns, hence the chair for it to rest in. If you know your computer well, you can tell when it's tired and sort of blue and in a funky mood. If such a condition seems imminent, turn rocker switch on for ten or twenty minutes. Your computer will love it and work all the harder for you. Remember that if you treat your computer well it will treat you well. When answer light has stopped flashing, turn master switch to *off* position. Machine will now re-cycle for the next question. Repeat procedure from beginning.

Exercise 4

Specific aim: To train the students to use the title, the picture and
                     their prior knowledge to anticipate the contents of
                     the text.
Skills involved: Anticipation.
Why?   By simply looking at the title and the
                     accompanying picture, one can often guess what
                     the text is about. This will allow us to ask ourselves
                     preliminary questions and expect to find some
                     answers in the text – which will greatly help the
                     process of reading. This technique is essential when
                     skimming (e.g. through a newspaper).

1 The text that you are going to read is entitled 'Keep off the grass'. Can
   you guess what the text might be about? Tick the boxes corresponding
   to what you think are possible ideas.
   ☐ Everday life in a large park
   ☐ Camping in the country
   ☐ Going for a picnic in London
   ☐ Going for a picnic in the mountains
   ☐ Interdictions and regulations
   ☐ How teenagers spend their week-ends
   ☐ Children playing in the streets
   Now discuss your answers with a partner. Explain why you think some
   of these ideas possible and some impossible. Whenever you think an
   idea is possible, try to imagine some of the points the article might
   mention.
   Can you think of further ideas about the contents of the article?

2 Now look at the pictures that accompany the text:

(photographs by (L) Mark Edwards and (R) Ron Chapman)

Do they help you reconsider your ideas and narrow down the
possibilities you had in mind?
Which of these possibilities would you now choose?

3 Let's suppose you have come to the conclusion that the text was about
'interdictions and regulations'. Choose a partner and discuss this
subject with him. You could consider the following points:
  – find examples of interdictions or regulations
  – which ones do you consider fair or good? Can you think of an
    interdiction which you find useless or unfair? Why?
  – how do you think regulations should be enforced (i.e. made
    effective)?

Exercise 5

Specific aim:
Skills involved: } Same as for exercise 4 but with titles only.
Why?

1 Look at these headlines, all taken from the same newspaper, and
choose the sentences that best describe the possible contents of the
articles:

Think before you jog...
  a) The pleasures of jogging.
  b) Statistics about the number of
     joggers.
  c) The dangers of jogging.
  d) The popularity of jogging in the
     U.S.A.

Injury cash for battered
wives soon
  a) Wives beaten by their husbands will
     soon get money as compensation.
  b) Beaten wives get together to raise
     money.
  c) Beating one's wife will soon be
     forbidden.
  d) Statistics about wives who were
     injured because they were beaten.

Tragedy of the slimmer
who loved nice clothes
  a) It is difficult to buy nice clothes when
     you're fat.
  b) A young person wanted to slim too
     much and died.
  c) The everyday problems of
     slimmers.
  d) The problem of a woman who
     bought too many clothes and ruined
     herself.

Cure that 'is worse than the problem'	a) A new drug has been discovered but it is far too expensive. b) A doctor criticizes the use of medicines in general. c) A widely used drug is found to cause more harm than good. d) People would face their problems better if they did not take drugs.
500 jobs to go	a) 500 jobs will be created as a factory opens. b) 500 persons will have to move to another town to keep their jobs. c) 500 jobs will be lost as a firm closes. d) The result of a study on the best 500 jobs.

Can you now speculate about the following titles?

It's fun to run at 80
Winning women
Call to end maximum penalties
Three of hearts

Exercise 6

Specific aim: To help the students to think about the key words or key ideas in the text.
Skills involved: Anticipation.
Why?   The students will be more ready (and find it easier) to read a passage if they have been prepared by thinking of the potential meanings and possible associations of some of the key words of the text. In this exercise, the students are given several words which do not necessarily appear in the text but which allude to the main events or ideas in the passage. Each student or group of students has a set of words and is asked to think of a story that might combine the ideas or events suggested by the words. This will lead the students to consider some possible associations between the words and even if no story in the class is remotely similar to the one that will be read, it will certainly help to motivate the students to read.

1 Work in groups of two. Look at the following words and think of a story that might combine them all. Then reorder the words according to the order in which they appear in your story. You can use any form of the verb and not necessarily the -ing one.

Examining	Sleeping	Rejecting
Rejoicing	Calling	Shutting up
Threatening	Plotting	Telling the truth
Eating	Fighting	Seizing

2 When you have decided upon a story, change partners and tell your story. Then listen to that of your partner. Ask each other as many questions as you can to learn further details or clarify some points.
3 Now read the text (see *The Unicorn in the Garden*, pages 215–16) and reorder the words according to what happens in the passage.
When you have finished, discuss the order you decided on with other groups.

Prediction and anticipation – further hints

– Matching titles of books and titles of chapters taken from those books.
– In order to help students develop a predictive strategy when reading, R. Young 'Predictive Reading', *MET*, Vol. 7, No. 3, suggests a way of dealing with a newspaper article:
  1 Give four photographs – corresponding to four different moments in the passage – to four groups and ask them to reorder them and invent a story illustrated by the pictures.
  2 Give the class a 'gapped text' which is interrupted after the conjunctions and link-words and ask the class to imagine what the text might be.

3.4 Skimming

Exercise 1

Specific aim: To prepare the students to skim by asking them to recognize the key sentences of a passage.

Skills involved: Identifying the main point or important
information.
Distinguishing the main idea from supporting
details.

Why? Training the students to recognize the key sentences
of a text is an essential preparation to skimming
since it will show them that (a) one sentence usually
sums up the gist of each paragraph and (b) this key
sentence often appears at the beginning of each
paragraph.

Here is the beginning of a short story by Roald Dahl (*The Way Up to
Heaven*). Skim through it and underline the sentence or the words that
best sum up the main idea of each paragraph (the key words or
sentences).

The Way Up To Heaven

All her life, Mrs Foster had had an almost pathological fear of missing a
train, a plane, a boat, or even a theatre curtain. In other respects, she was
not a particularly nervous woman, but the mere thought of being late on
occasions like these would throw her into such a state of nerves that she
would begin to twitch. It was nothing much – just a tiny vellicating muscle
in the corner of the left eye, like a secret wink – but the annoying thing was
that it refused to disappear until an hour or so after the train or plane or
whatever it was had been safely caught.

It was really extraordinary how in certain people a simple apprehension
about a thing like catching a train can grow into a serious obsession. At
least half an hour before it was time to leave the house for the station, Mrs
Foster would step out of the elevator all ready to go, with hat and coat and
gloves, and then, being quite unable to sit down, she would flutter and
fidget about from room to room until her husband, who must have been
well aware of her state, finally emerged from his privacy and suggested in
a cool dry voice that perhaps they had better get going now, had they
not?

Mr Foster may possibly have had a right to be irritated by this
foolishness of his wife's, but he could have had no excuse for increasing her
misery by keeping her waiting unnecessarily. Mind you, it is by no means
certain that this is what he did, yet whenever they were to go somewhere,
his timing was so accurate – just a minute or two late, you understand –
and his manner so bland that it was hard to believe he wasn't purposely
inflicting a nasty private little torture of his own on the unhappy lady. And
one thing he must have known – that she would never dare to call out and
tell him to hurry. He had disciplined her too well for that. He must also
have known that if he was prepared to wait even beyond the last moment
of safety, he could drive her nearly into hysterics. On one or two special
occasions in the later years of their married life, it seemed almost as though
he had *wanted* to miss the train simply in order to intensify the poor
woman's suffering.

Assuming (though one cannot be sure) that the husband was guilty,

what made his attitude doubly unreasonable was the fact that, with the exception of this one small irrepressible foible, Mrs Foster was and always had been a good and loving wife. For over thirty years, she had served him loyally and well. There was no doubt about this. Even she, a very modest woman, was aware of it, and although she had for years refused to let herself believe that Mr Foster would ever consciously torment her, there had been times recently when she had caught herself beginning to wonder.
(From Roald Dahl: *Kiss Kiss* (Penguin, 1963))

Exercise 2

Specific aim: To prepare the students to skim by asking them to give titles to short passages.

Skills involved: Skimming.
Identifying the main point or important information.

Why?   In itself, this exercise is not entirely an exercise in skimming since some of the passages will have to be read carefully in order to choose an appropriate title. However, the students can be encouraged to do the exercise as quickly as possible to see how quickly they can understand the gist of each article. Also, it is one way of drawing the students' attention to the importance of titles which are often sufficient to tell us whether or not the text is worth reading from our point of view.

Read the following articles as quickly as you can and decide which title is best suited to each of them.

SHERLOCK HOLMES would be proud of Dorothy Perry of Detroit, even though she tracked down a remarkably dim robber. Losing her handbag in a mugging, Ms Perry remembered that her purse held concert tickets as well as £40. She turned up at the show a few days later with a cop on her arm—and sure enough, the mugger was sitting in her seat.

A lucky meeting

Violence in Detroit

A clever policeman

A good detective

Daily Mail

A WEALTHY business man is giving £500,000 to help gifted children go to private schools.

Multi-millionaire Mr John James, 72, whose father was a miner, is sharing the cash between five Bristol schools— 61 years after he won a scholarship to the city's Merchant Venturers School.

The money will provide places for able children whose parents cannot afford the fees.

Ironically, Mr James's son David—who received £1,500,000 from his father in 1972—went bankrupt three weeks ago.

David, 35, blamed his failure on "bad judgment, bad timing, combined with lack of business acumen."

Daily Express

Business man gives £½ million to pay for bright children

A help to private schools

An unfortunate son

A gifted businessman

JESUIT priests have been invited back to China after 30 years' enforced exile, the order's Superior-General said yesterday. Through the French embassy in Peking it offered to reopen the former Jesuit Aurora University in Shanghai as a French-teaching medical school.

"They said they would welcome back the former professors," Father Pedro Arrupe said. "The Jesuits would be happy to return. and wish to serve China as they used to during the last 400 years." — Reuter.

The Guardian

New medical school in China

Jesuits to return to China

Diplomatic victory for France

Educational changes in China

By Our Science Correspondent
Hundreds of people made 999 calls to police stations throughout Britain early yesterday to report a fiery meteor. Many said they had seen a UFO.

P.c. John Forder. who was in a patrol car in the New Forest. reported a glowing light with a long orange tail. "After a second or two, it seemed to explode or disintegrate." It is thought to have fallen in the sea off the Isle of Wight.

About a million tons of meteoric rock and dust land on the earth each year. They are part of the primordial debris from which the solar system was formed some 5,000 million years ago.

The Daily Telegraph

Explosion in New Forest

UFO seen over Britain

Hundreds call police about meteor

Catastrophe near the Isle of Wight

Exercise 3

Specific aim: To show the students where to look for the main
                  information in the article.
Skills involved: Inference.
                  Predicting.
Why?   In order to be able to skim quickly and efficiently
                  through a text, students should know where to
                  look for the main information. This exercise aims at
                  showing them the importance of the first and last
                  paragraphs in an article and therefore to give them
                  the means of reading a newspaper more easily and
                  naturally, giving their whole attention only to what
                  they are really interested in.

Below, you will find the title and the first and last paragraphs of an article.
Can you find out what the article is about?

Travis Walton disappears

ONLY WEEKS after NBC had screened a programme on the Hill case in 1975, the strange tale surfaced of Travis Walton, an Arizona woodcutter who disappeared for five days in November 1975 after his colleagues claimed to have seen him taken aboard a flying saucer. As the Express recounted on February 24:

The moral is that UFOlogists should admit that there are two sides to even their best stories. And journalists should be more careful about trusting them.

The Sunday Times

The article tells us that:

☐ Travis Walton has never been found again.
☐ Travis Walton probably left in a U.F.O.
☐ There is no doubt that Travis Walton disappeared in a flying saucer.
☐ Travis Walton's friends probably killed him.
☐ Travis Walton and his friends probably lied, and he never really
  disappeared.

Exercise 4

Specific aim:
Skills involved: } Same as for exercise 3 but this time no possible
Why? } answers are provided.

On this page you will find the titles, the first paragraphs and the last
paragraphs of three articles.
Can you guess what each of them is about?

Teeth-prints make legal history

By Rob Rohrer

A HALF-EATEN Golden
Delicious apple, abandoned at
the scene of a fire, made legal
history last week in the Court
of Criminal Appeal when Karl
Johnson, a Southport dustman,
failed to have his conviction for
arson quashed.

People can lie
through their teeth, but their
teeth cannot lie."
(*The Sunday Times*)

How Ronnie Sharp shot from £8 to £295-a-week

RONNIE SHARP used to be an
unambitious part-time soccer
player in the Scottish League
with Cowdenbeath; his days were
divided between shift work down
the pit, soccer training and
sleep. On Saturdays came his big
day; the football match that
brought him £8 a week.

As his appearance on the football field becomes less youthful,
Sharp looks forward to managing a football club, or in his
homesick moments — running a
pub back in Scotland.

Frank Lodge

(*The Sunday Times*)

Fans run wild

SOCCER violence returned to Britain yesterday, the first day of the league season.

Arrests were made.

(*The Sunday Times*)

Exercise 5

Specific aim: To train the students to skim through a text.
Skills involved: Predicting.
                   Anticipating.
Why?   One way of skimming through a text is to look at
                   the beginning of each paragraph. The very first
                   words used often give us precious clues to the
                   discourse function as well as to the contents of what
                   follows.

The title, the first sentence and the first words of each paragraph of an
article have been given below. They should be enough to give you an
idea of the contents of the article. Tick the boxes corresponding to the
points that you think are mentioned.

Nuclear cloud spreads

PENNSYLVANIA came close to a nuclear catastrophe yesterday as the nuclear power station at Harrisburg started releasing radio-active steam into the air.
It all began ....
....
The probable cause ....
....
As in the 1950 catastrophe in ...
....

The situation today is still ......
....
However ....
....
Officials said ....
....
This happened just as ....
....
The new film describes ....
....
Let us hope ....
....

The article tells us/mentions:

no evidence
perhaps
yes

☐ ☐ ☐ other catastrophes of that kind have happened before
☐ ☐ ☐ why this accident happened
☐ ☐ ☐ the danger is now over
☐ ☐ ☐ the opinion of the workers in the station
☐ ☐ ☐ the opinion of the authorities
☐ ☐ ☐ a description of the accident
☐ ☐ ☐ a film was made of this accident
☐ ☐ ☐ a film about a nuclear catastrophe has just come out
☐ ☐ ☐ it should be a warning to all governments
☐ ☐ ☐ it is the first incident of this kind
☐ ☐ ☐ the situation should improve soon
☐ ☐ ☐ what the other dangers of a nuclear station are

Exercise 6

Specific aim: To train the students to skim through a text.
Skills involved: Predicting.
                    Anticipating.
Why?   The aim of this exercise is to encourage the weaker
                    students who tend to read slowly and never skim
                    through a text because they think there is too much
                    they do not understand. The idea here is to show
                    them that even a few words understood here and
                    there can be enough to understand what the passage
                    is about. In fact, it is what often happens when we
                    run our eyes over a text to get the gist of it.

You are skimming through an article in which most of the words are
unknown to you. Here are the ones you can understand, however:
professor
Institute of Biochemistry
hard-working man
results of experiments
published
confession
invention
different results
fraud
regrets it

Can you guess, from these few words, if the article is about
☐ a well-known professor who has just published his confessions
☐ a scientist who has admitted inventing the results of his experiments
☐ a scientist who has killed himself because he couldn't get the same
   results as everybody else
☐ a scientist who regrets the publication of the results of his experiments

Exercise 7

Specific aim: To train the students to skim through a text.
Skills involved: Predicting.
                    Anticipating.
Why?   Skimming through a text means that we do not
                    read each sentence, but rather we run our eyes over
                    the text, reading a few sentences here and there and
                    recognizing certain words or expressions as clues to
                    the function and ideas of what follows, thereby

making it unnecessary to read the text in detail. This exercise tries to re-create what happens when we are skimming through a text and aims to show students how much they can guess by simply looking at some of the sentences of the text.

In the following text, some paragraphs or sentences are missing. Read the whole passage and supply the missing sentences so as to get a coherent text.

A planned transport system?

In the past we have muddled through somehow over transport. Enormously bulky and heavy goods, which would be more suitable for rail, fill up the roads. On the other hand ....
....

Once quiet villages and country towns are filled with petrol fumes, and their inhabitants can hardly cross the road to get to a shop on the other side. In the cities ....
....

We have reached the point at which we must plan our transport. We must .... ;
we must plan and build roads to take an increasing volume of traffic, and arrange it so that our cities are not choked with cars and our villages ....
....
.... ?

One answer would be to make traffic tunnels underground leading to central car-parks, but this would be terribly expensive.
....

(From *Britain in the Modern World* by E. N. Nash and A. M. Newth)

Can you think of other answers?

Exercise 8

Specific aim: } Same as for exercise 7 but with a short story
Skills involved: } from which whole paragraphs have been taken
Why? } out. The students can be helped along by giving them several possibilities to choose from for each of the deleted passages.

The Model Millionaire is a short story by Oscar Wilde. Only short passages from it have been given below. But if you read them carefully they should allow you to get a general idea of what happens in the missing parts and to understand the story as a whole.
In order to check your understanding, can you *choose the answer or answers* that seem(s) most likely to you for each missing passage?

The model millionaire

PART I

a) In the first line of Part II, 'he' refers to the main character who has been presented at the beginning of the story. It is:
☐ Alan Trevor
☐ the Colonel
☐ Hughie
☐ a beggar

b) In Part I, the main characteristic in the description of the hero is that he is:
☐ not very handsome
☐ charming
☐ penniless and without a profession
☐ extremely intelligent

PART II

To make matters worse, he was in love. The girl he loved was Laura Merton, the daughter of a retired Colonel who had lost his temper and his digestion in India, and had never found either of them again. Laura adored him, and he was ready to kiss her shoestrings. They were the handsomest couple in London, and had not a penny-piece between them. The Colonel was very fond of Hughie, but would not hear of any engagement.

'Come to me, my boy, when you have got ten thousand pounds of your own, and we will see about it,' he used to say; and Hughie looked very glum in those days, and had to go to Laura for consolation.

PART III

In Part III, we are told that:
☐ Hughie unexpectedly meets his friend Trevor
☐ Hughie decides to pay a visit to his friend Trevor

PART IV

When Hughie came in he found Trevor putting the finishing touches to a wonderful life-size picture of a beggar-man. The beggar himself was standing on a raised platform in a corner of the studio. He was a wizened old man, with a face like wrinkled parchment and a most piteous expression. Over his shoulders was flung a coarse brown cloak, all tears and tatters; his thick boots were patched and cobbled, and with one hand he leant on a rough stick, while with the other he held out his battered hat for alms.

'What an amazing model!' whispered Hughie, as he shook hands with his friend.

'An amazing model?' shouted Trevor at the top of his voice; 'I should think so! Such beggars as he are not to be met with every day. *A trouvaille, mon cher*; a living Velasquez! My stars! what an etching Rembrandt would have made of him!'

'Poor old chap!' said Hughie, 'how miserable he looks!'

PART V	In the conversation in Part V: ☐ Hughie is sorry for the beggar because he is so poor ☐ Hughie envies the beggar ☐ Hughie tells Alan Trevor he works too much ☐ Hughie shows he is kind and generous
PART VI	'Well, I think the model should have a percentage,' cried Hughie, laughing, 'They work quite as hard as you do.' 'Nonsense, nonsense! Why, look at the trouble of laying on the paint alone, and standing all day long at one's easel! But you mustn't chatter; I'm very busy. Smoke a cigarette and keep quiet.' After some time the servant came in, and told Trevor that the framemaker wanted to speak to him.
PART VII	After Trevor leaves the studio: ☐ Hughie tells the beggar he admires him ☐ Hughie tells the beggar Trevor takes advantage of him ☐ Hughie gives money to the beggar ☐ Hughie gives his scarf to the beggar so that he won't be cold
PART VIII	Then Trevor arrived, and Hughie took his leave, blushing a little at what he had done. He spent the day with Laura, got a charming scolding for his extravagance, and had to walk home. That night he strolled into the Palette Club about eleven o'clock and found Trevor sitting by himself in the smoking-room drinking hock and seltzer. 'Well, Alan, did you get the picture finished all right?' he said, as he lit his cigarette. 'Finished and framed, my boy!' answered Trevor; 'and by the bye, you have made a conquest. That old model you saw is quite devoted to you. I had to tell him all about you – who you are, where you live, what your income is, what prospects you have –'
PART IX	In Part IX: ☐ Hughie is afraid the beggar will come to see him to beg for money ☐ Trevor pities the beggar ☐ Trevor thinks the beggar is romantic and doesn't pity him
PART X	'Alan,' said Hughie seriously, 'you painters are a heartless lot.' 'An artist's heart is his head,' replied Trevor; 'and besides, our business is

77

to realise the world as we see it, not to reform it as we know it. *A chacun son métier.* And now tell me how Laura is. The old model was quite interested in her.'

'You don't mean to say you talked to him about her?' said Hughie.

'Certainly I did. He knows all about the relentless Colonel, the lovely Laura, and the £10,000.'

'You told that old beggar all my private affairs?' cried Hughie, looking very red and angry.

PART XI

In this passage, Trevor tells Hughie:
- ☐ the beggar is in fact a rich and important person
- ☐ the beggar was furious because Hughie gave him something
- ☐ the beggar's real name is Hausberg
- ☐ the beggar used to be very rich but lost all his money the year before
- ☐ the beggar's clothes were just a disguise for the painting

---

PART XII

'I think you might have told me, Alan,' said Hughie sulkily, 'and not have let me make such a fool of myself.'

'Well, to begin with, Hughie,' said Trevor, 'it never entered my mind that you went about distributing alms in that reckless way; and when you came in I didn't know whether Hausberg would like his name mentioned. You know he wasn't in full dress.'

'What a duffer he must think me!' said Hughie.

'Not at all. He was in the highest spirits after you left; kept chuckling to himself and rubbing his old wrinkled hands together. I couldn't make out why he was so interested to know all about you; but I see it all now. He'll invest your sovereign for you, Hughie, pay you the interest every six months, and have a capital story to tell after dinner.'

'I am an unlucky devil,' growled Hughie. 'The best thing I can do is to go to bed; and, my dear Alan, you mustn't tell anyone.'

'Nonsense! It reflects the highest credit on your philanthropic spirit, Hughie. And don't run away. Have another cigarette, and you can talk about Laura as much as you like.'

However, Hughie wouldn't stop, but walked home feeling very unhappy, and leaving Alan Trevor in fits of laughter.

The next morning, as he was at breakfast, the servant brought him up a card on which was written, 'Monsieur Gustave Naudin, *de la part de* M. le Baron Hausberg.' 'I suppose he has come for an apology,' said Hughie to himself; and he told the servant to show the visitor up.

PART XIII

The man who comes
- ☐ wants Hughie to apologize to Baron Hausberg
- ☐ brings Hughie £1,000 from 'the beggar'
- ☐ brings Hughie £10,000 from 'the beggar'
- ☐ tells Hughie the Colonel has finally accepted his marriage with Laura

PART XIV

When they were married Alan Trevor was the best man, and the Baron made a speech at the wedding breakfast.

'Millionaire models,' remarked Alan 'are rare enough; but by Jove, model millionaires are rarer still!'

(From Oscar Wilde: *The Model Millionaire* in *Lord Arthur Saville's Crime and Other Stories* (Penguin, 1954))

Exercise 9

Specific aim:
Skills involved: } Same as for exercise 8 but this time no help is
Why? } given to the students.

Below, you will find several passages that represent about half of a short story by L. P. Hartley called *A High Dive*. After reading these passages can you guess what happens in the sections that were left out?

A high dive

The circus-manager was worried. Attendances had been falling off and such people as did come – children they were, mostly – sat about listlessly, munching sweets or sucking ices, sometimes talking to each other without so much as glancing at the show. Only the young or little girls, who came to see the ponies, betrayed any real interest. The clowns' jokes fell flat, for they were the kind of jokes that used to raise a laugh before 1939, after which critical date people's sense of humour seemed to have changed, along with many other things about them. The circus-manager had heard the word 'corny' flung about and didn't like it. Now they must change their style and find out what really did make people laugh, if people could be made to; but he, the manager, was over fifty and never good himself at making jokes, even the old-fashioned kind. What was this word that everyone was using – 'sophisticated'? The audiences were too sophisticated, even the children were: they seemed to have seen and heard all this before, even when they were too young to have seen and heard it.

'What shall we do?' he asked his wife.

....

....

....

'Those things upset everyone. I know the public came after it happened – they came in shoals; they came to see the place where someone had been killed. But our people got the needle and didn't give a good performance

79

for I don't know how long. If you're proposing another Wall of Death I wouldn't stand for it – besides, where will you find a man to do it? – especially with a lion on his bike, which is the great attraction.'

'But other turns are dangerous too, as well as dangerous-looking. It's *being* dangerous that is the draw.'

'Then what do you suggest?'

....

....

....

The manager stared at him.

'Can you now' he said. 'If so, you're the very man we want. Are you prepared to let us see you do it?'

'Yes,' the man said.

'And would you do it with petrol burning on the water?'

'Yes.'

'But have we got a tank?' the manager's wife asked.

'There's the old Mermaid's tank. It's just the thing. Get somebody to fetch it.'

While the tank was being brought the stranger looked about him.

'Thinking better of it?' said the manager.

'No, sir.' the man replied. 'I was thinking I should want some bathing-trunks.'

'We can soon fix you up with those', the manager said. 'I'll show you where to change.'

....

....

....

The manager was surprised and pointed to the ladder.

'Unless you'd rather climb up, or be hauled up! You'll find a platform just below the top, to give you foot-hold.'

He had started to go up the chromium-plated ladder when the manager's wife called after him: 'Are you still sure you want to do it?'

'Quite sure, madam.'

He was too tall to stand upright on the platform, the awning brushed his head. Crouching and swaying forty feet above them he swung his arms as though to test the air's resistance. Then he pitched forward into space, unseen by the manager's wife who looked the other way until she heard a splash and saw a thin sheet of bright water shooting up.

....

....

....

'Then I'm afraid we can't do business. But just as a matter of interest, tell us why you turned down our excellent offer.'

The man drew a long breath and breaking his long silence said,

'It's the first time I done it and I didn't like it.'

With that he turned on his heel and straddling his long legs walked off unsteadily in the direction of the dressing-room.

The circus-manager and his wife stared at each other.

'It was the first time he'd done it,' she muttered. 'The first time.'
Not knowing what to say to him, whether to praise, blame, scold or
sympathize, they waited for him to come back, but he didn't come.

'I'll go and see if he's all right', the circus-manager said. But in two
minutes he was back again. 'He's not there,' he said. 'He must have slipped
out the other way, the crack-brained fellow.'
(From *A High Dive* in *Two for the River and Other Stories* by L. P. Hartley)

Exercise 10

Specific aim: To train the students to skim through longer texts.
Skills involved: Skimming.
                   Anticipating.
                   Predicting.
Why?   This is a very common and useful activity which is
                   essential for, for example, choosing a book. We
                   rarely buy books simply by looking at the title and
                   author's name; we usually try to get some kind of
                   rough idea of what the book is about or of the way
                   it is written.

The following exercise is based on a collection of short stories
called *Modern Short Stories*, edited by Jim Hunter. But a similar
exercise can be done with any anthology.

Step 1: Look at the titles of the stories in this book and try to guess what
each story might be about. Then discuss your ideas with a friend.

Step 2: Skim through the book as quickly as you can, trying to find out
what each short story is about. Then try to match the titles in the
first column and the short descriptions in the second column.

1 Dylan Thomas: *The Peaches*

2 Geoffrey Dutton: *The Wedge-Tailed Eagle*

3 Katherine Mansfield: *Her First Ball*

4 Alan Paton: *Ha'penny*

5 Ted Hughes: *The Rain Horse*

6 James Thurber: *The Secret Life of Walter Mitty*

A A girl from the South of the United States goes North to join her fiancé. But she can't bear the life and the cold there and returns South.

B A poor, homeless boy in a reformatory invents a mother and a family for himself.

C A sailor returns home after being away 10 years, looking forward to seeing his family again. But when he arrives he finds that there has been a terrible catastrophe.

D A little boy sees his father operate on a young Indian woman who is having a baby.

81

7 James Hanley: *The Road*

8 Joyce Cary: *Growing up*

9 T. F. Powys: *Lie Thee Down, Oddity!*

10 Patrick O'Brian: *Samphire*

11 D. H. Lawrence: *Tickets, Please*

12 Ernest Hemingway: *Indian Camp*

13 F. Scott Fitzgerald: *The Ice Palace*

14 William Faulkner: *Go Down Moses*

15 Walter de la Mare: *The Wharf*

E A young boy visits his father who lives on a farm.

F A man comes back home and finds a change in his daughters.

G An 18-year-old country girl goes dancing for the first time.

H A woman remembers the time when she had a nervous breakdown.

I Twelve years later a man comes back to his home country but only finds disappointment and fear.

J Two Australian pilots decide to try and kill a large bird just for fun.

K A man's heroic dreams to escape from his boring and unsatisfactory life with his wife.

L A woman tries to kill her husband as they are gathering plants by the sea-side.

M The story of a perfect gardener who is also a saint and who chooses to do what is difficult and what may help others.

N A man tries to hide from an old Negro woman the fact that her grandson is going to be executed for murder.

O Several girls running a tramway line during the war decide to revenge themselves on the man who has not been faithful to them.

Skimming – further hints

– We do not necessarily skim through a text to get an idea of its contents. We may want to ascertain the structure of the passage, or the tone of the writer. It would therefore be interesting to use skimming exercises to cover these reading purposes as well.
– A variation of exercise 6 consists of giving a text and asking the students to underline all the words, expressions or sentences that they can understand. They will then be asked to use these elements to guess the main ideas of the passage.

3.5 Scanning

Exercise 1

Specific aim: To train the students to run their eyes over a text quickly in order to locate specific information.

Skills involved: Scanning.

Why? When we are trying to locate specifically required information, usually we need not read the whole text carefully. What we do is try to find in which paragraph the information we are looking for is likely to be, then read this paragraph with more attention.

One of your friends tells you she has found a perfect idea for the coming holidays and gives you the newspaper article where she found it. You read it quickly to learn more about this possibility.

This is what you want to find out:

The number of such houses

Price

Meals

How old the organization is

Name and address of the organization

Name of the founder

Number of people staying there each year

History takes a holiday

OUR FAMILY has just spent the weekend in a Gothic temple. It stands in the grounds of Stowe School, more than 200 years old and the work of the architect James Gibbs. It is one of more than a score of temples, follies and monuments placed to arrest and enchant the eye in the splendidly landscaped parklands that surround Stowe, the mansion.

Some of these vista-stopping set pieces have people living in them but most are empty and one or two are crumbling. But the Gothic temple has been beautifully restored and adapted as a holiday place by a discreet but extraordinarily effective organisation called the Landmark Trust, to whom the school has given a long lease.

Landmark started in 1965 by restoring one modest but attractive cottage in Cardiganshire. Now it has more than 60 buildings. Most are historic, some — like The Pineapple at Dunmore, Stirlingshire — bizarre, all attractive, and all, to a greater or lesser degree, previously unwanted.

Now each of them is structurally sound, sensitively restored, comfortable and convenient, at least for holiday use — and all very much wanted. More than 10,000 people stayed in "Landmarks" last year, and the trust is consantly having regretfully to turn people away — even though it almost never advertises.

At the start, the trust's founders were by no means sure it would work. John Smith—Coutts Bank director, former Conservative MP, National Trust council member and committed preservationist—had wanted for years to set up an organisation to preserve and *use* such attractive but neglected old buildings. He thought one good way would be to offer them as places for "mildly improving holidays." But he did not know whether the formula would catch on. It did. Demand for lettings has expanded almost exactly in line with the supply of buildings.

Getting old buildings used in this way is one of the things that makes Landmark different. People come and stay in them, sometimes for a couple of days, occasionally for several months at a time, but usually for one or two weeks. John Smith believes this is the key to appreciation.

"Simply opening a building to the public is very different from getting the public to stay in it. People get immeasurably more out of a building if they stay in it for a few days than if they simply dash up in a motor car."

The log-books visitors find and fill in at each Landmark property prove his point. "Warm days and moonlit nights . . . the comfort of owls and bells," wrote someone before us at the Gothic Temple.

"Repeated cries from above of 'Quick Mummy—it's a big ship!' are marvellous for legs and waistline," wrote one family staying at Luttrell's Tower, an 18th century folly on the Solent.

"We shall miss everyone in the snug, the log fire and the company, the beautiful walks and the welcome peace," testified visitors to the Harp Inn at Old Radnor. And our family, aged six to 42, found its Gothic weekend delightful and stimulating.

Rents of Landmarks are not cheap. They run from £4 a night for some in winter up to £150 a week in summer for the 8 bed, wonderfully positioned Fort Clonque at the tip of Alderney in the Channel Islands. The buildings range from a fully fledged Highland castle to a Victorian water tower in Norfolk, leased according to the Landmark handbook from a "public-spirited local landowner." The owner is not named, but the tower is not a million miles from Sandringham. They are almost all self-catering, but they are very well equipped. Electricity (or sometimes, in its absence, gas) is included; they are beautifully though modestly furnished; and each has local footpath maps and a shelf full of books chosen to help you enjoy your stay. Besides, careful

restoration of decaying or derelict properties is an expensive business.

The capital for this comes from another charitable trust set up by John Smith and his wife three years earlier, the Manifold Trust. Originally it existed to help local causes like village playing fields, church restoration appeals and Red Cross branches. But John Smith the banker made its money work and grow. In its first 14 years, Manifold distributed a staggering £3.8 million. Disbursements ranged from £1,000 to the Sail Training Association and £8,000 for pollution research at Nottingham University to £105,000 for HMS Belfast and £180,000 to the Maritime Trust.

The lion's share — currently about 70 per cent — goes, however, to Landmark to save and restore threatened or neglected buildings. Sometimes this is because they are unfashionable. When, on the urging of then Labour MP Peter Jackson, Landmark took on a cotton mill in Edale, there was very little interest in such industrial buildings.

"In general." says Smth. "we are not interested in any build-

ing that anyone else wants. Landmark isn't stamp collecting; it's a safety net."

A safety net that caught Lundy Island when the National Trust lacked the resources to administer it. A safety net that has saved 50 or 60 handsome and interesting buildings that would otherwise have crumbled. And a safety net that gives 10,000 people a year the pleasure of a very special experience.

Its founder used to include in his *Who's Who* entry the words: *Recreation—improving the view.* He has certainly preserved it. John Smith is not a trumpet-blowing chap, and Smith is a disguising sort of name. But since our landscape and townscape already rejoice in the lasting legacy of a "Capability" Brown and a "Greek" Thomson, future generations will surely give thanks for the enduring bequest of "Landmark" Smith.

● *Further information from: Landmark Trust, Shottesbrooke, Maidenhead. Berkshire.*
For The Landmark Handbook which gives details of all the trust's properties, send £1.00.

Tony Aldous

(*The Sunday Times*)

Exercise 2

Specific aim:
Skills involved: } Same as for exercise 1.
Why?

You're thinking of buying a cottage in the Cotswolds (or North Cotswolds) This is what you want:
- three bedrooms or more
- an old house you could modernize yourself
- in a small village
- price under £40,000

Look at the following page and circle the advertisement(s) corresponding to what you are looking for (if any).
Try to do this as quickly as you can.

ulate. Sitting room, kitchen/diner, 2 bedrooms, garage, delightful garden. £32,500. Legrand Brothers, 26, Market Sq., Blandford, Dorset (0258 51313).

AVON. Bristol 10 miles, M4/M5 3 miles. Magnificent detached house with outstanding accommodation. 3 Receptions, billiards room, luxury kitchen, 6 bedrooms, 2 bathrooms, sauna, solarium, central heating, outbuildings, garaging for 3 cars, extensive walled gardens with heated swimming pool, paddock with stabling, 2 bedroom bungalow. Substantial offers invited.—Bruton, Knowles & Co., 3/4, Ormond Terrace, Cheltenham. Tel.: (0242) 45081.

BEAUTIFUL BLACKMORE VALE, Dorset, in tranquil situation. Charming, spacious 17th century farmhouse, stone under thatched roof, many original features. Lounge 25ft dining room, 5/6 bedrooms, c.h., large outbuildings, about 1 acre. £65,000. Legrand Brothers, 26 Market Sq., Blandford, Dorset (0258 51313).

BEXHILL-ON-SEA. Well designed modern detached bungalow close Old Town, easy reach town centre and seafront. 27′ South lounge with open outlook, kitchen, 2 beds, bathroom, sep. W.C., garage, pleasant South garden. £27,500 freehold. Sole agents Abbott & Abbott, 9 Endwell Road, Bexhill (0424) 212233.

BEXHILL-ON-SEA. Excep. det. chalet bung. In quiet pos. Ent. hall, lnge, dngrm/bed 3, kit./bfst rm, bath., 2 sep. w.c.s, 2/3 beds, gas c.h., det. gge, pleas. gdns. £29,500 Fhld. E SHEATHER & Ptnr, 14, St Leonard's Rd. Tel. (0424) 210350 (3 lines).

BOURNEMOUTH, East Dorset, New Forest and coast. Free home finder with many. State requirements to ORMSTON'S 12, Poole Hill, BOURNEMOUTH and 12 offices. Tel. 0202-25671.

BOURNEMOUTH 7 MILES. ASHLEY HEATH. A remarkable contemporary house in semi-rural setting, outstanding architectural design with 3 bedrooms, gallery, 21ft. 6in. x 12ft. 9in. lounge/dining room, kitchen, car port, garage. Gas central heating, fully insulated. Natural terracotta flooring, fitted wardrobes and carpets. Many other features. Quoted £45,000 - £49,000 prior to Auction. Photographic brochure from LEGRAND BROTHERS, 22, Poole Hill, Bournemouth (0202) 291822

BOURNEMOUTH. Home on the Coast, from HAMMONDS Map and details senton application to 24, Poole Hill, Bournemouth 29422.

BRIDPORT outskirts, ¾ mile to sea: converted old world village Inn; carefully modernised: 4 double bedrooms: 4 receptions. 2 bathrooms: ½ acre mature garden facing south; outbuildings; mains services; ample street parking. Offers on £35,000. Phone Bridport 22718.

BUXTED, EAST SUSSEX (Victoria 70 minutes). Beautifully situated character house, secluded within its own landscaped gardens and grounds extending to about 3 acres, magnificent views to South Downs and Ashdown Forest. Entrance Lobby, Hall, Cloakroom, Sitting Room, Dining Room, Study, Kitchen. 4 Bedrooms, Bathroom, separate w.c. Integral Double Garage. Second Garage. Excellent Outbuildings. Delightful gardens with pond, lawns, paddock, small copse, flowering trees and shubs in great variety. Offers in region £77,500 invited for the Freehold. Sole Agents BRAXTON, WATSON AND COMPANY, UCKFIELD (0825) 3344.

CAMBRIDGE—Detached House 3 Beds. Good Garden. Garage. £32,000. Tel (0223) 50348.

ing-Stamford road). Stone built. Superbly modernised but retaining character. 3 reception rooms, 3 bedrooms, 2 bathrooms, double garage, separate playroom, 2 bedroomed Granny Flat and small secluded garden. £36,000. Tel: 0536 4823.

CHIPSTEAD. 19th century Lodge recently extended in grounds of about 3acres. including paddock & stables. 4 bedrms., bathrm., 3 rec. rms., brkfstrm/kitchen. Oil Ctl Htg. Large garage. £89,000. SUTCLIFFE & PTNRS. Chipstead, Surrey Downland 52251.

COTSWOLDS. In unspoilt village, 2 miles Chipping Norton, 6 miles Stow-on-the-Wold. Interesting detached small stone-built Period Cottage, having enormous potential for modernisation and enlargement, with garden and excellent small pasture paddock of about half-an-acre. Auction (unless sold) 1st June. TAYLER & FLETCHER, Estate Agents, Stow-on-the-Wold, Glos. (Tel. 0451 30383).

COTSWOLDS. 7 miles BROAD WATER COTTAGE SHERBORNE. Delightful well modernised cottage with superb unspoilt views across the Sherborne Brook Valley and Broadwater. Hall, Cloaks, 2 reception, kitchen, 3 beds, bath, garage. Lovely garden. Auction 12th June. RYLANDS. Telephone CIRENCESTER (0285) 3101/5.

COTSWOLD COTTAGE. Charming detached natural stone cottage property in a picturesque Cotswold Village with outstanding views. 2 Bedrooms, 19′ Sitting Room, Kitchen, Bathroom and attractive gardens. Offers in the region of £27,000. Further details from the owners Sole Agents Messrs. Coles, 11, Montpellier Terrace, Cheltenham. Tel. Cheltenham (0242) 27001.

DEVON. Lovely Dartmoor. 3-bed cottage with 3·3 acres, only 8 miles from Exeter. Auction June 6th. Full details from Leslie Fulford & Son, 6, Paris St., Exeter. tel. 52666.

DEVON/SOMERSET borders between Tiverton/Wellington. Charming detached country house with 3¼ acres garden/paddock. 3 bedrooms, bathroom, 2 reception and kitchen; garage and useful outbuildings. Absurdly low rates Auction 29th May (unless sold meanwhile). Illustrated details available from GRIBBLE, BOOTH & TAYLOR, Estate House, 12, Fore Street, Tiverton. Tel. 56041.

DORSET. Attractive Detached House in the Historic Hilltop Town of Shaftesbury famous for its views and walks. Ideal for retirement. Brick built with slate roof. 3 Bedrooms, Bathroom, Living Room, Dining Room, Kitchen. Manageable Garden with Greenhouse. Main Services. FOR SALE BY PUBLIC AUCTION 31st MAY, 1979. — CHAPMAN, MOORE & MUGFORD, Agents for West Country Property, 9, High Street, Shaftesbury, Dorset. Tel. 0747 2400

ESSEX/SUFFOLK BORDER. — Beautiful undulating countryside and unspoilt medieval villages. Properties from about £10,000 to £75,000. Please state requirements. — H. J. Turner & Son, 31a, FRIARS STREET, SUDBURY, SUFFOLK. tel. Sudbury 72833/4

EXETER, DEVONSHIRE. — UNIQUELY SITUATED COUNTRY HOUSE 5 minutes from city centre. 3 fine reception rooms, well kept kitchens, 5 principal bedrooms, 3 bathrooms, staff/granny suite. Oil central htg. Good garaging, stabling and other outbuildings. 4½ acres grounds. Offers invited from sole agents, The Lester Smith Partnership, 101, South St., Exeter (0392) 31276.

EALING, W.5. Det. 4 beds., 3 recpt., kit./bkfstrm., utility.

High Street, Blackpool Telephone (0253) 20087.

FINCHLEY/HENDON border. Mod. semi., 3 beds, 31ft. lounge, bathrm., 2 sep. w.c.s. Full gas C.H. Gge., gdn Freehold £38,000. Phone 346 8961.

FOLKINGHAM. A most charming village house with a classical Georgian Facade, situated in a delightful 17th Century Market Square, with views over rolling countryside to the rear.
Hall, 3 Reception Rooms, Domestic Offices, 5 Bedrooms, 2 Bathrooms, Box Room. Partial Central Heating. Former Brew House and Stable. Large walled Garden. Offers around £43,500. Strutt & Parker, Spitalgate House, London Road, Grantham. Tel. 0476 5886.

GLOS. Meyseyhampton, 7 miles East of Cirencester. Charming village house built 20 years ago. 4/5 bedrooms, 2 bathrooms, 2 reception, kitchen, etc. Mature garden with variety of fine trees and shrubs. About ½ acre. Offers over £60,000. W. H. Cooke & Arkwright, Berrington House Hereford (67213) or Rylands & Co., The Mead House, Cirencester (3101).

GRACIOUS DETACHED COUNTRY HOUSE in N. Dorset, natural stone under thatched roof, many fine features. Acquired by Henry VIII for Catherine Howard, since modernised, now in excellent order. Equally suitable for one family, or those with relatives seeking two adjoining self-contained units. 6 bedrooms, 2 bathrooms, 4 reception, 2 kitchens, cloakroom, garage, outbuilding, half-acre garden. £74,000. Legrand Brothers, 26, Market Sq., Blandford, Dorset (0258 51313).

GWENT (formerly Monmouthshire). A detached 2-bedroomed stone built bungalow, enjoying complete seclusion with unrivalled views over surrounding farmland. Situated within 5 mins. M4 access and Raglan village. Ideal holiday residence. Freehold. Offers invited around £10,000. Apply Digby Turner & Co., 21, Bridge Street, Usk, Gwent. Tel. Usk 2405

LIMPSFIELD: A delightful Detached Georgian Residence of Character fully modernised and renovated. 4 Bed. 2 Bath. 3 Rec. Clk. Utlyrm. Kit-Breakrm. Full Gas C.H. Gge. Almost ¼ Acre. Freehold. Offers in region of £65,000. Ibbett, Mosely, Card & Co., Oxted (tel. 2241), Surrey.

NEAR CREWKERNE, Somerset. A detached family house with paddock extending to nearly 1 acre in an edge of village position but with local shops, buses, etc., close by. Hall, living rom, dining room with inglenook fireplace, kitchen, bathroom, conservatory. 3 bedrooms. Gardens front and rear and paddock. Total area almost 1 acre. For Sale By Auction 16th May 1979. Price guide £20,000/£25,000. Gribble, Booth & Taylor, 1 Market Square, Crewkerne, Somerset. Tel: (0460) 73421.

NR. HORLEY, SURREY. Charming part period and fully modernised property with many fine features. 5 Beds. 3 Rec. 3 Baths. Bar. Sauna. C.H. ¾ acre. High walled garden. Offers over £75,000. Douglas-Smith & Co., High Street, Dormansland, Surrey. Lingfield 833817.

NR. MARLOW. Convenient M4/M40. Spacious Riverside Family House with superb Granny Annexe. 6 Beds. 2 Baths. Shower/Dressing Rm. 3 Recep 2 Kitchens. Clkrm. Double Garage, Oil C.H. 74ft. Direct River Frontage. Offers invited for the Freehold Price Guide

Market Square, Crewkerne. Tel.: Crewkerne (0460) 73421.

NEW FOREST. A spacious 5 year old family house in an elevated position on the edge of the New Forest within walking distance of the village centre and the main line railway station. Excellent views over open country. Cloakroom, L-shaped sitting/dining room, fully fitted kitchen, utility room, large television room (or fourth bedroom), three bedrooms, bathroom, gas-fired central heating, double garage and attractive walled garden. £59,500 FREEHOLD. Jackson & Jackson, The House on the Quay, Lymington, Hampshire. Telephone (0590) 75025.

NORTH COTSWOLDS, in charming unspoilt village 2 miles Stow-on-the-Wold. A high-quality and luxuriously appointed detached stone-built Bungalow Residence. Hall, Cloaks, Lounge, Dining Room, beautifully fitted Kitchen-Breakfast Room, Laundry Room, 3 fine Bedrooms, Bathroom, en suite Shower Room. C.H. Double Garage. Landscaped Garden of one-third Acre. Offers around £55,000 to include carpets, curtains and other extras. Tayler and Fletcher, Estate Agents, Stow-on-the-Wold. Tel. 0451 30383

NORTH-WEST HEREFORDSHIRE. Substantial family house in lovely rural position near Weobley with 1·3 acres. 4 bedrooms, bathroom, 2 reception rooms, kitchen, utility room, attics, mature garden, excellent outbuildings. Apply: W. H. Cooke & Arkwright, Berrington House, Hereford. (Tel: 67213.) Ref: TVB/RWD.)

OFFERS around £26,500 Heathfield, East Sussex. A particularly attractive detached bungalow, pleasantly and conveniently located. Hall, Sitting room, Kitchen/Breakfast room, 2 Bedrooms, Bathroom etc, gas central heating, Garage Workshop. Pretty Garden. Early Sale desired—recommended. Braxton, Watson & Co., Heathfield, tel. 2211.

PERTHSHIRE, COMRIE. Detached bungalow in picturesque village, comprising of hall; large L-shaped lounge/dining room, with picture window giving magnificent uninterrupted view to the hills; 3 bedrooms all with fitted wardrobes; master bedroom with toilet/wash-hand basin en suite; modern kitchen; bathroom with coloured suite; full central heating. Double Glazing. 80% floored loft with access by Ramsay ladder. Large heated single garage; ¼ acre flat easily maintained garden. Local amenities Golf, fishing (Salmon and Trout), bowls, 50 miles approximately from Glasgow and Edinburgh, Gleneagles 17 miles. Offers in excess of £32,000. For appointment to view please phone 076 47 538.

READING. Attractive Victorian house University area. 2 Rec., 4 Bed., 2 upper Bed., 3 WCs, gge, walled gdn. £45,000. Possession July. 0734 84294.

RENFREWSHIRE / NORTH AYRSHIRE border. Delightful Georgian family house with outbuildings and land. Beautiful rural location convenient to Glasgow and Central Belt. Viewing by appointment with the sole agents: R. & W. Hall, Chartered Surveyors, P.O. Box 48, Paisley. 041 889 8778/9.

ST. LEONARD'S-ON-SEA. — Gracious detached residence (1903) in attractive residential location. Main Hall, Clkrm. Kitchen Quarters, 2 Receptions, 6 Bedrooms, 2 Bathrooms. Garage Block, garden. Auction 6th June (Price Guide: £40,000.) BRAXTON WATSON & CO., BATTLE (04246 3333) SX.

SANDWICH BAY. Att. cottage-style bungalow near golf courses and private beach. 3

(*The Daily Telegraph*)

Radio 4 UK

200kHz/1500m
VHF: 92-95

6.0 am
News Briefing

6.10
Farming Today
6.25 Shipping forecast
long wave only

6.30 Today
Brian Redhead
with LIBBY PURVES
including at
6.45* Prayer for the Day
with
THE REV RICHARD HARRIES
7.0, 8.0 Today's News
Read by EUGENE FRASER
7.30, 8.30 News headlines
7.45* Thought for the Day

8.45 The School-mistress
A short story by
ANTON CHEKHOV
translated by
CONSTANCE GARNETT
Read by Geoffrey Beevers
Producer MAURICE LEITCH
8.59 Continental Travel
Information

9.0 News

9.5 Stereo
Baker's Dozen
Popular classics presen-
ted by Richard Baker
(Revised repeat of Satur-
day's broadcast at 7.30 pm)

10.0 News

10.5 From Our Own Correspondent
Producer PADDY O'KEEFFE
(Next edn: Mon 7.20 pm)

10.30 Daily Service
NEM, p 106; Teach me, O
Lord, the perfect way
(BBC HB 473); Psalm 23;
Matthew 24, vv 29-44 (AV);
The King of Love my
Shepherd is (BBC HB 475)

10.45
Morning Story
The Pagoda Room Victory
by MARGARET DANKS
Read by Eileen Barry
Producer JANE MARSHALL
BBC Birmingham

11.0
Down Your Way
Brian Johnston recently
visited Hastings in Sussex
Producer ANTHONY SMITH
BBC Bristol
(Revised rpt: Sun 5.15 pm)
11.40 Announcements

11.45
Listen with Mother
Story: Abigail Can't Sleep
by MOIRA MILLER
Presenters PAT GALLIMORE
and DAVID BRIERLEY
Written by RACHAEL BIRLEY
Producer JANET BOULDING

12.0 News

12.2 pm
You and Yours
Presenters Sue Cook
and George Luce

12.27 Stereo
The Enchanting World of Hinge and Bracket
(Broadcast Wed at 6.30 pm)
12.55 Weather; programme
news: long wave only

1.0 The World at One: News
Presenter
Julian O'Halloran

1.40 The Archers
(Broadcast Thurs 7.5 pm)
1.55 Shipping forecast
long wave only

2.0 News

2.2 Woman's Hour
from Birmingham
Introduced by
Maureen Staffer
Shakespeare Worldwide:
each year students from
all parts of the world
travel to Stratford-upon-
Avon to attend the Shake-
speare Summer School.
How is the Bard regarded
overseas? Does his appeal
change from country to
country? LIZ DANIELS re-
ports.
Tales from The Day Be-
fore Yesterday: HARRY
SOAN describes one of the
village characters he
knew in his youth.
Farmers in the Swim:
RICHARD CARRINGTON visits
a trout farm. He exam-
ines the techniques being
used and looks at the
prospects for this new
breed of farmers.
BBC Birmingham
Sabrina (4)

3.0 News

3.5
Afternoon Theatre
Till the End of the Plums
by JEREMY SANDFORD
This is a story of British
gypsies today and one
young gypsy in particular
who falls in love with a
gorgio, a non-gypsy girl.
with Andrew Branch
as Jim and
Petra Markham as Maggie
Ruben............ERIC ALLAN
Pub Governor.FRED BRYANT
Jim's mum.HILDA KRISEMAN
Prince........PETER BALDWIN
Jim's dad...GORDON DULIEU
Maggie's mum.EVA STUART
Other gypsies, gorgios,
police and security men:
JOE DUNLOP, KENNETH SHAN-
LEY, STEPHEN THORNE and
SHIRLEY DIXON
The play was recorded on
location in Epping Forest
and in the studio.
Directed by
RICHARD WORTLEY

4.0 News

4.5 Stereo
Vice Versa
Two modern poets, Roger
McGough and Brian Pat-
ten, talk to Michael Dean
about poetry, poets and
the pains and pleasures
of those who attempt to
' paint the colour of the
wind '.
Recorded before an in-
vited audience at The
Arvon Foundation, Tot-
leigh Barton, Devon
BBC Bristol

4.35 Story Time
Pigeon Post
by ARTHUR RANSOME
abridged in ten parts and
read by GABRIEL WOOLF (10)
Producer PAMELA HOWE
BBC Bristol

5.0 PM
with Robert Williams
and Gavin Scott
5.50 Shipping forecast
long wave only
5.55 Weather; programme
news

6.0 The Six O'Clock News
including Financial Report

6.30 Going Places
Railway Special
Presented by Barry Nor-
man live from the Golden
Hind High Speed Train
bound for Penzance,
plus Continental
Travel Informa-
tion.
Producer
GEOFF DOBSON
Editor ROGER
MACDONALD

FEATURE P15

7.0 News

7.5 The Archers
(Rptd: Mon at 1.40 pm)

7.20 Stereo
Pick of the Week
Margaret Howard presents
her selection.
Producer DAVID EPPS
(Repeated: Sat 10.30 am)

8.10 Profile
A personal portrait

8.30 Stereo
When Men and Mountains Meet
5: The Story of Alexander
Gardiner
with Joseph O'Conor
as Alexander Gardiner
Narrator John Rowe
with Fred Bryant
Godfrey Kenton
and Philip Sully
The most eccentric resi-
dent of Srinagar, the
capital of Kashmir, in the
1860s was a retired army
officer, Colonel Alexander
Gardiner. Eighty, or there-
abouts, six feet tall, and
dressed habitually in a
suit of tartan plaid, he
lived in oriental splen-
dour and to anyone pre-
pared to listen he would
tell his extraordinary
story – of his years rob-
bing and murdering in
the lawless tracts of Uz-
bekistan, of his tragic
marriage to an Afghan
princess, of his wander-
ings among the lofty
peaks of the Himalayas.
Was his story true, or
was it, as more than one
investigator came to be-
lieve, a colossal hoax?
A series of six program-
mes, adapted by JOHN
KEAY from his book When
Men and Mountains Meet.
Producer ALAN HAYDOCK
(Broadcast Thurs 11.0 am)

9.15 Letter from America
by Alistair Cooke
(Repeated: Sun 9.15 am)

9.30 Kaleidoscope
Presenter Paul Gambaccini
Producer CARROLL MOORE
9.59 Weather

10.0 The World Tonight: News
Douglas Stuart reporting

10.30 Stereo
The Grumbleweeds
Are you tired, bored and
listless? You're probably
watching too much tele-
vision. Listen instead to
the GRUMBLEWEEDS. You'll
still be tired, bored and
listless, but at least it
doesn't hurt your eyes.
Written by MIKE CRAIG and
RON McDONNELL
Producer MIKE CRAIG
BBC Manchester
(First broadcast on R2)

11.0
A Book at Bedtime
Some Do Not (10)
long wave only

11.15 The Financial World Tonight
long wave only

11.30 Travels of a Gentleman
3: Giro d'Italia
John Julius Norwich nar-
rates the third of six pro-
grammes tracing the
travelling habits of the
English abroad, from
Tudor times to the 19th
century. Readers LEONARD
FENTON, BRENDA KAYE and
PHILIP SULLY. Written by
MARY ANNE EVANS
Producer BRIAN COOK

11.45 Stereo
Just Before Midnight
Macbeth, or
Unlucky for
Some
A 13-minute
version of
SHAKESPEARE'S play by
JOHN WELLS, especially
written for recording at
the Edinburgh Festival
with
George Baker as Macbeth
Norma Ronald
as Lady Macbeth
and John Wells as a har-
assed Radio Director
The action of the play, as
is appropriate, takes
place in a BBC studio in
Edinburgh in front of a
passing audience.
First Witch/Son
AUDREY CAMERON
Second Witch/Nurse
MARGOT BOYD
Third Witch/Lady Macduff
GUDRUN URE
Duncan/First murderer/
Doctor............JACK MAY
Porter/First servant/Ban-
quo/Lennox/Malcolm
ROGER HAMMOND
Ross/Macduff/Second ser-
vant............FRASER KERR
Directed by GLYN DEARMAN

12.0 News
Weather report; forecast
followed by an interlude
12.15-12.23* am Shipping
forecast; Inshore forecast

VHF only
6.25 am Programme news

6.30-8.45 am
South West (& local MF):
Morning Sou'West
East:
Roundabout East Anglia

6.50-6.55, 7.50-7.55
Regional news; weather
North East and Cumbria:
Newstalk
with STUART PREBBLE

12.55-1.0 pm
(except London and SE)
Regional news; weather
1.55-2.0 Programme news

5.50-5.55
Regional news; weather

11.0-11.30
Study on 4
Children and Books
Five programmes
1: What's in it for Them?
AIDAN CHAMBERS looks at
ways of helping children
get the most from their
reading. With PROFESSOR
RICHARD HOGGART; MAR-
GARET SPENSER of the Lon-
don Institute of Educa-
tion; and poet ALAN
TUCKER. Series producer
JUDITH BUMPUS (Repeat)

(Radio Times)

86

Exercise 3

Specific aim:
Skills involved: } Same as for exercise 1.
Why?

Today is Friday and you are looking at the radio program to see what is on.

You would like to listen to a play, a novel or a short story. You will be away in the afternoon from 2 to 5 and you never listen to the radio late at night. (Not after 11 p.m.)

Quickly look at the programme and try to find out whether you will be able to listen to
– a play: ......
– a short story or a novel: ......

If you answer is yes, indicate at what time you will have to turn the radio on.

Exercise 4

Specific aim:
Skills involved: } Same as for exercise 1.
Why?

Consult the dictionary page to answer the following questions.
1 What is the simple past form of the verb 'to flow'? ....
2 What name is given to a rose that hasn't opened yet? ....
3 Is 'flown' the past participle of   ☐ flow
                                          ☐ fly
                                          ☐ flee
4 What word is 'flu' short for? ....
5 If you had to divide the word 'fluctuate' when writing it, which of the following divisions would be correct?
flu-ctuate fluc-tuate fluct-uate
fluctu-ate fluctua-te fl-uctuate
6 Flour is made from   ☐ seeds
                           ☐ flowers
                           ☐ vegetables
                           ☐ grains
7 What word is used to describe an exhibition of flowers?

....
8 A flue is used to carry   ☐ pipes
                                ☐ hot water
                                ☐ air

flour/fluff   330

flour /'flaʊə(r)/ *n* [U] fine meal, powder, made from grain, used for making bread, cakes, pastry, etc. □ *vt* [VP6A] cover or sprinkle with ∼. ∼**y** *adj* of, like, covered with, ∼.

flour·ish /'flʌrɪʃ/ *vi,vt* **1** [VP2A] grow in a healthy manner; be well and active; prosper: *His business is* ∼*ing. I hope you are all* ∼*ing*, keeping well. **2** [VP6A] wave about and show: ∼ *a sword.* **3** [VP2A] (of a famous person) be alive and active (at the time indicated): *When did the troubadours* ∼? □ *n* [C] ∼ing movement; curve or decoration, ornament in handwriting, eg to a signature; loud, exciting passage of music; fanfare: *a* ∼ *of trumpets*, eg to welcome a distinguished visitor.

flout /flaʊt/ *vt* [VP6A] oppose; treat with contempt: ∼ *sb's wishes/advice.*

flow /fləʊ/ *vi* (*pt, pp*∼ed) [VP2A,C] **1** move along or over as a river does; move smoothly: *Rivers* ∼ *into the sea. The tears* ∼*ed from her eyes. The river* ∼*ed over* (= overflowed) *its banks. Gold* ∼*ed* (= was sent) *out of the country.* **2** (of hair, articles of dress, etc) hang down loosely: ∼*ing robes; a* ∼*ing tie; hair* ∼*ing down her back.* **3** come from; be the result of: *Wealth* ∼*s from industry and economy.* **4** (of the tide) come in; rise: *The tide began to* ∼. ⇨ ebb. □ *n* (*sing* only) ∼ing movement; quantity that ∼s: *a good* ∼ *of water; a* ∼ *of angry words; the ebb and* ∼ *of the sea. The tide is on the* ∼, coming in.

flower /'flaʊə(r)/ *n* **1** that part of a plant that produces seeds. *in* ∼, with the ∼s out. '∼**-bed** *n* plot of land in which ∼s are grown. '∼ **garden**, one with ∼ing plants, not vegetables, etc. '∼**-girl** *n* girl who sells ∼s, eg in a market. '∼ **children**/

people, (colloq, in the 1960's) hippies favouring universal love and peace. '∼ **power**, the ideals of these people. '∼**·pot** *n* pot, eg of red earthenware or plastic, in which a plant may be grown. '∼ **show** *n* exhibition at which ∼s are shown (often in competition for prizes). **2** *the* ∼ *of*, the finest part of: *in the* ∼ *of one's strength; the* ∼ *of the nation's manhood*, the finest men. **3** ∼ *of speech*, ornamental phrase. □ *vi* [VP2A,C] produce ∼s: ∼*ing bushes; late-*∼*ing chrysanthemums.* **flow·ered** *adj* decorated with floral patterns: ∼*ed chintz.* ∼**y** *adj* (-ier, -iest) having many ∼s: ∼**y** *fields*; (fig) full of ∼s of speech: ∼**y** *language.* ∼**·less** *adj* not having, not producing, ∼s: ∼*less plants.*

flown /fləʊn/ *pp* of fly.

flu /fluː/ *n* (colloq abbr of) influenza.

fluc·tu·ate /'flʌktʃʊeɪt/ *vi* [VP2A,C] (of levels, prices, etc) move up and down; be irregular: *fluctuating prices;* ∼ *between hope and despair.* **fluc·tu·ation** /ˌflʌktʃʊ'eɪʃn/ *n* [U] fluctuating; [C] fluctuating movement: *fluctuations of temperature; fluctuations in the exchange rates.*

flue /fluː/ *n* [C] channel, pipe or tube for carrying heat, hot air or smoke to, from or through a boiler, oven, etc: *clean the* ∼*s of soot.*

flu·ent /'fluːənt/ *adj* (of a person) able to speak smoothly and readily: *a* ∼ *speaker;* (of speech) coming smoothly and readily: *speak* ∼ *French.* ∼**·ly** *adv* **flu·ency** /'fluːənsɪ/ *n* [U] the quality of being ∼.

fluff /flʌf/ *n* **1** [U] soft, feathery stuff given off by blankets or other soft woolly material; soft fur or down¹. **2** bungled attempt. ⇨ **2** below. □ *vt* **1** [VP6A,15B] ∼ *(out)*, shake, puff or spread out: ∼

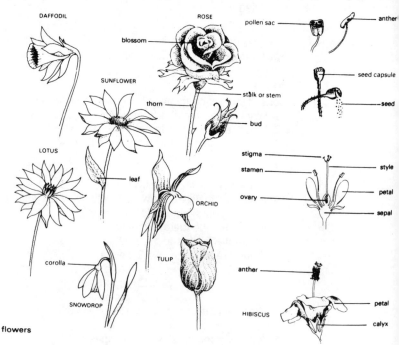

DAFFODIL
ROSE
blossom
SUNFLOWER
thorn
LOTUS
leaf
ORCHID
corolla
TULIP
SNOWDROP

pollen sac
anther
seed capsule
stalk or stem
seed
bud
stigma
stamen
style
ovary
petal
sepal
anther
petal
HIBISCUS
calyx

flowers

(From *Oxford Advanced Learner's Dictionary of Current English* by A. S. Hornby)

9 Which of the following words has different English and American
pronounciations? ☐ flown
☐ fluent
☐ flourish
☐ flour
10 You want to use the expression 'to be in the flower of one's strength'.
Can it be used in the plural (i.e. flowers)?

Scanning – further hints

- Similar exercises can be done with telephone directories, a page
of classified advertisements, train schedules, etc. When possible,
it is a good thing to set a time limit, trying to do so as naturally as
possible (e.g. you have a train to catch and you have only two
minutes to find someone's number in the telephone directory).
- Give the students a newspaper article and ask them to find what
information different persons (e.g. someone who is looking for a
job; a shopkeeper) might draw from it.

II · HOW THE AIM IS CONVEYED

1 Aim and function of the text

1.1 Function of the text

Specific aim: To train the students to recognize the function of the text.

Skills involved: Understanding the communicative value of the text.

Why?   It is impossible to understand a text if one is not aware of its function. When confronted by a new text students should be encouraged to find out its function *first*. The origin of the document, its presentation and layout are usually very helpful in determining its function, as can be seen in this exercise.

Match the following passages and their function:

We Request the Pleasure of your Company at a Party which will be given

at 21 Park Street, London

on June 19th. (7 p.m.)

1

Persuasion

Warning

Giving information

Giving directions

Invitation

Request

2

DO NOT USE K2r ON:
acetate • chamois • fur • latex • leather • plastic • rubber • suede • varnished surfaces • faille (rayon & cotton blend) • satin (rayon) • rayon • waterproofed fabrics.

3

Admission: Although the Museum of Fine Arts is a public museum, it is sustained not by government funds but by individual support. Membership subscriptions, gifts, and admission charges sustain this outstanding cultural resource.
Hours: Tuesday, 10 to 9; Wednesday through Sunday, 10 to 5. Closed Mondays, New Year's Day, July 4, Labor Day, Thanksgiving, December 24, and December 25.

Weekly Events and Schedule Changes: Dial A-N-S-W-E-R-S (267-9377) for a recorded listing. For further information call the Museum at (617) 267-9300.
Parking: Available off Museum Road adjacent to the building.

4

5

1. Squeeze K2r on the spot and work it in with your finger. (If spot contains water, dry it before using K2r.)

2. Let K2r dry completely to a powder. You may see a darkened area caused by the spot you are "lifting" out.

3. Brush away the powder and the spot is gone. No ring, no trace. Stubborn spots may need second application.

6

Unique and delicious salads and dressings, soup, magical frozen yogurt, juice and healthy shakes. Also hot vegetarian casseroles such as eggplant parmigiana and vegetable quiche.
Addresses:
1345 Avenue of the Americas
(55th St. between 6th and 7th Avenues)

1.2 Functions within the text

Specific aim: To train the students to recognize the function of sentences and utterances in a text.

Skills involved: Understanding the communicative value of sentences and utterances.

Why? Whereas a given text usually has one main function only, several language functions often appear within the text. It is sometimes easy to recognize the function (e.g. through the use of indicators such as an interrogative for a question) but in many cases it may prove more difficult (e.g. use of a statement to convey a suggestion). Exercises such as this one may help the students to become more conscious of the communicative value of utterances.

Read the following dialogue and match what the characters say and the functions listed underneath.

A Hello Jane!
B Hi Sue! How's life?
C Fine. But I've got to move next term. My room-mate's going and I can't find anyone else to share with.
D But why don't you keep looking? You've got another month and a half, haven't you?

E Yes, but I've never quite liked my room anyway. It's noisy and I'd much rather have something near your place.
F That's a good idea! It's really a lovely district to live in!
G Is it expensive?
H Rather, but if you start looking right away . . .
I Good, I will, and I'll give you a ring soon. Bye!
J Cheerio!

1 Demand for evidence
2 Agreement
3 Farewell
4 Asking for information
5 Greeting
6 Evidence (explanation)
7 Giving information

2 Organization of the text: different thematic patterns

2.1 Main idea and supporting details

Exercise 1

Specific aim: To sensitize the students to different ways of conveying the information in a paragraph.

Skills involved: Recognizing the technique used by the writer.

Why? Some exercises can be focused on the technique used by the writer in a given paragraph as a preparation to the study of the organization of a whole text. For instance, if one considers the opening paragraphs of most articles and stories, one finds that there are a number of types, e.g. starting with a question to catch the reader's attention, going directly to the main point, starting with an anecdote, etc.

Read the opening paragraphs of the suggested texts and decide which category they fall into.

	summary of the main point	question to hold the reader's attention	example	anecdote
It's like having a criminal record pages 187–8				
Faulty Winks pages 141–2				
Traveller gets $450 award page 210				
Programming people pages 28–9				
Botany Bay pages 47–8				

A similar exercise can be done with any paragraph in a text. This

93

will familiarize the students with the different possibilities of conveying a message (e.g. use of comparison, contrast, examples) as well as with the most common types of expansions. It will then be easier for the student to grasp the general organization of a given text.

Exercise 2

Specific aim: To train the students to consider the structure and coherence of a passage.

Skills involved: Understanding relations between parts of a text.

Why?   In this exercise students are asked to find out which sentence is out of place in the paragraph. This will oblige them to consider the topic of the passage and to find out (a) whether all sentences relate to this topic, and (b) whether the sentences follow each other naturally and logically.

Read the following passages and in each of them underline the sentence which does not belong.

In 1816, when she was 19, Mary Wollestonecraft was staying in Switzerland with her future husband – Shelley – and Lord Byron. They had read German short stories and decided to try to write their own. The result was a tale written by Mary and called 'Frankenstein'. It is the story of a scientist who creates a monster which will eventually destroy its creator. It was probably one of the first works of science-fiction. Mary's mother, Mary Godwin, had been one of the first feminists.

Mandrakes are plants that grow in Southern Europe. People used to associate them with magic and witchcraft. Mandrake juice was used by witches in lotions supposed to cause hallucinations. The flowers of the mandrake are white and the berries bright yellow. According to popular belief mandrake roots induced fertility in women and also grew under the gallows after a man had been hanged.

Exercise 3

Specific aim: To train the students to recognize the topic
sentences and the relation of the other sentences to
them.

Skills involved: Understanding relations between parts of a text.
Distinguishing the main idea from supporting
details.
Recognizing indicators in discourse.

Why? In order to read efficiently, one must be able to
recognize the topic sentences of the text, since they
carry the main information. One must also be able
to recognize the indicators which announce the
function of the sentences that are expansions of the
topic sentence (e.g. indicators announcing an
example, a restriction, a consequence, etc.) All the
questions in this exercise aim at drawing the
students' attention to these relations within the
text.

I don't know why UFOs are never sighted over large cities by hordes
of people. But it is consistent with the idea that there are no space
vehicles from elsewhere in our skies. I suppose it is also consistent with
the idea that space vehicles from elsewhere avoid large cities. However,
the primary argument against recent extraterrestrial visitation is the
absence of evidence.

Take leprechauns. Suppose there are frequent reports of leprechauns.
Because I myself am emotionally predisposed in favor of leprechauns, I
would want to check the evidence especially carefully. Suppose I find
that 500 picnickers independently saw a green blur in the forest.
Terrific. But so what? This is evidence only for a green blur. Maybe it
was a fast hummingbird. Such cases are reliable but not particularly
interesting.

Now suppose that someone reports: "I was walking through the
forest and came upon a convention of 7,000 leprechauns. We talked for
a while and I was taken down into their hole in the ground and shown
pots of gold and feathered green hats. I will reply: "Fabulous! Who else
went along?" And he will say, "Nobody," or "My fishing partner."
This is a case that is interesting but unreliable. In a case of such
importance, the uncorroborated testimony of one or two people is
almost worthless. What I want is for the 500 picnickers to come upon
the 7,000 leprechauns . . . or vice versa.

The situation is the same with UFOs. The reliable cases are
uninteresting ant the interesting cases are unreliable. Unfortunately,
there are no cases that are both reliable and interesting.
(From Carl Sagan: *Other Worlds* (Bantam, 1975))

1 Give a title to the passage.
2 If you had to pick out *one sentence* in the whole passage to sum up the main idea, which one would you choose?
3 Find the topic sentence of each paragraph.
4 Which words of the first paragraph do the second and third paragraph develop?
   2: ....
   3: ....
5 Find at least one instance of:
   – an illustration: ....
   – a restatement of an idea just mentioned: ....
6 What words are used to introduce the two illustrations given in the text?
   ....
   What words are used to introduce the conclusions drawn from these illustrations? ....
7 The following points are all mentioned in the text. Next to each of them, write down M if you think it represents a *main idea* in the passage and S if you think it is only a *non-essential, supporting detail*:
   – Space vehicles from elsewhere avoid large cities.
   – The primary argument against recent extraterrestrial visitation is the absence of evidence.
   – The author is emotionally predisposed in favour of leprechauns.
   – The fact that 500 picnickers saw a green light in the forest is terrific.
   – The green blur might have been a hummingbird.
   – Cases such as that of the picnickers are not interesting.
   – Someone said the leprechauns took him down their hole.
   – The man said his fishing partner was with him.
   – The reliable cases are uninteresting and the interesting cases are unreliable.

Exercise 4

Specific aim:
Skills involved: } Same as for exercise 3.
Why?

Calculator, calendar and clock

Even the cheapest and least complicated digitals are minor miracles of modern technology. They replace the traditional hands, springs and cogs with flickering digits and electronic circuits.

Some just display hours, minutes and seconds, but many function like baby computers. At the push of a button you can check the time in New York or New Dehli, see exactly how long Mario Andretti takes to lap a race track, set a small but shrill alarm, or even programme the watch, months in advance, to flash out a reminder about birthdays and other special dates. Some digitals have calendars that 'know' all about leap years and will remain accurate well into the 21st century.

Quartz, one of the world's most common minerals, lies at the heart of every digital watch. Almost a century ago, scientists discovered that quartz crystals vibrate at an absolutely constant frequency when an electric current is passed through them. But quartz digital watches did not become practical until miracles of miniaturisation were developed to save weight and room in spacecraft. The typical watch crystal, powered by a battery the size of a fingernail, vibrates 32,768 times every second. The vibrations are fed into a tiny 'chip' – little bigger than the end of a match – which is crammed with more than a thousand transistors and other components. This microscopic maze is the watch's 'brain' and can be designed to store a remarkable amount of information. But its most important single function is to keep dividing the vibrations by two until the quartz is pulsing precisely once every second.

Battery, crystal and chip combine to produce remarkably accurate watches whose timekeeping rarely strays by more than one or two seconds each month. They also tend to be very reliable, thanks to the absence of all the ticking machinery packed into a conventional clockwork watch.

If you fancy a digital watch, ask yourself how many of the tricks it performs are likely to be of genuine value. It makes no sense to spend extra money on what could become gimmicks once the novelty has worn off. (From *The Observer Magazine*)

Below, you will find the topic sentence of each paragraph of the text. Write underneath each of them
a) what expansions appear in the rest of the paragraph
b) what kind of relation these expansions have to the topic sentence (e.g. illustration, cause, consequence, supporting detail, rewording of the same idea, etc.)

TS 1 Even the cheapest and least complicated digitals are minor miracles of modern technology.

expansions	relation to TS

TS 2 many function like baby computers.

expansions	relation to TS

TS 3 Quartz, one of the world's most common minerals, lies at the heart of every digital watch.

expansions	relation to TS

TS 4 Battery, crystal and chip combine to produce remarkably accurate watches . . .

expansions	relation to TS

TS 5 If you fancy a digital watch, ask yourself how many of the tricks it performs are likely to be of genuine value.

expansions	relation to TS

Exercise 5

Specific aim: To train the students to find out the main idea of a passage.

Skills involved: Distinguishing the main idea from supporting details.

Why?   When the main idea of a paragraph is not actually stated, that is to say when there is no such thing as a topic sentence, the students may find it more difficult to decide what the general meaning of that paragraph is. It is therefore necessary to train them to find out the main ideas in passages of that type.

The first agent Leamas lost was a girl. She was only a small link in the network; she was used for courier jobs. They shot her dead in the street as she left a West Berlin cinema. The police never found the murderer and Leamas was at first inclined to write the incident off as unconnected with her work. A month later a railway porter in Dresden, a discarded agent from Peter Guillam's network, was found dead and mutilated beside a railway track. Leamas knew it wasn't coincidence any longer. Soon after that two members of another network under Leamas' control were arrested and summarily sentenced to death. So it went on: remorseless and unnerving.
(From J. Le Carré: *The Spy Who Came In From The Cold* (Pan Books, 1964))

The main idea of this passage is that
a) the police couldn't stop the murders of Leamas' men.
b) Leamas couldn't understand why so many people were killed.
c) Leamas knew someone was killing his agents.
d) the murders of Leamas' agents were savage and cruel.

The Hotel Taft was on a hill in one of the better sections of town. A wide street curved up past large expensive homes until it neared the top of the hill, then there was an archway over the street with a sign on the archway reading Taft Hotel and as it passed under the archway the street turned into the entranceway of the hotel. Benjamin drove slowly under the archway, then up the long driveway until he came to the building itself. He had to slow his car and wait in a line with other cars, most of them driven by chauffeurs, stopped by the entrance of the building for a doorman to open

the door for their passengers. When Benjamin was beside the entrance an attendant appeared at his car and pulled open the door.
(From C. Webb: *The Graduate* (Penguin, 1968))

The main idea of this passage is that
a) Benjamin was going to stay in the Taft Hotel.
b) The hotel Benjamin went to was a luxurious one.
c) There was an attendant waiting for Benjamin in the hotel.
d) Benjamin was impressed by the quality of the hotel.

Exercise 6

Specific aim: To train the students to discriminate between general and specific statements.
Skills involved: Distinguishing the main idea from supporting details.
Why?   Training the students to distinguish between generalizations and specific statements will often help them to find the main idea of a passage more quickly.

Look at the following statements and classify them according to their degree of generality.
a) Cats are extremely intelligent animals.
b) Siamese cats are believed to be more intelligent than others.
c) My neighbour's Siamese cat is exceptionally intelligent.
d) Some Siamese cats are just as intelligent as dogs.
e) My neighbour's Siamese cat can do all kind of tricks.

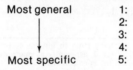

Most general   1:
                      2:
                      3:
                      4:
Most specific   5:

Exercise 7

Specific aim: ⎫
Skills involved: ⎬ Same as for exercise 6.
Why?   ⎭

On the following page you will find a number of statements. Decide first which ones are generalizations and second which ones are more specific statements. Then match the generalizations and the examples.
a) When I was young I could think of nothing but becoming a policeman.
b) Do you know the name of the product for which Scotch Tape is but a brand name?
c) The aim of advertisers is to create consumer wants.

d) The youths who attacked X in Chicago last week had all seen the ABC movie three nights before.
e) All children cherish a dream.
f) If the people who originally built many of our Eastern cities had been able to predict the automobile, there would certainly be less traffic problems nowadays.
g) Violence on TV is probably more harmful than we think.
h) Many of the problems one finds in city and suburban life result from a lack of proper planning.
i) So effective has brand advertising become that, for some products, the most familiar brand name is used to cover all similar items.
j) A producer of paper handkerchiefs recently launched a campaign to convince people they needed one box of tissues in each room of their house.

Generalizations:						
Specific statements:	↑	↑	↑	↑	↑	↑

Exercise 8

Specific aim: To help the students to find out how the text and the paragraphs are organized.
Skills involved: Understanding relations between parts of a text.
Why?   Matching paragraphs and their main ideas or function is a simple and useful way of sensitizing the students to the way the different points of a text are organized.

Tit-for-tat Hindi letter irks doctor

A NORTH Wales family doctor was not amused when his letter in Welsh to a local hospital was answered in Hindi.

Dr Carl Clowes, of Llanaelhern, Gwynedd, sent a middle-aged woman patient with a knee injury for x-ray, along with a referral note describing the symptoms, to the Caernarvon and Anglesey hospital at Bangor. The reply, signed by a Dr L. J. Price and written in Hindi, arrived by post.

Dr Price later described the letter as 'a bit of fun'. He was not Welsh-speaking and his two Indian colleagues in the casualty department certainly did not understand Welsh. 'It's a bit of fun really, our way of asking Dr Clowes to write to us in English. We do not always have time to get his letters translated, especially as many nurses do not speak Welsh.'

Dr Clowes is unrepentant. 'This is an insult not only to myself and my patient but to the Welsh language. All my patients are Welsh-speaking and it is their first language. It is a matter of principle in an area where the vast majority of people are Welsh-speaking.' He has complained to the health authorities and to his MP.

Mr Robert Freeman, administrator of the Gwynedd area health authority said yesterday that Welsh and English were equally valid. 'But a lot of our medical staff are English or foreign, although we do try to ensure that there is always a competent Welsh speaker on hand in the casualty department.' Dr Clowes could continue to write his letters in Welsh and in future he would receive a reply in Welsh.

(Ann Clwyd, *The Guardian*)

Match the paragraphs and the ideas.
para. 1 The facts
para. 2 The Welsh doctor's opinion
para. 3 Dr Price's opinion
para. 4 Summary of the article
para. 5 Conclusion of the 'case'
What is the common structure of paras. 3, 4 and 5?
 first sentence =
 rest of the paragraph =

Exercise 9

Specific aim: To help the students to find out how the text is organized.

Skills involved: Distinguishing the main points of the text and completing a diagram.

Why?   One way of drawing the students' attention to the way the text is organized is to give them a skeleton structure of the text which they are asked to complete. For instance, the following outline for the text entitled 'Just Call Him 181213 3 1234 5' simply indicates that the text is made up of an introduction and two parts, each of them divided into a number of sub-parts (or containing a number of points).

Decide what the main points of the text are and complete the skeleton structure given below.

Just Call Him 181213 3 1234 5

BY 1975, nine years ahead of Orwellian projections, every West German citizen may be officially known to his government by a twelve-digit number. The government has sent the Bundesrat (upper house of parliament) a proposal that would identify each person by six digits indicating his birth date, a seventh his sex and the century of his birth, the next four to distinguish him from others born on the same day, and the last a "control" number — which would make Chancellor Willy Brandt Number 181212 3 1234 5 or something very close to that. The number will follow a person from birth until 30 years after his death when,

presumably, he would be expunged from the computers.

The government explains the move on the grounds that its voluminous registration system is being computerized. It also hopes to eliminate the confusing snarls that sometimes arise in a country where many people have the same surname (there are 600,000 Müllers alone in West Germany). Israel and the Scandinavian countries already have such systems, and a number of others, including Japan, are preparing to follow suit.

As most Germans seem to see it, bureaucratization is already so pervasive that the new system could not be any worse. "We are already over-numbered," wrote Munich's respectable *Süddeutsche Zeitung*, "and who would have objections to a simpli-

GOETHE & SCHILLER BY THE NUMBERS

fication of the system?'' As it is, anyone moving from one city to another in West Germany must fill out an 18-inch-long questionnaire, in triplicate, first to deregister and then again to reregister. But not everyone is pleased with the name-to-number switch. In an opinion poll about the change, 31% protested. ''I have been a number long enough as a soldier and a prisoner of war,'' said a retired policeman. ''I want to keep my name.''

(*Time*)

Introduction:
I
   A
   B
   C
II
   A
   B

Exercise 10

Specific aim: ⎫ Same as for exercise 9 but this is an easier version
Skills involved: ⎬ of the exercise since the different points of the
Why?   ⎭ text, out of order, are given together with the
               skeleton outline of the structure.

Can you reorder these different points in the skeleton structure given below?

Reactions against the project in Germany
Reasons given by the government
Presentation and explanation of the project
Supporting argument: the example of other countries
Reactions in favour of the project in Germany

What German people think of the idea
The project will reduce the possibility of errors
Computers are being used nowadays in registration

Introduction:

I
  A
  B
  C

II
  A
  B

2.2   Chronological sequence

Exercise 1

Specific aim: To help the students to understand the chronological sequence in a text.

Skills involved: Selective extraction of relevant points from the text.

Why?   This exercise will oblige the students to refer back to the text to check in what order the events took place and it is one way of drawing their attention to the chronological organization of the passage.

(See 'It's like having a criminal record' pages 187–8). After reading the text complete the sentences with one of the following words: before, after, when, since, while, during, as soon as

a)   Michael left school .... getting his A levels.

b)   .... he was at the London School of Economics, Michael did not work very hard.

c)   .... entering the Warburg Institute, Michael Godfrey brilliantly got his degree.

d)   .... his year in Canada, Michael thought that getting a job was no problem.

e)   .... his year in Canada, Michael found it was very difficult to get a job.

Exercise 2

Specific aim: To help the students to study the chronological
                  sequence in a text.
Skills involved: Understanding relations between parts of a text.
Why?   In order to be able to rebuild a passage whose
                  different parts are given out of order, the students
                  will have to study the time adverbs, the system of
                  reference and the chronology of events which help
                  to make the text coherent.

Can you reorder the following frames so as to get a coherent story?

a)

b)

c)

d)

© 1962 United feature Syndicate Inc.

(From *Nobody's Perfect Charlie Brown* by Charles Schultz)

The right order is: ....

It is also possible to combine this exercise with a matching exercise
(see pages 135ff). The speech balloons are then cut out and both the
text and the pictures are presented out of order and have to be
reorganized. For such an exercise cartoons in which the pictures are
more or less interchangeable obviously must be avoided.

Exercise 3

Specific aim:
Skills involved: } Same as for exercise 2.
Why?

Here is a recipe for sherry trifle. But the instructions are not in the right order. Can you reorder them?

Serves 8   Time taken: 45 minutes
Chill for several hours

Ingredients
6 trifle sponge cakes   100g ratafias
raspberry jam   1½dl sweet sherry

For the custard:
6 egg yolks
50g castor sugar   a few drops of vanilla essence
3½ tsp flour   toasted flaked almonds
½l cream

a) Draw off the heat, add the vanilla essence and allow to cool for a few moments.
b) Split the sponge cakes and spread with jam.
c) Separate the egg yolks into a basin. Add the sugar and cornflour. Mix the ingredients.
d) Pour over the soaked sponge cakes and leave until cold. Chill for several hours. Then sprinkle with the toasted flaked almonds just before serving.
e) Cut in pieces and place them in a large dish. Add the ratafias and pour over the sherry.
f) Heat the cream in a saucepan until very hot, then draw off the heat and gradually stir into the egg mixture. Mix well and put the custard into the saucepan. Put over low heat and stir until it thickens. Do not let it boil.
g) Set aside for 30 minutes while preparing the custard.

The right order is: ....

Exercise 4

Specific aim:
Skills involved: } Same as for exercise 2.
Why?

Here is the opening page of a novel by Charles Webb, *Love, Roger* (Penguin, 1970). But the various sentences or paragraphs have been jumbled. Can you reorder them?
a) The man looked over at her, then back at me. 'She's just leaving.'
b) I got there just as it was closing. On the other side of the glass doors a man was turning a key in the lock. 'Sir?' I said.
c) 'I thought you were open till six.'
d) 'I have some stationery to pick up,' I said. 'I could just run in, pick it up, then run out.'
    'We're closed,' he said.
e) The reason I had to go to Filene's was to pick up some stationery with my name on it, which I had ordered a few weeks before. During the middle of the afternoon I called up to find out if the stationery was ready, and I should have found out how late the store was open.
f) I stepped nearer and moved my shoe ahead so the door stuck on it. 'I had a letter to write tonight. I wanted to be able to write it on personalized stationery.'
g) 'Five-thirty.'
h) He pointed at some letters on the door that said the store closed at five-thirty, then turned and started walking away.
i) The woman took her bag and started over towards the door. As she approached, the man opened it for her, then stood and held it as she walked out.
j) 'Sir?' I said again, putting my face up the crack between the doors. 'We're closed,' he said.
k) I pointed over to one of the counters inside where a woman was being handed a package. 'I see a customer in there,' I said.
l) He stopped, turned around and came partway back towards the doors. 'We're closed,' he said.

Exercise 5

Specific aim:
Skills involved: } Same as for exercise 2 but the sentences of two
Why? different stories have been jumbled.

Here are two very short stories. But the sentences of each story are out of order and the two stories have been mixed. Can you separate the sentences belonging to story 1 from those belonging to story 2 and then reorder the sentences so as to get two meaningful stories.
a) His friend was upset and told him to hurry up.
b) 'When I make out my report it will be easier to write "King Street" as the place of occurrence.'
c) 'Whatever are you doing that for?' asked a bystander.

d) Two burglars broke into a bank.
e) He replied: 'Don't worry. It will take a bit longer, but we'll drive the fingerprint department crazy.'
f) The policeman replied with a knowing look:
g) One went up to the safe, took off his shoes and socks and started moving the combinations with his toes.
h) A horse had dropped dead in a street named Nebuchadnezzar Street and a policeman was laboriously dragging it round the corner into the next street.

Story 1: ....
Story 2: ....

2.3 Descriptions

Exercise

Specific aim: To help the students to find out how a description is organized.

Skills involved: Selective extraction of relevant points from a text. Understanding relations between parts of a text.

Why? Some texts – mainly descriptive ones – are organized so that the reader may visualize the scene. But this can be done in many different ways. The aim of this exercise is to make the students aware of the way the information is presented in such texts.

Read the following passages and decide which type(s) of organization they represent.

down ↓ up	up ↓ down	outside ↓ inside	inside ↓ outside	details ↓ general impression	general impression ↓ details
1					
2					
3					
4					
5					

Can you think of other ways the details could be organized?

1
Howards End,
Tuesday.

Dearest Meg,
It isn't going to be what we expected. It is old and little, and altogether

delightful – red brick. We can scarcely pack in as it is, and the dear
knows what will happen when Paul (younger son) arrives tomorrow.
From hall you go right or left into dining-room or drawing-room. Hall
itself is practically a room. You open another door in it, and there are the
stairs going up in a sort of tunnel to the first floor. Three bedrooms in a
row there, and three attics in a row above. That isn't all the house really,
but it's all that one notices – nine windows as you look up from the front
garden.
(From E. M. Forster: *Howards End* (Penguin 1941))

2 The largest building, in the very centre of the town, is boarded up
completely and leans so far to the right that it seems bound to collapse at
any minute. The house is very old. There is about it a curious, cracked
look that is very puzzling until you suddenly realize that at one time, and
long ago, the right side of the front porch had been painted, and part of
the wall – but the painting was left unfinished and one portion of the
house is darker and dingier than the other. The building looks
completely deserted. Nevertheless, on the second floor there is one
window which is not boarded; sometimes in the late afternoon when the
heat is at its worst a hand will slowly open the shutter and a face will
look down on the town.
(From C. McCullers: *The Ballad of the Sad Café* (Penguin, 1963))

3 I entered. It was a very small room, overcrowded with furniture of the
style which the French know as Louis Philippe. There was a large
wooden bedstead on which was a billowing red eiderdown, and there
was a large wardrobe, a round table, a very small washstand, and two
stuffed chairs covered with red rep. Everything was dirty and shabby.
There was no sign of the abandoned luxury that Colonel MacAndrew
had so confidently described.
(From W. Somerset Maugham: *The Moon And Sixpence* (Pan, 1974))

4 The house itself was long and low, as if a London house holidaying in
the country had flung itself asprawl; it had two disconnected and roomy
staircases, and when it had exhausted itself completely as a house, it
turned to the right and began again as rambling, empty stables, coach
house, cart sheds, men's bedrooms up ladders, and outhouses of the
most various kinds. On one hand was a neglected orchard, in the front
of the house was a bald, worried-looking lawn area capable of
simultaneous tennis and croquet, and at the other side a copious and
confused vegetable and flower garden . . .
(From H. G. Wells: *Marriage* (Macmillan and Co, 1912))

5 Woodleigh Bolton was a straggling village set along the side of a hill.
Galls Hill was the highest house just at the top of the rise, with a view
over Woodleigh Camp and the moors towards the sea . . . The house
itself was bleak and obviously Dr. Kennedy scorned such modern
innovations as central heating. The woman who opened the door was
dark and rather forbidding. She led them across the rather bare hall and
into a study where Dr. Kennedy rose to receive them. It was a long,
rather high room, lined with well-filled bookshelves.
(From Agatha Christie: *Sleeping Murder* (Bantam, 1976))

Descriptions – further hints

The same kind of exercise can easily be done by asking the students to compare several portraits (e.g. the description can go from top to bottom, from general appearance to details, from the most striking features to the less striking ones, etc.)

2.4   Analogy and contrast

Exercise 1

Specific aim: To help the students to understand comparisons
                     made in the text.
Skills involved: Understanding relations between parts of a text.
Why?   Asking the students to fill in a comparison table is a
                     good way of clarifying the analogy or contrast
                     developed in the passage.

1   Read the text called 'The Classification of Species' and fill in the table below:

e.g. class	vehicles
order	
family	
genus	

2   Can you draw a tree diagram to represent the different types of vehicles? Think of as many branches as you can besides the ones mentioned in the text.

The Classification of Species

The group *species* is the starting point for classification. Sometimes smaller groups, *subspecies*, are recognized, but these will not concern us until we discuss evolution. There are many larger groups: genus, family, order, class, phylum, and kingdom.

Let us begin with the first seven species. We belong to the genus *Homo* and to these more inclusive groups: (1) the family Hominidae (hoh·MIN·ih·dee), which includes, in addition to *Homo*, extinct men not of the genus *Homo*, and (2) the order Primates (pry·MAY·teez), which includes also the lemurs, monkeys and apes. The three cats – lion, house cat, and tiger – belong to the genus *Felis*. In general we can think of a *genus* as a group of closely related species. The three cats also belong to the family Felidae (FEE·lih·dee). Generally a *family* includes related genera (in the table, this is shown only in the case of the two genera of robins).

The first seven species, different enough to be put in three orders, are yet

Common name	Species name	Genus	Family	Order	Class	Phylum	Kingdom
Man	Homo sapiens	Homo	Hominidae	Primates	Mammalia	Chordata	Animalia
Lion	Felis leo	Felis	Felidae	Carnivora			
House cat	Felis domesticus	Felis	Felidae				
Tiger	Felis tigris	Felis	Felidae				
Dog	Canis familiaris	Canis	Canidae	Carnivora			
Gopher	Thomomys bottae	Thomomys	Geomyidae	Rodentia			
Gopher	Spermophilus tridecimlineatus	Spermophilus	Sciuridae	Rodentia			
American robin	Turdus migratorius	Turdus	Turdidae	Passeriformes	Aves		
European robin	Erithacus rubecula	Erithacus	Turdidae				
Gopher turtle	Gopherus polyphemus	Gopherus	Testudinidae	Chelonia	Reptilia		
Green frog	Rana clamitans	Rana	Ranidae	Salientia	Amphibia		
Bullfrog	Rana catesbeiana	Rana	Ranidae				
Paramecium	Paramecium caudatum	Paramecium	Parameciidae	Holotricha	Ciliata	Protozoa	

alike in many ways. All are covered with hair, they nurse their young with milk, and their red blood cells are without nuclei. Because of these and other resemblances they are combined in a still more inclusive group, Class Mammalia (ma·MAY·lih·ah). A *class*, therefore, is composed of related orders.

Biologists have classified all of the known animals and plants in the way just described. Their system of classification not only shows how organisms are related to one another, but it also conveys much information about the organisms themselves. This can be brought out by analogy. Suppose you are told that object X belongs to a group 'vehicles'. Even if you have never seen this particular X you would be able to make some very general predictions about its structure and function. It would probably have wheels or runners, be used for carrying objects or people, and so on. If you were then told that X belongs to a more specific group, 'vehicles with internal combustion engines', you could make more specific predictions. It would probably have spark plugs and pistons and use a fuel derived from petroleum. If you were told that X is an 'automobile' you would be able to make still more specific predictions. Finally, if you were told that X is a 'Ford automobile' you would know a great deal more about it. The group, Ford, might be thought to correspond to the group, genus, in biological classification. The many kinds of Fords would correspond to the various species within a genus.

(From *Biological Science, An Inquiry into Life* by Biological Sciences Curriculum Study)

Exercise 2

Specific aim:
Skills involved: } Same as for exercise 1.
Why?

Read the following text and complete the table given below.

Imagine a piece of land twenty miles long and twenty miles wide. Picture it wild, inhabited by animals small and large. Now visualize a compact group of sixty human beings camping in the middle of this territory. Try to see yourself sitting there, as a member of this tiny tribe, with the landscape, your landscape, spreading out around you farther than you can see. No one apart from your tribe uses this vast space. It is your exclusive home-range, your tribal hunting ground. Every so often the men in your group set off in pursuit of prey. The women gather fruit and berries. The children play noisily around the camp site, imitating the hunting techniques of their fathers. If the tribe is successful and swells in size, a splinter group will set off to colonize a new territory. Little by little the species will spread.

Imagine a piece of land twenty miles long and twenty miles wide. Picture it civilized, inhabited by machines and buildings. Now visualize a compact group of six million human beings camping in the middle of this territory. See yourself sitting there, with the complexity of the huge city spreading out all around you, farther than you can see.

Now compare these two pictures. In the second scene there are a hundred thousand individuals for every one in the first scene. The space has remained the same. Speaking in evolutionary terms, this dramatic change has been almost instantaneous; it has taken a mere few thousand years to convert scene one into scene two.
(From Desmond Morris: *The Human Zoo* (Corgi Books, 1970))

	scene 1	scene 2
land		
human beings		
other living creatures		
your feelings		
what people do		

2.5   Classification

Exercise 1

Specific aim: To help the students to understand a text based on a classification.

Skills involved: Understanding relations between parts of a text.

Why?   It is important to encourage the students to draw tree diagrams to visualize the information contained in a text. It will help them to see at once the main points of the text and the relations between them. Obviously, tree diagrams are particularly well adapted to texts based on classifications.

Read the following passage and complete the tree diagram below with the words given underneath.

Anthropology

We shall outline the four major subfields of anthropology that have emerged in the twentieth century: physical anthropology, archeology, linguistics and cultural anthropology.

Physical anthropology deals with human biology across space and time. It is divided into two areas: paleontology, the study of the fossil evidence of the primate (including human) evolution, and neontology, the comparative biology of living primates, including population and molecular genetics, body shapes (morphology), and the extent to which behavior is biologically programed.

Archeology is the systematic retrieval and analysis of the physical remains left behind by human beings, including both their skeletal and cultural remains. Both the classical civilizations and prehistoric groups, including our prehuman ancestors, are investigated.

Linguistics is the study of language across space and time. Historical linguistics attempts to trace the tree of linguistic evolution and to reconstruct ancestral language forms. Comparative (or structural) linguistics attempts to describe formally the basic elements of languages and the rules by which they are ordered into intelligible speech.

Cultural anthropology includes many different perspectives and specialized subdisciplines but is concerned primarily with describing the forms of social organization and the cultural systems of human groups. In technical usage, ethnography is the description of the social and cultural systems of one particular group, whereas ethnology is the comparison of such descriptions for the purpose of generalizing about the nature of all human groups.

(From D. E. Hunter and P. Whitten: *The Study of Anthropology* (Harper and Row, 1976))

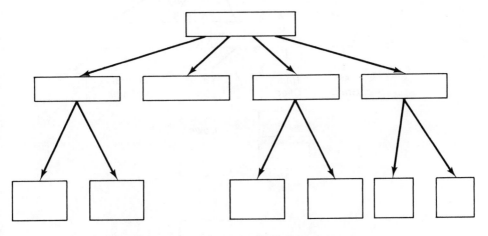

ethnology
archeology
structural linguistics
physical anthropology
neontology
anthropology

historical linguistics
cultural anthropology
linguistics
paleontology
ethnography

Exercise 2

Specific aim:
Skills involved: } Same as for exercise 1 but some of the boxes have
Why? } been filled to help the students.

After reading the text on pages 143–6, can you complete the following tree diagram where some of the boxes have been left empty?

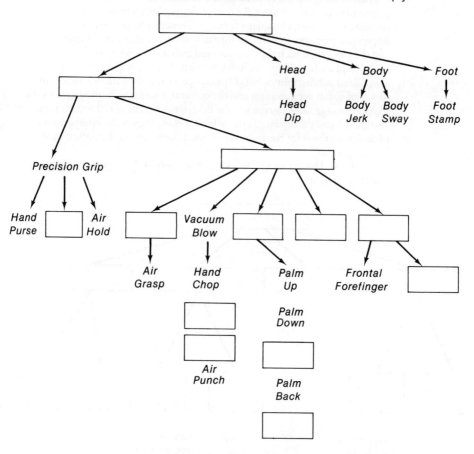

Exercise 3

Specific aim:
Skills involved: } Same as for exercise 2
Why?

Read the text on page 155 which describes eighteenth-century houses in London. Then complete the diagram below showing the different types of housing.

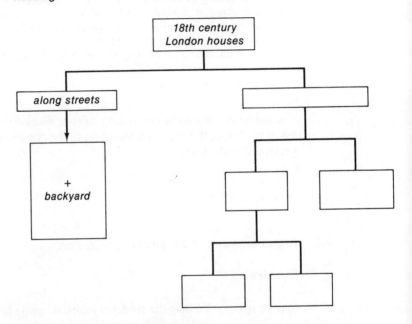

Exercise 4

Specific aim:
Skills involved: } Same as for exercise 1 but no frame is given this
Why? time.

In the following passage, Bertrand Russell explains one of the examples Plato gives of the method of division. After reading the passage, can you draw a tree diagram to represent the various categories mentioned in the text and find an example of what could appear at the end of each branch of the tree.

The term to be defined is angling. To begin with, angling is an art, so that the arts constitute the first category. We may divide them into arts of production and arts of acquisition, and angling evidently belongs to the latter. Acquisition is now divided into cases where its objects give consent,

and where they are simply captured. Again, angling belongs to the second of these. Capture can be divided into open and concealed, angling being of the latter kind. The things taken can be inanimate or living; angling is concerned with living things. The animals in question may live on land or in a fluid, and again the term to be defined belongs to the second class. Inhabitants of fluids may be birds or fish, fish may be caught by net or by striking, and you may strike by night or day. Angling is done in daylight. We may strike from above or below, and angling is the latter kind. Retracing our steps and collecting all the differences, we define angling as the art of acquiring by concealed capture animals that live in water, catching by day and striking from below. The example is not to be taken too seriously, it is chosen because the sophist may also be taken as an angler, his quarry being the souls of men.
(From Bertrand Russell: *Wisdom of the West* (Macdonald, 1959))

Classification – further hints

The students can also be given three or four diagrams or trees and asked to choose the one corresponding to the classification presented in the text.

2.6 Argumentative and logical organization

Exercise 1

Specific aim: To help the students to discriminate between 'for' and 'against' arguments in a text.
Skills involved: Understanding the communicative value of sentences.
            Understanding more or less explicitly stated information.
Why?   In many argumentative passages, the various arguments presented can be found throughout the text, so that all the reasons given in favour of the point being discussed as well as those against it are not necessarily found together. An exercise of this type can be useful to help the students think about the meaning and value of the ideas expressed in the text.

In the following text, several arguments are presented for or against canned food. Decide whether the arguments contained in the underlined sentences are for or against food canning.

One of the first men to make a commercial success of food conservation was Henry John Heinz. He started by bottling horse-radish, and he was so successful that in 1869 he founded a company in Pittsburgh, USA. Like other Americans of his generation, Heinz made his name a household word throughout the western world. <u>At last, man seems to have discovered how to preserve food without considerably altering its taste.</u> } a

The tins of food (Heinz tins!) which Captain Scott abandoned in the Antarctic were opened 47 years after his death, and the contents were not only edible, but pleasant.

The main argument against conserved foods is not that the canning of food makes it taste different; rather, people complain that <u>the recipes which the canning chefs dream up are tedious or tasteless. But</u> } b

<u>any recipe is tedious or tasteless when it is eaten in great quantities. And a</u> } c

company like Heinz can only produce something if it is going to be eaten in great quantities. The tomato is very pleasant to eat when it is freshly picked. A regular diet of tomatoes alone could well prove tedious. The canning companies try to cook the tomato in as many ways as possible. The Heinz factories in Britain use millions and millions of tomatoes every year. They claim that if all the tomatoes were loaded on to 15-ton lorries, the line of lorries would stretch for 60 miles.

But <u>there are many people who do not like to eat food out of season.</u> They like their } d

food to be fresh, and they like to cook it themselves in "the old-fashioned way". But <u>it is very difficult for modern man to realise what it is like to live without the advantages of pre-packaged and canned food.</u> } e

European society in its present form could not cope without modern methods of food processing. Imagine your local supermarket without all the cans of pre-packaged foods. <u>There wouldn't be much variety left,</u> } f

and <u>what was left would have to be increased enormously in order to give the same amount of food.</u> } g

<u>The supermarket would turn into a chaos of</u> rotting } h

vegetables, stale bread and unhealthy meat. <u>The health problems would be insurmountable,</u> unless we } i

all went back into the country to support ourselves.

So next time you reject canned food as being tasteless or unimaginative, remember that you can only afford to eat fresh food because canned food exists.

Epicurus

(From *Current 9*)

Arguments for: ....

Arguments against: ....

Exercise 2

Specific aim: } Same as for exercise 1 but the students have to
Skills involved: } draw up a list of all the arguments presented in
Why? } the text.

You're thinking of having your windows double glazed. You want to
consider all the aspects of the problem before making up your mind.
Read the following article and draw up a list of all the points you can find
for and against double glazing.

Double Glazing

Presumably you have already insulated your roof and walls if you are considering double glazing? In an 'ordinary' home you lose 25 per cent of heat through the roof and 35 per cent through the walls, so they must be your priorities unless your house is made of windows.

New buildings now have to meet new standards of insulation and are often fitted with double glazing when built, especially since the Government's Save It campaign. Usually this factory-made double glazing does not just add to the comfort but is very well designed and actually looks quite good.

Still, it's a difficult decision to double glaze an existing home, since you're going to have to spend a lot of money on what, in an ordinary small house with smallish windows, will save you about 10 per cent of the heating bill. And that's if you install sealed units.

Of course there are other benefits besides the financial one. The room will be much more comfortable. You won't get a chilly feeling when sitting near the window and draughts will be fewer. So on the whole, if the wherewithal exists, double glazing is not a foolish enterprise, though even good double glazing won't be as effective as a brick wall!

Double glazing is not just 'Double Glazing'. There are several ways of achieving it. You can install Replacement Windows with two sheets of single glass or twin-sealed units. Or you can have Secondary Windows, either hinged to the existing window or sealed to it. Secondary windows are cheaper, can often be installed by the owner, but are not likely to be so efficient as replacement windows.

The simplest form of DIY double glazing is the applied frame method which means fixing a second pane of glass directly on to the original frame using beading or special frame sections. The most important thing is that the second leaf should be completely sealed, and that the seal should be long-lasting.

Points to check are: that condensation will not occur between the two panes; that you will be able to open 'openable' windows (or that you're prepared to give up that luxury); that you will (or won't) want to be able to clean the window and that you have some other form of ventilation.

If you think that by double glazing

you automatically insulate against sound too — think again. To have a noise insulating effect the two leaves will need a gap of 110 mm or 200 mm (the wider the gap the better) so double glazing with noise insulation needs to be specially made. It is more difficult to make it look nice and to fit it into the existing window openings. With this gap it won't work as well for heat insulation unless thicker glass is used. So unless you live directly under Concorde's flight path it will hardly be worth insulating for sound.

(From *The Observer Magazine*)

Exercise 3

Specific aim: To help the students to understand the organization of a discursive passage.

Skills involved: Understanding relations between parts of a text.

Why?   The exercise consists of completing a diagram which visualizes the organization of the whole text and also indicates (in small boxes) the link-words or indicators that introduce the different parts or arguments. This kind of exercise usually requires a close study of the text, but it can be made more or less difficult by the following adaptations:
  – one can give a partly-filled frame to the students and ask them to complete it
  – one can give everything except the link-words (or give only the link-words)
  – one can give the frame only
  – advanced students can be asked to draw the diagram themselves.

After reading the text called 'The last bus to Donington-on-Bain' can you complete the diagram that follows?

The last bus to Donington-on-Bain

JOHN FRYER reports on the local problems of a national crisis—how people without cars can move about in the country

LAST MONDAY the little village of Donington-on Bain, deep in the Lincolnshire wolds, lost its last contact through public transport with the outside world. Once, Donington (pop. 236) boasted its own railway station. That closed a generation ago, and on April 1 the two bus services, to Lincoln in one direction and Louth in the other, were withdrawn. Now the villagers of Donington, a third of whom do not own a car, face a three-mile trek for the nearest bus route.

Lincolnshire is not good bus country, with the population scattered around in little pockets over the flat, rich farmland. The buses have to cover long distances from place to place carrying only a few passengers at a time. The bus companies argue that they don't make enough money on these journeys, and that even using the

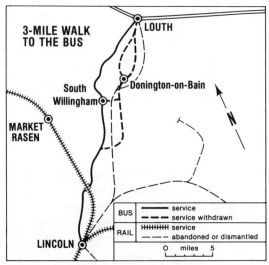

money they make on the busy routes to pay for the less busy ones they can't make ends meet. So they cut back the services. There are fewer buses. Fewer people find the service they need. For some the car has taken over.

In 1952 21% of people travelled by rail, 45% by bus and 34% by car. In 1970 9% went by rail, 14% by bus and 77% by car.

But what about the 14% who still use the buses? What are they going to do when the services stop?

It came as a shattering blow to Donington-on-Bain. "They've got no right to leave us here without a bus," said Eva Traves, a 56-year-old housewife who has lived in the village for 36 years. "We've ever such a lot of elderly people here. How are they going to get out?

"My husband Ron was in hospital at Louth recently and I visited him every day. I couldn't do that now, unless somebody took me in their car. The nearest bus is at South Willingham, three miles away."

Donington's local councillor, Charles Turner, was one of the first to be hit by the lost service. Unlike Ron Traves, who rides on a scooter to the local gravel pit to work, he cannot drive. "There were two committee meetings in Louth this week," he said. "I couldn't get there." Turner says that some 35 per cent of the Donington people, especially in the old people's bungalows and the council houses, do not have a car.

All hope, however, is not lost. Louth Rural District Council is trying to persuade a local firm to run a bus service to and from Donington two days a week. The trouble is that it will not do so unless the council underwrites the costs at the rate of £7 a day. The council has refused, but its clerk, Bryan Spence, is trying to talk the firm into having a few experimental runs to see what happens.

Unless something is done, the drain of people from the villages to the towns will continue, which cannot be healthy. If there are more people in the villages it will be easier to justify running buses to them. Many councillors seem to cling to the mistaken belief that all villagers are two-car families, when in fact many do not even have one.

(*The Sunday Times*)

Organization of the text

Here is a possible way of completing the diagram.

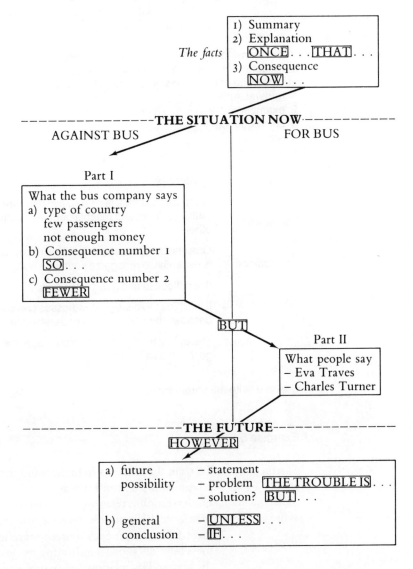

1) Summary
2) Explanation
   ONCE . . . THAT . . .
3) Consequence
   NOW . . .

The facts

— — — — — — — — — — — — — THE SITUATION NOW — — — — — — — — —

AGAINST BUS   FOR BUS

Part I

What the bus company says
a) type of country
   few passengers
   not enough money
b) Consequence number 1
   SO . . .
c) Consequence number 2
   FEWER

BUT

Part II

What people say
– Eva Traves
– Charles Turner

— — — — — — — — — — — — — — — THE FUTURE — — — — — — — — — — — — —
HOWEVER

a) future   – statement
   possibility   – problem THE TROUBLE IS . . .
                 – solution? BUT . . .

b) general   – UNLESS . . .
   conclusion   – IF . . .

Exercise 4

Specific aim: To train the students to understand the logical
                  relationships within a text.
Skills involved: Understanding relations between parts of a text.
Why?   This is a complex exercise since the students must
                  first relate the sentences to their function within the

text, and then decide which words could introduce each part. This will oblige them to actively re-create the author's reasoning.

In the following text, the sentences have been separated from their introductory link-words and both have been jumbled. All you know is that the following points appear in the text, in this order:
1 general truth
2 example
3 consequence
4 restriction
5 conclusion

Link-words:	*Sentences*:
However	In the Carlisle trial, last year, two different witnesses, both intelligent and reliable persons, contradicted each other.
This is why	
But	
For instance	One should always bear in mind that additional evidence is essential to recognize someone guilty.
	It is difficult to find good witnesses.
	It is difficult to disregard witnesses completely, partly because they can help us understand the truth.
	The police tend to look for more dependable proofs of guilt, such as fingerprints.

Can you write the paragraph?

Exercise 5

Specific aim:	To train the students to understand the logical relationships within a passage.
Skills involved:	Understanding relations between parts of a text.
Why?	When working on this exercise, students will be forced to consider each sentence carefully and look for 'clues' or 'signals' indicating its possible place in the text and its relationship with the other passages.

Can you reorder the following sentences so as to form a coherent paragraph?
a) We should not dismiss Malthus too quickly, however.
b) But certain directions of developments are clear and suggestive of our future problems.
c) There are few people today who agree with the Malthusian theory in its original form.
d) It is hard enough to understand those we already face.

e) A large part of the world population still lives in hunger, just above starvation level.
f) No one can predict exactly what our main problems will be in the next generation or two.
g) The reason may be that he didn't know about the advances in technology and transportation which have increased food production and made it possible to use in one part of the world what has been produced in another.
h) One certainly will be the difficult balance between man and the natural resources on which he depends.
i) Because of these historical facts, the English economist Robert Malthus declared in 1798 that population tends to grow more quickly than food supplies.
j) Despite the enormous increase of the world population since his day, his theory is no longer feared.
k) Time after time, the population of certain areas has developed so quickly that there was not enough food available, which brought about starvation and social disorders.
l) In the foreseeable future, world food production will be enough for the population.

Now look at the text again and underline all the words and expressions that helped you find the articulation of the passage.

Exercise 6

Specific aim: ⎫ Same as for exercise 3 but the text is more
Skills involved: ⎬ complex and its organization is both
Why? ⎭ argumentative and logical.

Read the following text and complete the diagram.

Tighten Your Belt

The fact is that the energy crisis, which has suddenly been officially announced, has been with us for a long time now, and will be with us for an even longer time. Whether Arab oil flows freely or not, it is clear to everyone that world industry cannot be allowed to depend on so fragile a base. The supply of oil can be shut off at whim at any time, and in any case, the oil wells will all run dry in thirty years or so at the present rate of use.

New sources of energy must be found, and this will take time, but it is not likely to result in any situation that will ever restore that sense of cheap and copious energy we have had in the times past. We will never again dare indulge in indiscriminate growth. For an indefinite period from here on in, mankind is going to advance cautiously, and consider itself lucky that it can advance at all.

To make the situation worse, there is as yet no sign that any slowing of the world's population is in sight. Although the birthrate has dropped in some nations, including the United States, the population of the world

*How the aim is conveyed

seems sure to pass six billion and perhaps even seven billion as the twenty-first century opens. The food supply will not increase nearly enough to match this, which means that we are heading into a crisis in the matter of producing and marketing food.

Taking all this into account, what might we reasonably estimate supermarkets to be like in the year 2001?

To begin with, the world food supply is going to become steadily tighter over the next thirty years – even here in the United States. By 2001, the population of the United States will be at least two hundred fifty million and possibly two hundred seventy million, and the nation will be hard put to expand food production to fill the additional mouths. This will be particularly true since the energy pinch will make it difficult to continue agriculture in the high-energy American fashion that makes it possible to combine few farmers with high yields.

It seems almost certain that by 2001 the United States will no longer be a great food-exporting nation and that, if necessity forces exports, it will be at the price of belt-tightening at home.

This means, for one thing, that we can look forward to an end to the 'natural food' trend. It is not a wave of the future. All the 'unnatural' things we do to food are required to produce more of the food in the first place, and to make it last longer afterward. It is for that reason that we need and use chemical fertilizers and pesticides while the food is growing, and add preservatives afterward.

In fact, as food items will tend to decline in quality and decrease in variety, there is very likely to be increasing use of flavouring additives. Until such time as mankind has the sense to lower its population to the point where the planet can provide a comfortable support for all, people will have to accept more artificiality.

Then, too, there will be a steady trend toward vegetarianism. A given quantity of ground can provide plant food for man or it can provide plant food for animals which are later slaughtered for meat.

In converting the tissues of food into the tissues of the feeder, up to 90 percent is used for reasons other than tissue maintenance and growth. This means that one hundred pounds of plant food will support ten pounds of human tissue – while one hundred pounds of plant food will support ten pounds of animal tissue, which will then support one pound of human tissue. In other words, land devoted to plant food will support ten times as many human beings as land devoted to animal food.

It is this (far more than food preferences or religious dictates) that forces overcrowded populations into vegetarianism. And it will be the direction in which the United States of 2001 will be moving – not by presidential decree, but through the force of a steady rise in meat prices as compared with other kinds of food.

This, in turn, will come about because our herds will decrease as the food demand causes more and more pastureland to be turned to farmland, and as land producing corn and other animal fodder is diverted to providing food directly for man. And in the suburbs, lawns and gardens will be converted into vegetable plots as was done during World War II. They will be 'survival gardens,' rather than 'victory gardens.'

Another point is that it is not only energy that is in short supply. A shortage of oil means a shortage of plastics; a shortage of electricity means a shortage of aluminium. We are also experiencing a shortage of paper and most other raw materials.

This means that, for one thing, our generosity in wrapping, bagging and packaging will have to recede. There will have to be at least a partial return in supermarkets to the old days where goods were supplied in bulk and ladled out in bags to order. It may even become necessary to return bags, as we once returned bottles, or pay for new ones.

A decline in per-capita energy use will make it necessary to resort to human muscle again, so that the delivery man will make a comeback (his price added to that of the food, of course). Since energy shortages will cause unemployment in many sectors of the economy, there will be idle hands to do the manual work that will become necessary.

From an energy-saving standpoint, it would make far more sense to order by phone and have a single truck deliver food to many homes, than for a member of each home to drive an automobile, round-trip, to pick up a one-family food supply.

To be sure, it will not all be retrogression. Even assuming that Earth is in a desperate battle of survival through a crisis of still-rising population and dwindling energy reserves, there should still continue to be technological advances in those directions that don't depend on wasteful bulk-use of energy. There will be continuing advances in the direction of 'sophistication', in other words.

Most noticeably, this will mean a continuing computerization and, where possible, automation of the economy.

By 2001, we can imagine devices that will make the phoned-in order more versatile and more precise. We might imagine a centralized supermarket catalog, issued once a year, that lists, with description and price, all that is in stock. If you want peas, you will very likely get peas in a plain package, minimally marked – or just a bag, filled by a computerized device responding to the size of your order.

(From an article by Isaac Asimov)

A possible way of completing the diagram is shown on page 126.

Argumentative and logical organization – further hints

– When using diagrams, the students can be asked to number the paragraphs of the text and, under each of the boxes in the diagram, write down the number(s) of the corresponding paragraph(s).
– The students can be asked if all the boxes of such a diagram are equally important and if some of them could be taken out without changing the main idea of the passage.
– The following procedure can also be of interest: After the students have filled the diagram with the help of the text, they can be asked to write a text again, looking only at the diagram. (Obviously this should be done with shorter texts.) It can then be interesting to compare the various texts produced in the class.

Here is a possible way of completing the diagram.

The facts:
a) Energy crisis
difficult to depend
on oil

new sources of energy
can't solve the problem

To make matters worse

b) Population growth

Question:
What will
supermarkets
be like
in
2001?

To begin with — LESS FOOD

for one thing → no more 'natural' foods

unnatural elements
help produce more
food → food will decline
in quality → flavouring
additives

too → tendency to vegetarianism

land better used
for cultivation
than breeding animals

Another point is — LESS ENERGY

less plastics, aluminium, paper

use of human muscle

this means that — less packaging

home
deliveries
again

To be sure/ Still — COMPUTERIZATION

3 Thematization

Exercise 1

Specific aim: To train the students to recognize how the arrangement of the information in the passage can determine the order of the words in the sentences.

Skills involved: Understanding relations between parts of a text.

Why?   One unconsciously rewrites sentences so that old information – that is to say information which is already known – will come first and new information will be taken in last. It is important to be aware of this distribution of the information to be an efficient reader as it will help to find out new information more quickly.

Read this short passage and fill in the following table to show how the information is distributed within the text.

In 1970, a film called *M.A.S.H.* came out and people started talking about a new, very different pair of actors: Elliott Gould and Donald Sutherland. Why? Because they were very funny, in a new and original way. They acted very naturally. *M.A.S.H.* is about the chaotic daily life of a mobile surgical unit of the US army behind the front, during the Korean war. The reason behind the chaos in the *M.A.S.H.* unit was the determination of two surgeons, Hawkeye (Donald Sutherland) and Trapper (Elliott Gould) to keep everybody's spirits up in spite of the war. This they did by playing various practical jokes and elaborate tricks.

(From *Current 8*)

Here is the complete table.

Sentences	Theme *(what is given or already known)*	Theme *(what is new)*
1.	*In 1970, a film called M.A.S.H.*	*a different pair of actors*
2.	*They*	*funny / original*
3.	*They*	*acted originally*
4.	*M.A.S.H*	*chaotic life of a mobile surgical unit*
5.	*The reason behind the chaos*	*keep everybody's spirits up*
6.	*This*	*playing jokes and tricks*

Exercise 2

Specific aim:
Skills involved: } Same as for Exercise 1 but the students are asked
Why?   to choose the best possibility.

Complete the following passage with the sentences which seem
preferable to you.

In 1970, a film called *M.A.S.H.* came out and people started talking about
a new, very different pair of actors: Elliott Gould and Donald Sutherland.
Why? Because they were very funny, in a new and original way. They
acted very naturally.
a) The chaotic life of a mobile surgical unit of the US army behind the
   front, during the Korean war, is the subject of *M.A.S.H.*
b) *M.A.S.H.* is about the chaotic daily life of a mobile surgical unit of the
   US army behind the front, during the Korean War.
c) It is the Korean war, and the chaotic life of a mobile surgical unit of the
   US army behind the front, which is the subject of *M.A.S.H.*

a) In order to keep everybody's spirits up in spite of the war, two surgeons, Hawkeye (D.S.) and Trapper (E.G.) created chaos in the *M.A.S.H.* unit.
b) The two surgeons who are determined to create chaos in the *M.A.S.H.* unit to keep everybody's spirits up in spite of the war, are Hawkeye (D.S.) and Trapper (E.G.)
c) The reason behind the chaos in the *M.A.S.H.* unit was the determination of two surgeons, Hawkeye (D.S.) and Trapper (E.G.) to keep everybody's spirits up in spite of the war.

a) This they did by playing various practical jokes and elaborate tricks.
b) Various practical jokes and elaborate tricks were the method they chose to do this.

Exercise 3

Specific aim:
Skills involved: } Same as for exercise 2.
Why?

A Decide which sentence is most acceptable in the given context.
  1 You do not agree with your wife about the date when your sister Irene came to see you.
    a) Irene came to stay with us during the Christmas holidays.
    b) It was Irene who came to stay with us during the Christmas holidays.
  2 You can't find your gloves. Your friend says:
    a) The waste-paper basket is near your gloves.
    b) Your gloves are near the waste-paper basket.
  3 You know someone phoned last night and you have asked your parents who it was. They answer:
    a) Edith phoned last night.
    b) The person who phoned last night was Edith.

B Here are pairs of sentences which differ by their thematic structures. Find a context to explain each sentence.
  1 a) Peter probably left the parcel.
    b) The parcel must have been left by Peter.
  2 a) She never gave the books to me.
    b) The books to me she never gave.

(Exercises of this type are suggested by Enkvist in *Some Aspects of Applications of Text Linguistics.*)

III · UNDERSTANDING MEANING

1 Non-linguistic response to the text

1.1 Ordering a sequence of pictures

Exercise

Specific aim: To help the students to understand the chronological sequence in the text by reordering accompanying photographs.
Skills involved: Selecting relevant points from a text. Relating the text to a document.
Why? This exercise is important in showing the students that understanding a text often implies visualizing the information contained in it.

Dear Tom,

Here we are, just back from the Deep South and I can't wait to tell you all about our marvellous trip. But what about you? How did you like Colorado?

Did you get our card from St. Martinville? It was sweet of you to take us to the airport, Tom. Anyway, we had a good flight to New Orleans and spent the evening walking in the town, and even doing some shopping as some of the shops were still open!

The next morning we visited some beautiful old houses in the French Quarter, some of those with the beautiful wrought iron balconies ... we even had coffee outside. We met some very nice people from Kansas and they took us for a drive in the afternoon. We even visited one of the cemeteries: a very old one, and it's so damp there that the graves are built up on top of each other instead of under the ground. We had a delicious meal at Antoine's in the evening (I would have liked to go for brunch but we were too busy for that) and ended up at a jazz concert.

From there we travelled by bus all the way up North through Mississippi. You know how I'd dreamed for years of visiting Faulkner's village in Oxford. It was very late when we got there but we were lucky to meet a charming old man in charge of the bus depot and he told us everything about Oxford – which is very small – where to stay, and eat, and everything. We found a little café kept by a Greek right in front of the Courthouse and had supper there. The next morning, we walked around Oxford: there's just the Courthouse in the centre of the village – it's a kind of meeting-place, people go there and talk and sit on the benches nearby. And then we visited Faulkner's home – a beautiful wooden house in the middle of a park.

Our next stop was Columbus, further East, not far from Alabama. It's really one of the most beautiful places I've ever seen so far: it has dozens of lovely ante-bellum houses with white columns and rocking chairs and huge parks.... we could have spent days there but we'd planned to come back to New Orleans along the Mississippi, so we went down to Natchez. I must say I was a bit disappointed. I must have built up a lot of dreams around Old Man River and I'm afraid I didn't find it very impressive .... what you can see of it anyway for it's usually hidden by trees overgrown by what they call 'kutu': it's a kind of creeping plant that covers everything ... like the jungle. And I don't know if it's pollution or what, but the smell was simply dreadful! But I did enjoy a trip we took on a steamboat in St. Francisville. We saw some very charming villages all along the river, just as you see them in picture books, with old wooden houses all along the main street.

So you see, we had a wonderful time though it was short. But it was so hot and humid that I'm not sure I would have liked to stay there for weeks. .... I was going to forget: we had an afternoon free before flying back home and we took a bus to the Mississippi Delta : it's called Venice. It wasn't really what we'd expected but it was very interesting and different from what we'd seen before : lots of swamps with trees growing in the middle, wild flowers growing everywhere and a lot of fishing villages ...

I've enclosed some of the pictures we took. You can keep them as I'm having others printed.

I hope you're all very well. I'll write again soon but I hope to hear from you and your holiday before that.

Lots of love,

Pat

Here are the photos that Pat sent to Tom. Can you put them back in the order in which they were taken? (Write a number next to each of them.)

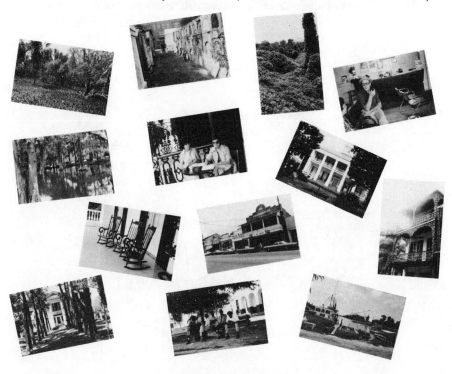

1.2 Comparing texts and pictures

Exercise

Specific aim: To help the students to understand implied and stated information through comparing the information contained in the text to that of a picture.

Skills involved: Extracting relevant points from a text. Relating the text to a document.

Why? It is common, when reading a text, to compare its contents to situations or events we are familiar with. Comparing a story to a drawing or document is therefore a very natural activity. It will also encourage the students to refer back to the text for similarities and differences.

The following exercise can be done after reading Roald Dahl's short story *Mrs Bixby and the Colonel's Coat*.

Now that you have read the short story, look at the following drawing. Are there any common points between the two?
In what way does the cartoon differ from the story?

1.3 Matching

Exercise 1

Specific aim: To help the students to understand the main information in the text through the identification of the corresponding diagram.

Skills involved: Selecting relevant information from the text. Relating this information to diagrams.

Why? In this particular text, it is important to understand the family relations described by the writer of the letter. This exercise will
- help the students by forcing them to read some parts of the text again to check details
- familiarize them with the use of diagrams to sum up the contents of a text – a skill essential to a good reader.

Read the letter and choose the family tree that corresponds to Gwenda's family.

Freetown,
New Zealand,
4 May

Dearest Gwenda, [Miss Danby had written]

I was much disturbed to hear that you had had some worrying experience. To tell you the truth, it had really entirely escaped my memory that you had actually resided for a short time in England as a young child.

Your mother, my sister Megan, met your father, Major Halliday, when she was on a visit to some friends of ours at that time stationed in India. They were married and you were born there. About two years after your birth your mother died. It was a great shock to us and we wrote to your father, with whom we had corresponded, but whom actually we had never seen, begging him to entrust you to our care, as we would be only too glad to have you, and it might be difficult for an Army man stranded with a young child. Your father, however, refused, and told us he was resigning from the Army and taking you back with him to England. He said he hoped we would at some time come over and visit him there.

I understand that on the voyage home, your father met a young woman, became engaged to her, and married her as soon as he got to England. The marriage was not, I gather, a happy one, and I understand they parted about a year later. It was then that your father wrote to us and asked if we were still willing to give you a home. I need hardly tell you, my dear, how happy we were to do so. You were sent out to us in charge of an English nurse, and at the same time your father settled the bulk of his estate upon you and suggested that you might legally adopt our name. This, I may say, seemed a little curious to us, but we felt that it was kindly meant – and intended to make you more one of the family – we did not, however, adopt that suggestion. About a year later your father died in a nursing home. I surmise that he had already received bad news about his health at the time when he sent you out to us.

I'm afraid I cannot tell you where you lived while with your father in England. His letter naturally had the address on it at the time, but that is now eighteen years ago and I'm afraid one doesn't remember such details. It was in the South of England, I know – and I fancy Dillmouth is correct. I had a vague idea it was Dartmouth, but the two names are not unlike. I believe your stepmother married again, but I have no recollection of her name, not even of her unmarried name, though your father had mentioned it in the original letter telling of his remarriage. We were, I think, a little resentful of his marrying again so soon, but of course one knows that on board ship the influence of propinquity is very great – and he may also have thought that it would be a good thing on your account.

It seems stupid of me not to have mentioned to you that you had been in England even if you didn't remember the fact, but, as I say, the whole thing had faded from my mind. Your mother's death in India and your subsequently coming to live with us always seemed the important points.

I hope this is all cleared up now?

I do trust Giles will soon be able to join you. It is hard for you both being parted at this early stage.

All my news in my next letter, as I am sending this off hurriedly in answer to your wire.

Your loving aunt,
Alison Danby

P.S. You do not say what your worrying experience was?
(From Agatha Christie: *Sleeping Murder*

Miss Danby. . . Megan × Major Halliday × young woman
                                                              \
                                    Giles × Gwenda

Miss Danby. . . Megan × Major Halliday × young woman
                                |
                       Gwenda × Giles

Megan × Major Halliday . . . Miss Danby
       |
Gwenda × Giles

Key
×   married to
· · ·   brother/sister
| son/daughter

Exercise 2

Specific aim: To help the students to understand the important information in the text by asking them to match information in the text and routes on a map.

Skills involved: Extracting relevant points from the text. Relating the text to a map.

Why?   This kind of exercise will help the students to read the text accurately since some of the routes are very similar. They will therefore have to refer back to the text constantly. Also, trying to trace a route on a map is the most natural activity when reading an article on geography or explorations.

The early explorers

Hernando de Soto, the Spanish governor of Cuba, was the first white man to reach the banks of the Mississippi. On 3 June 1539 he landed with 730 men and 237 horses at Tampa Bay in Florida. He took possession of the area in the name of the King of Spain, and marched inland in search of gold and rubies. His compatriots Coronado and Alvarez de Pineda had already penetrated the mysterious North American continent. The former, starting from Mexico, travelled across part of the south-west in a vain attempt to discover the seven mythical cities of Cibola; the latter explored the gulf, landing in Texas. Members of these expeditions had brought back rumours of fabulous treasure, and de Soto, who had taken part in the conquest of Peru, believed the undiscovered lands beyond Florida to be a new Eldorado of incredible wealth.

For two years his little band wandered in all directions, killing Indians, destroying and plundering their villages, crossing rivers, mountains and deserts, but the gold proved elusive, search where they might. On 8 May 1541, when half his company had succumbed to disease, privation and Indian arrows, de Soto, following the sound of a herd of wild pigs, found himself on the shores of an immensely broad, muddy river. It was so wide that one could scarcely discern the other bank clearly; in the water could be seen trunks of trees from the green forests lining the river. The expedition encamped; a Franciscan friar intoned the *Te Deum*, and de Soto gave the river the name of Rio Grande.

With the cross and the sword
The 'great river' was the Mississippi. From the point where he had chanced upon it de Soto organized further marches in all directions, but instead of gold he found only mosquitoes – and died of malaria a year later. His men sold his slaves by auction and buried him, but afterwards dug up his body and flung it into the Mississippi, to persuade the Indians that the 'son of the Sungod', as they called him, had not died but had gone on a voyage to the Indian Olympus. The waters closed over the explorer's corpse, and as years went by the river with its great and constant deposit of alluvium, slowly obliterated every trace of the expedition. The exact spot at which de Soto discovered the Mississippi is therefore unknown. The inhabitants of Memphis claim that it was on the site of their city, but historians believe it to have been some 40 miles (65 km) to the south.

Subsequent explorers were discouraged by de Soto's fate, and it was a hundred and thirty years before white men again set eyes on the great river. This time it was discovered by Frenchmen from the north. In 1665 a Jesuit missionary, Claude Allouez, stationed on the remote shores of Lake Superior, heard from Indian nomads of the existence of a mighty river which they called the 'Misi Sipi'.

Eight years later in 1673 the governor of New France invited the merchant Louis Jolliet and the Jesuit, Jacques Marquette to go in search of the river, since if it crossed the continent from east to west it would be a trade route of the first importance. In May 1673 Jolliet and Marquette set out in two canoes from Lake Michigan: they followed the Wisconsin river to the Mississippi and navigated the latter as far as Arkansas. Finding that its course lay southward to the Gulf of Mexico, where the Spaniards were believed to be, the explorers returned to Quebec, where they received an enthusiastic welcome. It was not until 1681, however, that their expedition was followed up, this time by Robert Cavalier, sieur de La Salle.

La Salle, realizing that the great river cut the continent in half from north to south, had the ambitious plan of constructing a chain of forts and trading posts along it which would enable the French to dominate the entire American fur trade. He set out in December 1681 with 23 Frenchmen and 28 Indians. La Salle was a man of grandiose ideas, and Henri de Tonti, his second-in-command – a specialist in fortifications – was well fitted to carry them out.

La Salle reached the mouth of the Mississippi in April 1682, having found no trace of the Spaniards, and annexed the whole river basin – which he baptized Louisiana – to the dominions of Louis XIV. Later, in a second trip to the mouth of the river, he was driven by a storm onto the coast of Texas. There he tried to found a new colony, but his men mutinied and he was murdered. Tonti thereupon assumed command, building a chain of forts and until his death in 1704 effectively acted as ruler of the Lower Mississippi basin.

The source of the Mississippi

One of the most exciting attempts to find the source was made by the Italian Constantino Beltrami. Aged 44, in Italy he had been a rather staid gentleman – a magistrate and student of the classics. In the New World, however, he developed an obsession for exploration – not so much for reasons of scientific curiosity but in response to romantic dreams nourished by literary and mythological study. Setting out from St Louis in 1823, he travelled as far as Fort Snelling by boat and then proceeded up river by canoe, accompanied by three Indians. The journey was an adventurous one through lakes, bogs and swamps; many of the Indian chiefs whom the travellers encountered were adorned in macabre fashion with white men's scalps. On 23 August 1823 Beltrami came to a small lake in what is now northern Minnesota, which he called Lake Julia in memory of a woman he had loved, and which he proclaimed to be the source of the Mississippi. His romantic self-comparison to Icarus, the Phoenicians, Marco Polo and Columbus, however, was not calculated to satisfy geographers, for he had no compass or sextant with which to determine his location. Weary and famished, attired in animal skins and with a hat made of bark, he returned in a birchwood canoe all the way to New Orleans. There he related his travels and as a result, he was acclaimed in Europe and became a member of several academies, while Lafayette and Chateaubriand honoured him with their friendship. In America, on the other hand, many regarded him as an impostor.

Nine years after Beltrami, The United States Superintendent of Indian Affairs for Michigan – Henry Rowe Schoolcraft – named a remote glacial

Non-linguistic response to the text

lake in Minnesota 'Itasca', from the Latin words *veritas* (truth) and *caput* (head, or source), proclaiming it the true source of the Mississippi.

His claim that Lake Itasca was the source of the river was accepted for many years, but many geologists now disagree. Accurate recent surveys show that a spring flows into it from Elk Lake, and that this in turn is linked with yet other lakes, which may be collectively regarded as the source of the great river.

(From *The Mississippi* edited by A. Miller)

After reading the text and looking at this map, can you match the explorers and their routes? Be careful! One of the explorers has not been mentioned in the text.

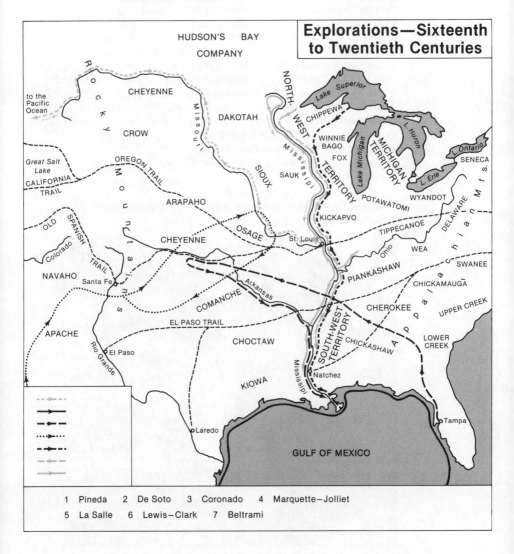

Explorations—Sixteenth to Twentieth Centuries

1 Pineda 2 De Soto 3 Coronado 4 Marquette–Jolliet
5 La Salle 6 Lewis–Clark 7 Beltrami

139

Exercise 3

Specific aim: To help the students to understand the main
information in the passage by asking them to
identify the corresponding diagram.

Skills involved:
Why?   } Same as for exercise 2.

Triangular trade routes

Because the colonies had an unfavourable balance of trade with Britain,
they had a constant need for specie to pay for imported British goods. To
obtain specie, colonial merchants developed trade through various
triangular trade routes, many of which violated the Navigation Acts since
they involved direct trade with foreign nations. One popular route took
colonial-made rum to West Africa where it was exchanged for slaves – as
well as gold. The slaves were then taken to the West Indies and sold for
sugar, molasses, and gold. The molasses and sugar were shipped to the
colonies and distilled into rum. Another profitable route took colonial fish,
grain and lumber to the West Indies. Here they were exchanged for sugar
and molasses, which then went to Britain to be exchanged for
manufactured goods needed in the colonies.
(From R. Curry, J. Sproat, K. Cramer: *The Shaping of America* (Holt,
Rinehart and Winston))

**Which of the following maps correspond(s) to the triangular routes
described in the text?**

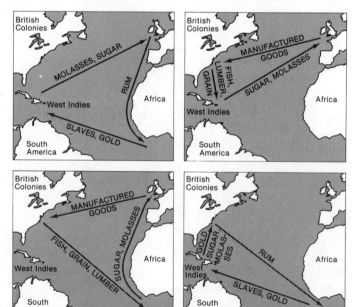

Exercise 4

Specific aim: To train the students to use the stated or implied information in the text to relate characters to pictures.

Skills involved: Extracting relevant points from the text.
Making inferences.
Relating the text to pictures.

Why? When reading about a person, one cannot help imagining what he or she looks like. The text may contain some hints or even a physical description, but we usually build up a mental portrait of the person through the general impression conveyed by the text.

Besides making the students read the text accurately, looking for relevant details, this exercise will also help them to define and discuss the 'mental portraits' the article suggests to them.

Match the following comments with the photographs of the people who made them.

LIFESPAN: HEALTH

Faulty winks

More than 500 million sleeping pills are dispensed in Britain every year. They can help in a crisis, but they interfere with natural sleep and reduce dreaming. *Colleen Toomey* talked to seven people who suffer from insomnia and manage without drugs, and asked them what they did when they could not sleep. Some of the replies will suprise you . . .

● **Peter Cook , writer, entertainer**
Age, 40; married, two children. "I watch *It's a Knockout* – it puts me into a deep sleep. Watching television programmes about people trying to be me – that puts me to sleep."

● **J. B. Priestley , writer**
Age, 83; married to Jacquetta Hawkes, author and archaeologist. "I've had a good deal of trouble in my time. Years and years ago I would write half the night, but I have given that up all together. Occasionally I will eat a digestive biscuit before going to bed. I think it helps to settle your tummy. A good deal of sleeplessness comes from tummy upsets, and the digestive biscuit will sometimes settle it."

● **Erin Pizzey, founder of Chiswick Women's Aid** Age, 38; separated, two children. "I drink ice-cold Dom Perignon champagne in a hot bath. It really works and I do it as often as I possibly can afford to – which isn't very often. I sleep early, but wake up at about 3 o'clock and can't get back to sleep. Then I read."

● **Chad Varah , founder of the Samaritans,** now Chairman of Befrienders International. Age, 65; married, five children. "I do something to keep myself faintly amused, like read Jane Austen. Otherwise I will get up and do something that needs to be done. Losing one night's sleep isn't going to be the end of the world.

● **The Very Rev Martin Sullivan Dean of St Paul's Cathedral**
Age, 67; married. "I once read this years ago about a man in Sing Sing prison and never thought about it again until I couldn't sleep. Lie on your back quite still. Let your arms relax like a spaniel's paw and drop your lower jaw. Close your eyes. Look at the inside of the eyelids, otherwise images appear. Imagine a beautiful scene like English springtime. Breathe in slowly. As you exhale, say the word 'Peace'. I used this when I was under pressure."

● **Roland Moyle Minister of State for Health**
Age, 49; married, two children. "I didn't suffer from insomnia until the Abortion Bill Com-

mittee started. I was only getting half-an-hour naps. To go to sleep, I just think about next year's Abortion Bill and that sends me off to sleep. The thought looms of how much sleep we will get then and I go straight off. Sometimes I play through a soccer match in my mind. I've always been successful and gone to sleep."

● **Janet Suzman, actress**
Age, 38; married to Trevor Nunn, artistic director of the Royal Shakespeare Company. "I suffer from insomnia so frequently that it makes me ill. It's awful; prolonging soliloquies without the benefit of an audience. I usually go up to my 'insomnia room' – it's the attic. I read *Mill on the Floss* – it's exhaustingly emotional. Sometimes I have a terrible revenge syndrome: if I can't sleep why should the neighbours? I would love a soundproof insomnia chamber where you wouldn't have to tip-toe."

(*The Sunday Times*)

Exercise 5

Specific aim: To help the students to reach a detailed understanding of the text by asking them to match drawings and passages in the text.

Skills involved: Understanding stated information. Relating it to drawings.

Why? One often reads texts describing gestures or movements and it is natural to try and visualize them. The exercise will also require a close scrutiny of the text since some of the gestures described differ only by a small detail.

The following text describes a number of gestures involving the hands and that we often make when speaking. Sixteen 'postures' are described in the passage (they have been capitalized). Can you find which of the drawings they correspond to? (Number the postures from 1 to 16 and write the appropriate number next to each picture.)
Which of the gestures has no corresponding picture? ....
....

Baton Signals

Actions that emphasize the rhythm of words

Baton Signals beat time to the rhythm of spoken thoughts. Their essential role is to mark the points of emphasis in our speech, and they are so much an integral part of our verbal delivery that we sometimes gesticulate even when talking on the telephone.

It is possible to make a detailed classification of these beating postures and then to study their natural history in the field. Here are some of the most important types:

1. The Vacuum Precision-grip. The human hand has two basic holding actions – the precision-grip and the power-grip. In the precision-grip it is the tips of the thumb and fingers that are used; in the power-grip the whole hand is involved. We employ the precision-grip when holding small objects delicately and manipulating them with accuracy, as when writing or threading a needle. When batoning during speech, we often adopt a precision-grip hand posture, even though the hand in question is empty. In other words, we perform the precision-grip in vacuo. This form of baton reflects an urge on the part of the speaker to express himself delicately and with great

exactness. His hand emphasizes the fineness of the points he is stressing.

There are two popular versions of the Vacuum Precision-grip: the Hand Purse and the Thumb-and-forefinger Touch. In the HAND PURSE the tips of all five digits are brought together until they touch in a tight circle, like the mouth of a string-closed purse.

In the THUMB-AND-FOREFINGER TOUCH, the tips of only these two digits are brought into contact with each other. This appears to be the most popular form of the Vacuum Precision-grip, requiring slightly less muscular effort than the Hand Purse.

2. The Intention Precision-grip. In this baton posture, the hand makes the intention movement of delicately taking hold of an imaginary, small object, but does not follow the action through to the point where the thumb-tip and finger-tips meet. It is an AIR HOLD posture and the mood it reflects is more one of a quest for precision than precision itself. There is usually an element of questioning or uncertainty on the part of the gesticulator, as if he is searching for something. The hand, beating the air, almost closes on the answer, but not quite.

3. The Vacuum Power-grip. We employ the power-grip for crude, forceful manipulations such as grasping or hammering. The digits are curled tightly around the held object. When this is done in vacuo, the result, in mild cases is a bent hand and, in strong cases, a tight fist.

In the HAND BEND posture the curled fingers only lightly touch the palm. This is a rather insipid baton posture, reflecting neither precision of thought, nor forcefulness. The Tight Fist, in contrast, although it lacks delicacy, does signal considerable determination and strength of thought.

4. The Intention Power-grip. The speaker who is seeking control and is striving in his speech to master the situation, but has not yet done so, performs his batons with his hand held in the frozen intention movement of the power-grip. This is the AIR GRASP posture, with the digits stiffly spread and slightly bent. The hand grasps at the air but does not follow through.

5. The Vacuum Blow. The hand acts, not as a holding machine, but as a blunt instrument. Instead of gripping, grabbing, or grasping, it chops, jabs or punches. But again it does this in

vacuo, chopping, jabbing or punching the air rather than a solid object.

The HAND CHOP, with the straight hand rigid and slashed downwards through the air like an axe, is the baton posture of the aggressive speaker who wants his ideas to cut through the confusion of the situation, to an imposed solution. A special variant of the Hand Chop is the HAND SCISSOR, where the forearms cross over each other horizontally, then both chop outwards. The Hands Scissor baton adds a strong flavour of denial or rejection to the mood of the speech. It is as if, with this variant, the speaker is cutting his way through a hostile barrier, negating the opposition by striking it away from him, both to the left and to the right.

The HAND JAB baton, where the fingertips are prodded sharply towards the listener, is also aggressive, but here the aggression is more specific. It has to do with the listener rather than with the general problem.

The AIR PUNCH is the most aggressive of the baton postures, and when the hand is beaten in the air as a clenched fist there is little doubt of the mood of the performer. There is a similarity between this type of batoning and the Tight Fist of the Vacuum Power-grip, but it is usually possible to distinguish between them. The Tight Fist shows the hand gripping the air, while the Air Punch shows it punching into the air. In both cases the hands may beat time aggressively, but only in the Air Punch is there a sense that the fists are delivering blows.

6. The Hand Extend. Instead of imaginary gripping or hitting, the batoning hand may simply be extended in front of the body and held there in a rather neutral posture, fingers together and flat. The important clue in such cases is the direction of the palm. THE PALM UP: the imploring hand of the beggar. Hand batons in this posture beg the listener to agree. THE PALM DOWN: the restraining hand of the cool-headed. Hand batons of this type reveal an urge to damp down or lower the prevalent mood – to control it by reduction. THE PALM FRONT: the repelling hand of the protester. The hand faces forwards as if to protect the speaker or push away some imaginery object approaching from the front. The mood reflected is one of rejection. THE PALM BACK: the embracing hand of the comfort-seeker. This baton is usually performed with both hands

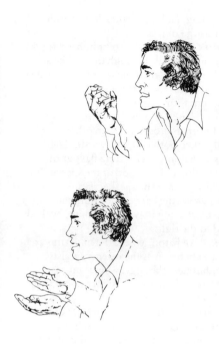

at once, palms towards the chest. They are held in front of the body as if embracing an invisible companion. Their posture reflects an attempt to embrace an idea, to encompass the concept under discussion, or to pull the other person metaphorically closer to the speaker. THE PALM SIDE: the reaching hand of the negotiator. The hand is held out in the hand-shake position, where it beats the air in a baton-action that seems to reflect the urge to stretch out and touch the companion. The predominant mood appears to be a strong desire to bridge the gap between speaker and listener – to 'reach' the other person's mind with the idea being expressed in words.

The Hands together. If the speaker joins his left and right hand in some sort of hand-to-hand contact, this tends to replace batoning. Instead of beating time to his thoughts, he now enjoys the comforting sensation of 'holding hands with himself' while continuing to talk.

The Forefinger Baton. Hand batons usually employ all the digits working together, but there is one common baton posture in which a single digit – the forefinger – plays a dominant role. This is the extended-forefinger posture.

There are two popular versions: the FRONTAL FOREFINGER BATON and the RAISED FOREFINGER BATON. In the frontal case the forefinger is jabbed towards the listener or towards some object under discussion. Pointing at an object may be merely a way of emphasizing the importance of that object for the discussion, but pointing directly at a listener is an assertive, authoritarian act and when it becomes extended as a rhythmic baton, the impact on the listener is one of open hostility or domination. The jabbing forefinger may only assault the air, but the listener can almost feel it stabbing into his ribs.

(From *Manwatching* by Desmond Morris)

Exercise 6

Specific aim:
Skills involved: } Same as for exercise 5 but this time the students
Why?   match descriptions of houses and their pictures.

Match the descriptions of the houses with the photographs.

1

2

3

5

SOUTHERN CALIFORNIA

San Diego—Sunny, Warm and Dry.

COLONIAL STYLE TOWN HOUSE

5 bedrooms, 3 bathrooms
3 reception rooms,
including one of 34 ft.
drawing room, kitchen,
utility room, sun room.

Mahogany panelling in
drawing room and
dining room.

Polished oak floor
throughout. **A**

Gas-fired central heating.

2 car garage.

£34,000 OR TRADE W

4

AN INTERESTING PERIOD COTTAGE
with potential in a Village
position facing open farmland

3 large bedrooms,
bathroom, hall, cloakroom,
lounge, dining room,
kitchen. **C**

Pretty garden and well
hedged field—about
2 ACRES.

B

Fine residentia: 5 bed house,
with 3 receps., brkfst. room, 2
wc's, kitchen and service areas.
Oil CH. Further accom. potential: outbuildings and well kept
grounds. Excellent as old
people's home or private
residence. £24,950. Ref.: 165.

MILLER AND CO.,
57 FORE STREET
REDRUTH (215594)
OFFICES COVERING
CORNWALL

D

CORNWALL—ST. IVES

MODERN PERIOD STYLE GRANITE RESIDENCE
with fine views

4 bedrooms,
bathroom,
3 reception rooms,
cloaks,
well fitted kitchen.
Charming spiral stairs

Garage.

Main services.

Price to include some
valuable curtains and
carpets.

E

HIGHLY INDIVIDUAL BUNGALOW RESIDENCE
in delightful grounds of **1 ACRE**

2 reception rooms, study, excellent kitchen,

4 bedrooms, 2 bathrooms.

Double garage, workshop, outbuildings.

Heated swimming pool. Superb gardens.

Exercise 7

Specific aim:	Same as for exercise 5 but this time it is the text
Skills involved:	which is jumbled and the pictures which are in
Why?	the right order. The pictures will therefore help
	to reorganize the text.

Look at the jumbled instructions on page 105. These drawings represent the main stages in making sherry trifle. Can they help you reorder the set of instructions?

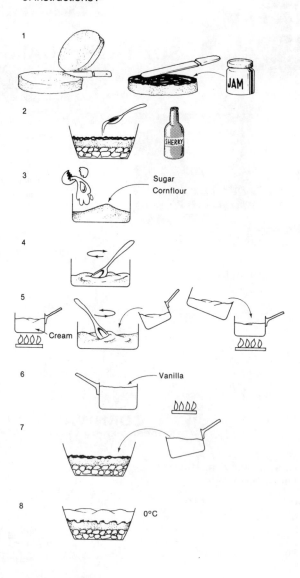

Exercise 8

Specific aim: To help the students to recognize the main
information of the text by asking them to match
articles and headlines.

Skills involved: Identifying the main idea of the text.

Why?   Finding the proper headline for an article means
you have understood the main point of the article.
This exercise will lead the students to consider the
text globally after they have read it and to try to
sum up its most important information.

Match the articles with their headlines.

VICAR Laurie Parsons—" I'm pushing 60 "
—was sponsored by his villagers at Radford
Semele, Warwickshire, to put his feet up
and rest instead of taking part in a charity
walk yesterday. The village paid £50 for
his day of rest.

ALMOST ONE in six of the
major advertisements carried
in national and regional newspapers and magazines in Britain
breaches in some significant
way the advertising industry's
own voluntary code of practice,
which demands that ads be legal,
decent, honest and truthful."

What is disturbing the OFT is
that a study of advertising in
Britain and Germany done four
years ago by the European union
of consumer groups found almost
exactly the same faults in
British advertising, as does the
present inquiry. The advertising industry, in other words,
does not seem to be improving

GOVERNMENT action to insist on the use
of clean petrol was urged yesterday by the
Bishop of Birmingham, Hugh Montefiore,
who said lead pollution from vehicle fumes
is threatening the health of thousands of
children. He was speaking at a diocesan
synod in Birmingham Cathedral.

Ten-year-old Mark Johnson,
who disappeared after his canoe
capsized in the river Goyt near
Stockport on Friday, was found
safe and well yesterday. After
reaching the bank, he got lost
in woods and sat down waiting
to be found.

A NEW computer system could provide a solution to Europe's
traffic problems. The new system,
to be tested next year over 100
kilometres of German motorway,
involves a dashboard computer
linked to roadside information
terminals which provide the driver
with regular details of hazards,
weather conditions, speed limits and
imminent traffic jams.

The driver simply punches into
a keyboard (on his dash) the code
for his destination, and the radio
aerial on the underside of his car
automatically picks up signals from
the induction loops embedded in
traffic lanes at each motorway inter-
section. (New Scientist, Volume 80,
Number 1123.)

IF YOUR dog or cat sleeps with you
in bed then the chances are that
your sleep cycles coincide.

Studies at Harvard, using time-
lapse photography of people asleep,
have shown that regular sleeping
partners, including pets, tend to
move around or remain still together. This synchronisation would
appear to extend even to dreaming.
(Sleep Research, Volume 5, Page
120.)

MALE STUDENTS can get away
with bad handwriting in their
essays, but not girls.

Ray Bull and Julia Stevens, of
North East London Polytechnic's
psychology department, have come
to this conclusion after 72 school-
teachers marked the same essays.
The essays differed in presentation
—some markers were given good
handwriting, others poor handwriting and others got typewritten
copies. Each marker also had the
photo of a different " author "
attached to his copy.

On its own, the attractiveness of
the " author," whether male or
female, made no difference. Men
got the same marks, regardless of
presentation. But the girls were
marked down for poor handwriting.
Curiously, the attractive girls got
the highest marks for good handwriting, while the unattractive did
best with typed copies. (Journal of
Occupational Psychology, Volume
51.)

TERRY GRIPTON, of Stafford, yesterday
failed to break the world shouting record.
He managed only 108½ decibels on a sound-
level meter, two-and-a-half below the record.
His wife said: " I'm not surprised he failed.
He's really a very quiet man and doesn't
even shout at me."

Easy riding

Cat naps

Boy sits tight

Nothing to shout about

Children 'at risk'

How ads
failed
the test

The cost of
scrawling

Vicar's £50 sit-in

The Sunday Times

Matching – further hints

- Besides matching paragraphs, characters or events to pictures or drawings, the students can also be asked to match the information given in the text to graphs or charts. With longer texts it is also possible to give the students several diagrams representing the evolution of the text and to ask them to select the one that reflects the structure of the passage.
- The students can also be asked to match
  a) parts of a text and dates or events
  b) parts of a text and a list (e.g. instructions, a menu, rules)
  c) questions and answers of an advice column.
- See also exercise 4, question 3 on page 163.

1.4 Using illustrations

Exercise 1

Specific aim: To help the students to understand a text by giving them a picture of what is being described or referred to.

Skills involved: Relating the text to a document.

Why? Whenever there is a direct reference to a picture, a scene or a landscape, the reader is usually expected to know this picture or scene and it is therefore only natural to provide it. Illustrations are also aids to the comprehension of words and ideas.

The two poems that follow are inspired by the same painting by Brueghel.
1 Read the poems, referring back to the painting to follow the poets' descriptions.
2 Compare the two poems. Which aspects of the painting are emphasized in each of them?

Landscape with the Fall of Icarus

According to Brueghel
when Icarus fell
it was spring

a farmer was ploughing
his field
the whole pageantry

of the year was
awake tingling
near

the edge of the sea
concerned
with itself

sweating in the sun
that melted
the wings' wax

insignificantly
off the coast
there was

a splash quite unnoticed
this was
Icarus drowning

William Carlos Williams

Musée des Beaux Arts

About suffering they were never wrong,
The Old Masters: how well they understood
Its human position; how it takes place
While someone else is eating or opening a window or just
    walking dully along;
How, when the aged are reverently, passionately waiting
For the miraculous birth, there always must be
Children who did not specially want it to happen, skating
On a pond at the edge of the wood:

They never forgot
That even the dreadful martyrdom must run its course
Anyhow in a corner, some untidy spot
Where the dogs go on with their doggy life and the
    torturer's horse
Scratches its innocent behind on a tree.

In Brueghel's *Icarus*, for instance: how everything turns
    away
Quite leisurely from the disaster; the ploughman may
Have heard the splash, the forsaken cry,
But for him it was not an important failure; the sun shone
As it had to on the white legs disappearing into the green
Water; and the expensive delicate ship that must have seen
Something amazing, a boy falling out of the sky,
Had somewhere to get to and sailed calmly on.

W. H. Auden

Exercise 2

Specific aim:
Skills involved: } Same as for exercise 1.
Why?

Read the following passage, making use of the picture to follow Mark Twain's description of a steamboat on the Mississippi river.

The Boys' Ambition

When I was a boy, there was but one permanent ambition among my comrades in our village on the west bank of the Mississippi River. That was, to be a steamboatman. We had transient ambitions of other sorts, but they were only transient. . . .

Once a day a cheap, gaudy packet arrived upward from St. Louis, and another downward from Keokuk. Before these events, the day was glorious with expectancy; after them, the day was a dead and empty thing. . . . I can picture that old time to myself now, just as it was then: the white town drowsing in the sunshine of a summer's morning; the streets empty, or pretty nearly so; one or two clerks sitting in front of the Water Street stores. . . ; a sow and a litter of pigs loafing along the sidewalk. . . ; two or three lonely little freight piles scattered about the 'levee'; a pile of 'skids' on the slope of the stone-paved wharf, and the fragment town drunkard asleep in the shadow of them; two or three wood flats at the head of the wharf, but nobody to listen to the peaceful lapping of the wavelets against them. . . .

'S-t-e-a-m-boat a-comin'!' and the scene changes! The town drunkard stirs, the clerks wake up, a furious clatter of drays follows, every house and store pours out a human contribution, and all in a twinkling the dead town is alive and moving. Drays, carts, men, boys, all go hurrying from many quarters to a common center, the wharf. Assembled there, the people fasten their eyes upon the coming boat as upon a wonder they are seeing for the first time. And the boat *is* rather a handsome sight, too. She is long and sharp and trim and pretty; she has two tall, fancy-topped chimneys, with a gilded device of some kind swung between them; a fanciful pilothouse, all glass and 'gingerbread'. . . ; the paddle-boxes are gorgeous with a picture or with gilded rays above the boat's name; the boiler deck, the hurricane deck, and the texas deck are fenced and ornamented with clean white railings; there is a flag gallantly flying from the jack-staff; the furnace doors are open and the fires glaring bravely; the upper decks are black with passengers; the captain stands by the big bell, calm, imposing, the envy of all; great volumes of the blackest smoke are rolling and tumbling out of the chimneys – a husbanded grandeur created with a bit of pitch pine just before arriving at a town; the crew are grouped on the forecastle; the broad stage is run far out over the port bow, and an envied deck hand stands picturesquely on the end of it with a coil of rope in his hand; . . . the captain lifts his hand, a bell rings, the wheels stop; then they turn back, churning the water to foam, and the steamer is at rest. Then such a scramble as there is to get aboard, and to get ashore, and to take in freight and to discharge freight, all at one and the same time; and such a

yelling and cursing as the mates facilitate it all with! Ten minutes later the steamer is under way again, with no flag on the jack-staff and no black smoke issuing from the chimneys. After ten more minutes the town is dead again, and the town drunkard asleep by the skids once more.
(From Mark Twain: *Life on the Mississippi* (Signet, 1961))

1.5   Completing a document

Exercise 1

Specific aim:	To help the students reach a detailed comprehension of the text through completing a diagram.
Skills involved:	Relating a text to a document.
Why?	The map will help the students since the text refers to it. But instead of leaving the students free to relate the text to the map (which would then be a mere illustration), one guides them by giving them several words used in the text to describe places and which they must relate to parts of the map. This is an accuracy activity requiring a close scrutiny of the passage.

Read the following description of eighteenth-century houses in London and study the map at the same time. Then, using arrows, show at least one example of what each of the words next to the map refers to.

Consider the main components of the map. The streets are lined with narrow-fronted houses whose sites stretch back to twice their width or more, and which have a tiny patch of courtyard or garden – rarely more than the size of a large carpet – at the back. These houses form by far the most numerous units. But they do not cover the whole area. They are merely the breastworks of inner areas, where alleys, courts, yards, and closes meet each other in an inscrutable topographical jig-saw. These hinterlands, contained both the best and the worst of mercantile London. At one extreme there was the long, broad, paved court, with a fine house fitting the end, equally good houses along the sides, and an entry to the main street wide enough for a coach or cart. At the other extreme was the miserable, unpaved alley, hastily built in the garden of a once affluent house as a means of producing rent from the labouring class which clustered around the advancing standard of capitalism. The hinterlands, in fact, belonged to the Londoner who did not require a shop-front; on the one hand, the merchant who was not a retailer, on the other, the man who had nothing to sell but the labour of his hands.

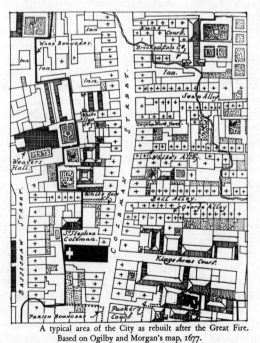

narrow-fronted houses

courtyard

fine house fitting the end

inner areas

paved court

miserable, unpaved alley

A typical area of the City as rebuilt after the Great Fire.
Based on Ogilby and Morgan's map, 1677.

(From John Summerson: *Georgian London* (Pelican, 1969))

Exercise 2: Parts (a) and (b) are matching exercises. Part (c):

Specific aim: To help the students reach a detailed understanding
of the text through completing a diagram.

Skills involved: Relating a text to a document.

Why?   The idea behind this exercise is the same as for
exercise 1 but it is slightly more difficult since the
students now have to provide the right words to
describe the diagrams.

The exploitation of steam

Of all the many factors which contributed to the Industrial Revolution, the
most revolutionary and the most impressive was not coal but
steam-power. J. L. and Barbara Hammond said that steam-power
'declared the triumph of industry and the glory of man'. From clumsy and
inefficient beginnings it was quickly improved to open up tremendous
possibilities for industrial progress. The limitations of muscle-power are
obvious, and though water had served well to work bellows and hammers
in iron works, or to turn machinery like the water-frame and the mule in
the textile industry, it could only be applied in a limited way in Britain. For
water-power is most useful in a land with many fast-flowing streams and,
apart from areas like the Pennines, Scotland, and Wales, this country's
rivers flow slowly. The Alpine area of Europe, and much of the United
States relied on water-power for much longer than Britain, and
hydro-electricity has brought water back into its own in many parts of the
world. The geographical imitations of Britain's water-power, however,
necessitated finding an alternative solution to the problem.

When water vaporizes it expands 1,800 times. The idea of harnessing
this energy is far from new. It was probably used by Hero of Alexandria in
the 1st century B.C. to open temple doors or to pour libations apparently
by magic. Hero's writings were rediscovered during the Renaissance and
many people, including, for example, the Marquis of Worcester (1601–67),
experimented with devices using steam. Regretfully, therefore, we must
dismiss the old myth that steam-power was born in the mind of a bright
Scots lad called James Watt as he sat one winter's evening watching his
mother's kettle boil on the hearth. Watt's contribution to steam is
incalculable, but steam-pumps had been used in Britain for over seventy
years before he began his work.

The first steam-engine used in industry was invented by Thomas Savery
(1650–1715), Called 'The Miners' Friend or an engine to raise water by
Fire', it was patented in 1698 and worked on simple principles. It pumped
water from wells quite efficiently and was used successfully in Cornish
copper-mines, but its limitations were revealed when it was tried in the
Broadwater Collieries in Staffordshire in 1706 and was found to be capable
of pumping water up no more than 100 feet. When greater pressure was
used the boiler burst. Thereafter, Savery's engine was used to supply water
in gentlemen's houses or to work fountains – tasks it could perform
effectively, though not quite safely as there was no pressure-gauge.

It was Thomas Newcomen (1663–1729), a Dartmouth blacksmith and
ironmonger, who produced the first steam-pump to be used widely in

industry. It was known as an 'atmospheric engine' because, in contrast to Savery's engine, the steam in the cylinder was not used to drive the pump but only to create a partial vacuum when condensed. Ordinary air pressure drove the piston into the cylinder and this raised the pump which was connected to the piston by a see-sawing cross-beam. A large piston meant that it was possible to gain more force without increasing steam pressure and this made Newcomen's engine much more powerful than Savery's.

The first engine was made about 1706 but it was a clumsy affair. The piston did not fit tightly into the cylinder and condensation, which was achieved by pouring cold water on the outside of the cylinder, was far from complete. Moreover, the tap controlling the passage of steam into the cylinder was worked by hand seven or eight times a minute. These difficulties were ironed out by 1720; water was now sprayed into the cylinder to improve condensation, the operation of the taps had been made automatic, and a safety-valve had been fitted to eliminate the danger of explosion.

The improved engine soon became standard equipment in most large mines, and it was also used to pump water into canals and to supply drinking-water in towns. It is difficult to know exactly how many were in use by the second half of the 18th century but in 1767 fifty-seven were found around Newcastle, and there were eighteen in Cornish mines in 1780. (From *The Industrial Revolution* by Keith Dawson)

After reading the text, decide:
a) Which drawing represents Savery's steam-engine and which one represents Newcomen's.
b) Which description fits which engine.

The water in the boiler is heated to make steam, which passes, when the valve is opened, into the tank. The tank is then doused with water from a pipe above, and the steam condenses, creating a partial vacuum. Thus, water is drawn up the up pipe, and forced out.	Water is heated in the boiler to make steam, which passes into the cylinder and forces the piston up, assisted by the counter weight. Water is then admitted into the cylinder. The steam condenses and creates a partial vacuum, thus drawing the piston back down again. A see-saw motion is set up which is used to drive a pump.

c) After reading the descriptions and looking at the drawings, can you supply the missing words or explanations on the drawings?

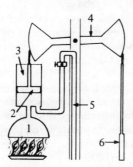 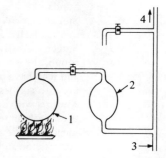

III *Understanding meaning*

Exercise 3

Specific aim: To help the students to understand the relations
                   between the characters in a passage by asking them
                   to draw a sociogram.
Skills involved: Transcoding information to diagrammatic display.
Why?   To be able to draw such a sociogram, one has to
                   understand the relations between all the characters
                   in the passage. In the case of many psychological
                   studies, such an exercise can help the students to
                   visualize the main information they have found in
                   the text.

The following passage sums up the beginning of Carson McCullers's
novel, *The Heart is a Lonely Hunter.* After reading the text, can you draw
a sociogram to represent the relations between the different characters in
the story?
Use thick arrows to indicate feelings of love or friendship and thin arrows
to show dislike or hatred.

Singer, a deaf-mute about thirty-two years old, has been living in a
Southern town for ten years working as an engraver. Living with him is
another deaf-mute, a Greek named Antonapoulos. The latter is gross,
greedy, cretinous, but Singer adores him, attributing to him intelligence
and sympathy that he does not possess.

When Antonapoulos's odd behavior becomes intolerable and he is sent
to the state insane asylum 200 miles away, Singer is distraught. He moves
into a furnished room in a house run by the Kellys, a large, impoverished
family. He begins taking his meals at the New York Café, a restaurant
owned by Biff Brannon, a lonely man filled with a tenderness that finds no
outlet. Biff's wife, Alice, treats him with contempt, especially since he has
become impotent.

Singer soon becomes, without his willing it or understanding it, a
magnet for four unfulfilled, spiritually restless people. First there is Jake
Blount, a five-foot, huge-fisted, raging wanderer who goes on periodic
drunks. Jake is maddened by the hopelessness of people, their refusal to
learn what they can do to improve their miserable lot. He goes from place
to place in the South, always unheeded or misunderstood. Singer seems to
him to comprehend and even to share the emotions that drive him. On
Sundays, when he is free from his job as a carnival mechanic, Jake comes to
Singer's room to talk tumultuously of his experiences, his hopes, his ideals.

Mick Kelly, a gangling fourteen-year-old girl, is another who finds in
Singer a sensitive understanding of things she cannot fully articulate. A bit
rough, she is nevertheless a girl who loves her little brothers until it hurts,
and who has a passion for music that leads her to sacrifice her lunches in
order to take lessons from a more fortunate girl who can play the piano.
Music is with her always – little tunes that go through her head and that she
tries, without technical knowledge, to put down on paper. She comes to
identify music and Singer, and she worships the deaf-mute for his apparent
compassion and, she supposes, empathy.

Dr. Benedict Copeland, a tubercular Negro physician, also feels that
Singer shares his ideals. The doctor is filled with suppressed fury at the
brutality of white men and at the ignominy of his race. He has always
striven to invest his people with a sense of mission – freedom to serve
humanity as equals and receive their due. He names his children Karl
Marx, Hamilton, William, and Portia, but they reject his ambitions for
them and remain content with their trivial round of pleasures. Only
Singer, different from all other white men he has known, will respond to
his impassioned statement of purpose which has alienated his wife whom
he loved but who rejected him and drove his children from him.

Finally Biff Brannon, inquiring and skeptical, a searcher but not a
devotee, comes often to see Singer. Restless, unceasingly interested in
penetrating beneath the surface, feminine in spite of his hirsute masculine
appearance, Biff is misinterpreted by Jake who cannot understand that Biff
feels an affinity for him though not for his beliefs, and by Mick who
distrusts him intuitively and feels that he harbors animosity toward her.
Biff, in fact, likes freaks and children. He likes freaks, his wife once sharply
informed him, because he is a bit of a freak himself. He has a secret
fondness for perfume, which he dabs under his ears, and he keeps a
complete file of newspapers dating back twenty years to World War I. He
likes children, too, in an ambiguous fashion, varying from a tender
parental longing for children of his own to a diffuse sexual longing for
Mick.

(From Abraham H. Lass: *A Student's Guide to 50 American Novels*
(Washington Square Press, 1960))

Here is what the diagram would look like in this case.

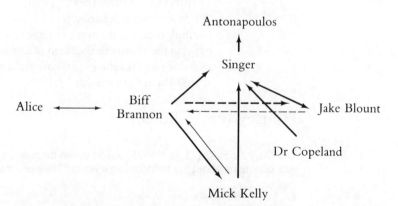

Sociograms – further hints

It is also possible to use other kinds of arrows to symbolize other
relations between characters (e.g. indifference, jealousy, envy, etc.)

A first step in this exercise might be to give only the 'frame' of the sociogram, i.e. the arrows, and to ask the students to fill in the names.

e.g.

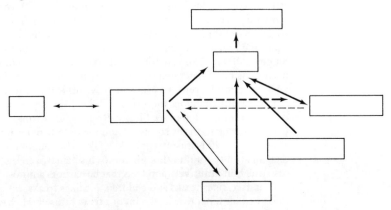

Exercise 4: Questions 1 and 3 are exercises in completing a document and matching. Question 2:

Specific aim: To help the students to understand the main idea in the text by asking them to transfer the information given into percentages.

Skills involved: Transcoding information into figures.
Identifying the main idea of a text.

Why?   When analysing the answers to a questionnaire, it is normal to divide them into categories and to express the results in the form of percentages. This exercise requires the global comprehension of the main idea in each answer.

Housewives' Choice

The *Daily Express* (11 April 1979) asked seven housewives to answer ten vital questions about the forthcoming election. Here are their answers:

1
1. I've never really thought about it.

2. Mr Callaghan. A woman wouldn't be strong enough.

3. I haven't really thought about Mrs Thatcher's image, I don't think Mr Callaghan's is very good at the moment but he's never really been given a chance. Leaders are important and they should be of good character.

4. The rising price of food, clothing, heating, rates and mortgage.

5. I have to go out to work to help with the cost of living.

6. Yes, it is time whoever gets in to start putting laws down to curb unions.

7. Yes, I think each child has a better chance as schools are now.

8. Bring back hanging for murder and stricter sentences.

9. Try to bring down the prices on different things such as food and clothing. Stop strikes and be firmer.

10. They won't have any effect. I'm proud to be Welsh but I don't believe in Welsh Nationalism.

2
1. Yes.
2. Mrs Thatcher because I feel she knows about finance from personal experience, e.g. shopping, etc.
3. I think public image matters a lot at election time. I don't think Mrs Thatcher's image is very impressive. She seems too gentle. Mr Callaghan seems a very nice person, but he's a fence sitter.
4. Rising cost of food and clothes.

5. The family budget's been affected —and we're always getting complaints about the price of beer.
6. Yes, and over stepping the mark.
7. Yes, although teachers should have more authority in discipline.
8. Bring back hanging for murder, child rape and terrorism.
9. Freeze prices. Further investigations into social security scroungers.
10. They've lots of good ideas but they haven't got the strength.

3
1. Yes.

2. Mr Callaghan. It would be bad for this country if another Government took over at this time. He has been a fair Prime Minister.

3. Mrs Thatcher appears a ruthless woman, he seems a fair man. I think leaders matter because the overall policy of the party comes through them.

4. The main problem has been the rising cost of foodstuffs though those seem to have been stabilising over the past six months.

5. By having to increase the amount I spend on food.

6. No, if the trade unions didn't have power there would be even more people on very low wages.

7. Yes, I think the comprehensive system is very good, but classes could be smaller.

8. People who have committed serious offences and been given long or life sentences rarely serve them. I think this should be treated more seriously.

9. Curb prices, lower income tax but don't then collect it back through VAT or something else. More money in education.

10. The minority parties aren't a force to be considered.

4
1. What we want is a good leader, regardless of sex.
2. Mr Callaghan. He has been a good Prime Minister. He has previous experience and is more likely to be able to deal with the unions.
3. Mrs Thatcher seems condescending Mr Callaghan seems to have his feet firmly on the ground, he's realistic and doesn't make extravagant promises. I vote both for the party and the leader.
4. Inflation and rising prices—particularly food. Teachers salaries have not kept pace with inflation.
5. I have had to take a part-time job to help our monthly budget. Before I could stay at home full-time to bring up my children. We've

had to cut down on spending— fewer clothes and outings and less entertaining. We have adjusted our diet to less meat and less expensive foods but it's probably more basic and healthy now.
6. Yes.
7. Yes I believe in the comprehensive system but it must be tightened up so that the more able children are not creamed off.
8. No. The present system seems adequate.
9. Reduce inflation and keep tighter controls on rising prices. Spend more money on education and medical services.
10. I don't think they have any effect.

5
1. Yes.
2. Mrs Thatcher. She is a warm understanding person who believes in what she says. He only says what he thinks the majority will want to hear.

3. Mrs Thatcher strikes me as someone who has thought out her policies. Mr Callaghan's image is of power at any cost. Party leaders do matter but they shouldn't.

4. Price rises, falling education standards, too many petty regulations, having more and more of my responsibilities given to the state. Over-burdened health service.

5. Gas bills and rates which I think are based on an unfair system. I make as many clothes as possibly

myself.
6. Yes, it's strike first, talk later. Common sense doesn't prevail.
7. No, we must train people for the future.
8. More policemen on the streets with a better career structure for the police. More muggers caught and stiffer penalties.
9. Don't treat housewives as separate people, we have the same problems as the rest of society. Treat bringing up the next generation as our most important task. More law and order, better education and less interference.
10. I think the more choices of parties we have, the better.

ten vital election questions

6
1. Yes.
2. Mrs Thatcher. It's about time a woman had a chance.
3. She comes across as an intelligent and thinking woman. His image isn't very good. I think leaders are important ; they put across what the party are going to do.
4. The cost of food and rising prices in general.
5. I used to save the salary from my part-time job. Now it has to go into the housekeeping to maintain our standard of living.
6. Yes, but they're still necessary.
7. No.
8. Yes.
9. Bring down tax and see that people on strike do not get State benefit.
10. You can't have fence sitters running the country.

7
1. I do not think the gender matters.
2. At the moment I'm not sure — they both seem to be dangling the carrot at the housewife.
3. Mrs Thatcher does seem the Iron Maiden, rather school-teacherish with strong opinions. Burly Mr Callaghan is rather a let down sometimes but he seems unflappable in a crisis. But I put policies before leaders' personalities.
4. Inflation taxes and rising crime. Five years ago I spent £25 a week on food, now it's £38.
5. My standard of living used to be a great deal better. Now there's not so much of the good life.
6. Yes, they disrupt my life with power cuts, transport stoppages and shortages of household goods.
7. No. We should have the right to choose to pay fees if we want.
8. G r e a t e r   deterrents to the criminal
9. Reduce inflation, lower taxes, curb crime, and encourage enterprise in private industry.
10. The Liberals will never be strong enough to attract me—and I don't want to see Great Britain fragmented.

| 1 |
| 2 |
| 3 |
| 4 |
| 5 |
| 6 |
| 7 |
| 8 |
| 9 |
| 10 |

1 After reading these answers, can you work out what the ten questions were?

2 How would you state the results of the interviews?
Write down the answers given as briefly as you can and write
percentages or figures in front.
e.g.1: Yes: four (57%) Don't know or Doesn't matter: three (43%)
1:..
2:..
3:..
4:..
5:..
6:..
7:..
8:..
9:..
10:...

3 Here are some details about each of the seven housewives who
answered the questions. Can you match the people and the answers?
What details helped you in each case?

A **MRS HEATHER WARDLE**, 26, of Coventry, husband works for Massey Fergusson, baby 10 months. Votes Labour because they represent the working class and believes they will win the election.

B **MRS JANET LAND**, 34, from Chadwell Heath, Essex. Three children aged between four and nine. Married to a technical college lecturer and votes Tory because "people who work hard should be rewarded for their efforts."

C **MRS RITA SMITH**, 36, from F o r m b y, Liverpool. Teenage son and daughter. Married to a superintendent at Ford's and has a part-time job. Votes Tory and believes the past five years have been "a disaster."

D **MRS KAREN FEAKIN**, 31, from East Dulwich, London. Two children, girl, five, and boy three, and another baby due in the summer. Married to a teacher and has a part-time teaching job herself. Votes Labour because of "their concern for lower socio-economic groups" but believes the Tories will win the next election.

E **MRS KIM WESTON**, 36, runs a pub with her husband in York. Two teenage children. A floating voter who wants "an improvement on the past five years."

F **MRS MARLYN WATT**, 31, from Hellensburgh, Strathclyde, Scotland. Two daughters, four and seven. Married to a surveyor. Describes her politics as "Don't know" with Tory leanings. Not at all sure who will win the election.

G **MRS SANDRA WHITE**, 36, a miner's wife from Hengoed, Mid-Glamorgan. Two daughters, 12 and 14. Votes Labour because "we get a better deal."

163

1.6   Mapping it out

Exercise 1

Specific aim: To help the students to understand the main
information (or details) of a text by asking them to
trace a route on a map.

Skills involved: Transcoding information to diagrammatic display.

Why?   It is natural when reading about a precise itinerary
to visualize it in one's mind or to use a map to trace
it on. By providing a frame (i.e. the diagram) this
exercise will help the students, while it will at the
same time force them to a very accurate reading of
the passage, searching for relevant details.

Read the following passage and indicate on the diagram:
a) All that Iverson can see in de Groot's room (e.g. door, furniture, etc.)
b) de Groot's movements (use arrows).

The two rooms were separated by a heavy door. It was firmly locked and
paper had been stuffed into the keyhole. By the time Iverson had scraped
out the paper – using the curved blade of his nail scissors – it was past
midnight. De Groot would soon be back for he had left his table lamp on
when he went out at eleven.

Iverson switched off his own light and went back to the now open
keyhole. Looking through, he could see almost the whole of de Groot's
room, except the two corners to his immediate left and right. But straight
in front of him, in the square mirror overhanging the bed, he could see the
reflection of these two corners: to his left, the entrance door; to his right,
the shiny wardrobe, half blocking the window. The two rooms were in
every way identical and must have been a single large room before changes
were made to the hotel.

He was about to move away from the door when he heard the sound of
de Groot's key and a voice saying in Hungarian 'goodnight'. In the mirror,
Iverson could see de Groot's back. He shut the door, turned the key twice,
took off his jacket and threw it onto the bed. Then he crossed to the
window, looked out for a second over Budapest, and closed the curtains.
And even once they were closed, he pulled again, twice, at the imitation
red velvet drapes, as if determined to block out all light from outside.
There was a moment of silence as he looked back over his shoulder at the
mirror, waited and listened. Iverson dared not move. De Groot's eyes
seemed to be fixed on the empty keyhole. But, no, he had noticed nothing.
He crossed to the bed, sat down, and took off his shoes. Then he lay back
and poured himself a glass of water from the carafe on the table to his left.
For a while he lay there, thinking, with the empty glass in his hand. He
seemed to be making some calculation. Finally, he sat up, pulled his jacket
towards him and took out an envelope from the inside pocket. Iverson
recognized the envelope: it was the same one as had been given to all
delegates to the congress, and it contained 900 Hungarian forints – for local

expenses. De Groot took out the notes and began counting. He had already reached thirty-five when suddenly he stopped, listened, and then switched out the light.
(by A. Duff)

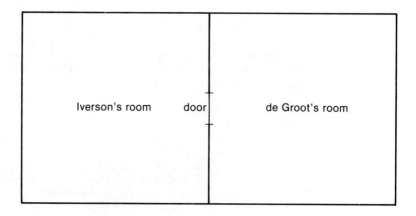

Exercise 2

Specific aim:
Skills involved: } Same as for exercise 1.
Why?

A friend of yours is coming to visit Boston where you live. You think she should follow the 'Freedom Trail' along which the main places of historic interest in Boston can be seen. All you have is a map of Boston and a little guidebook that tells you how to follow the Freedom Trail.
Can you trace the route your friend should take on the map and indicate where the main places of interest are (write down on the map the numbers corresponding to those of the guidebook).

Here is what the guidebook says:

Start from Boston Common (1), bought in 1634 to train the troops and feed the cattle. In the center of the Common, you will see the 'Old Elm' on which 17th century witches and pirates were hung. Then walk to the corner of Beacon Street and Park Street. Just opposite the Common, you will find the State House and Archives (2) built in 1795 and where the Constitution of 1780 and other famous historical records are kept. You must also see the Hall of Flags while you are there. When leaving the State House, follow Park Street along Boston Common and at the corner of Park Street and Tremont Street you will see Park Street Church (3), which Henry James called 'the most interesting mass of brick and mortar in America.' Next to the Church on Tremont Street is the 'Granary burying ground' (4), the most famous of Boston's cemeteries. Three of the men who signed the Declaration of Independence, Paine, Hancock and Adams are buried there.

Go along Tremont Street and turn right in School Street. Just on your left you will find King's Chapel (5), the first Unitarian Church in America, and next to it the site of the first public school in Boston (6). The site is now occupied by the City Hall and on its lawn you will see the first statue of Boston, that of Benjamin Franklin. (7) Go on down School Street and at the corner of Washington Street, on the left, you will see the Old Corner Book Store (8) where some of the best-known American writers used to meet: Hawthorne, Longfellow, Emerson, Harriet Beecher-Stowe . . .

Turn right on Washington Street, then take the first street on the left (Milk Street) and you will find the 'Old South Meeting House' (9) on your left. In this house which also served as a church, some of the most important events in the history of our nation (such as the Boston Tea Party) were planned. Follow Milk Street and turn left on Devonshire Street. At the end of that street, where Court and State Streets meet, stands the 'Old State House' (10), the real cradle of Independence since it was there that the Colonial government had its seat. It was from its east balcony that the Declaration of Independence was first read and it was just east of it that the Boston Massacre was fought. It is now marked by a ring of cobble-stones on the pavement (11). Another Hall, Faneuil Hall (12) can be found on the square just east of Government Center, on Congress Street.

From there, just pass under the John Fitzgerald Expressway until you reach North Street. At the North-West corner of Richmond and North Streets, stands the oldest house in Boston, Paul Revere's home (13), built in 1677. In the house you will find many historic exhibits about the life and skill of Paul Revere.

To finish your visit of Boston's Freedom Trail, turn right in Richmond Street, then right again in Hanover Street, left in Prince Street, then right again. On your right, just after Tileston Street, you will see the Old North Church which is Boston's oldest church and which played an important part during the Independence War.

(Between 7 a.m. and 6 p.m. on weekdays, special Freedom Trail buses can take you back to Boston Common for 20c.)

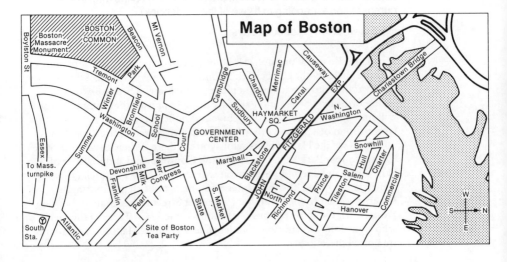

Map of Boston

Non-linguistic response to the text

Exercise 3

Specific aim:
Skills involved: } Same as for exercise 1.
Why?

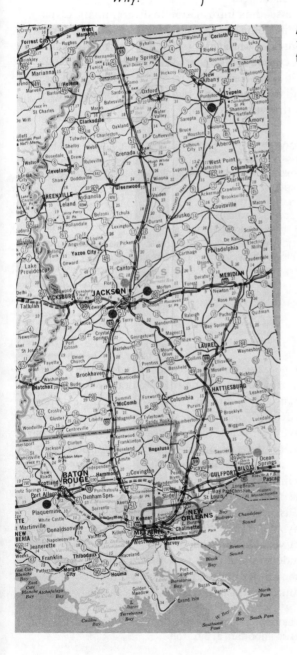

After reading the letter on pages 130–3, can you trace on the map the route followed by Pat?

Exercise 4

Specific aim: To help the students to 'see' the text as a scene from a play and to visualize the comings and goings of the characters.
Skills involved: Transcoding information to diagrammatic display.
Why?   While doing this exercise, the students will become conscious of the number of indications given in the passage about the characters' movements. It will help them to visualize the scene and it should later lead to a better appreciation of the technique used by the writer.

1 Read the short story 'Cat in the Rain' by Ernest Hemingway and try to consider it as a one-act play.
2 Underline all the expressions at the beginning which could serve as directions for the setting.
3 How many scenes can you find?
4 Fill the diagrams opposite with crosses to show where the characters are and arrows to show where they are going.
5 Can you now find in the type of dialogue, the style, the descriptions, some more indications showing this story is built like a play?

Exercise 5

Specific aim: To help the students to understand specific information by asking them to draw a diagram.
Skills involved: Transcoding information to diagrammatic display.
Why?   In order to understand a text, it is often essential to have a very clear idea of what certain objects look like or of the arrangement of a room or of the situation of a house, to mention only a few examples. Asking the students to draw a diagram of the object or a map to show the situation of the house is the best way of ensuring that the students pay attention to details. In addition, the comparison between the different diagrams drawn by the students should lead to interesting discussions since many descriptions are vague on certain points and admit of various interpretations.

Read Roald Dahl's story *Mrs Bixby and the Colonel's Coat* and draw the pawn ticket which is so important in the story.

Here are the completed diagrams.

Sea and square

2nd floor bedroom

Scene 1

Scene 2

Scene 3

Scene 4

Scene 5

Exercise 6

Specific aim: ⎫
Skills involved: ⎬ Same as for exercise 5.
Why? ⎭

Read the following passage and complete the diagram to show how the
guests are arranged around the table.

In the centre of the table was a small silver vase with four roses, deep red
roses, tidily arranged (for James Curry was a man who loved precision)
like the four points of the compass – North, South, East and West. And
around this rose-pointed compass the guests were arranged. Finding the
right arrangement had not been easy, but James Curry had hit on a simple
solution: to put the 'talkers' opposite each other, and the 'non-talkers'
between them. Like this, he was sure at least that the conversation would
be directed towards the centre – towards the silver vase – and not away
from it. On this basis, he had divided his guests into those who talked 'too
much' and those who talked 'too little'.

Now, as he looked down the long table, he saw with satisfaction that his
planning had been well done. He was right. The 'talkers' were talking, the
'non-talkers' listening. He felt a scientist's pride at having distributed his
forces so well. At each corner of the table was a talker; between each talker
were two non-talkers; and, at either end, like two magnetic poles, the host
and hostess, James and Maureen Curry.

Two conversations were going at once. He sat back and listened. 'It's
not the first time; things have disappeared before . . .' Joan Fowles, who
with every word moved her knife closer to his fork, was explaining her
'theory' to the Davidsons. While from the opposite corner, Anton
Vinogradoff (whom Maureen had playfully called 'my left-hand man') was
explaining *his* theory to the Monroes: 'A professional thief would never
have used dynamite . . .' Silent and respectful, the two married couples
stared at each other over the roses. But before they could say anything,

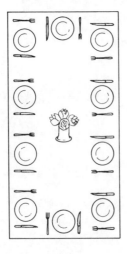

two other voices had broken into the conversation. Patrick Marsh, like a warm wind from the South-East, with a cheerful: 'Well, they didn't take everything, did they?' And Joan Glazenby, like a sharp blast from the North-West, with a cold: 'How d'you know it was *they*?'

James Curry was pleased. This was what he had hoped for. The arrangement could not have been better planned.

(by A. Duff)

Exercise 7

Specific aim:
Skills involved: } Same as for exercise 5.
Why?

Read the following passage and draw a map showing where Midwich is. Indicate all the roads and neighbouring villages mentioned in the text.

Midwich lies roughly eight miles west-north-west of Trayne. The main road westward out of Trayne runs through the neighbouring villages of Stouch and Oppley, from each of which secondary roads lead to Midwich. The village itself is therefore at the apex of a road triangle which has Oppley and Stouch at its lower corners; its only other highway being a lane which rolls in a Chestertonian fashion some five miles to reach Hickham which is three miles north.

(From John Wyndham: *The Midwich Cuckoos* (Penguin, 1960))

Mapping it out – further hints

Instead of transferring written information into a map or a drawing, students can also be asked to draw graphs, flow-diagrams or tables with figures.

1.7   Using the information in the text

Exercise 1

Specific aim: To help the students to understand the text by asking them to use the information contained in it to make decisions.

Skills involved: Using the information contained in the text. Scanning.

Why?   Many texts do not simply bring us information or ideas, they tell us what to do and influence our behaviour. The best and most natural way of dealing with such texts is to ask the students to do what they would naturally be supposed to do after reading the text, for instance, folding a piece of paper in the case of origami instructions, or trying a recipe. If it is difficult to carry out the required actions, as in the case of the following text, one can prepare a questionnaire to see how the students would have reacted.

Read this extract from the regulations of Regent's Park.

REGENT'S PARK

THE PARKS REGULATION ACTS, 1872 and 1926

REGULATION †
The figure of 30 miles an hour is amended
to 30 miles an hour by The Regent's Park (First
Amendment) Regulations, 1960, dated 20th July,
1960.

REGULATIONS

made by the Commissioners of His Majesty's Works and Public Buildings pursuant to the Parks Regulations Acts, 1872 and 1926.

B.—BATHING, FISHING and SKATING.

1. Bathing and fishing are prohibited.
2. No unauthorised person shall go upon any ice when prohibited by notice, and no person shall enter any enclosed section of ice without the written authorisation of the Commissioners or shall wilfully break or damage the ice or throw stones or rubbish or act so as to be likely to endanger the safety or interfere with the comfort and convenience of persons using the ice for skating or otherwise.

GENERAL REGULATIONS

1. No unauthorised person shall enter into or remain in any part of the Park during any time appointed for closing of same.
2. No person shall wilfully interfere with the comfort or convenience of any other person using or enjoying the Park.
3. No alms, donations, contributions or subscriptions of any kind shall be made or given, solicited or collected in the Park.
4. No unauthorised person shall sell or offer for sale or hire in the Park any article, commodity, pamphlet, programme or thing.
5. No person shall in the Park, exhibit, distribute, sell or offer for sale any indecent print, picture, book or article.
6. The letting or placing of chairs for hire without the licence in writing of the Commissioners is prohibited.
7. No unauthorised person shall walk upon any shrubbery, flower-bed or lawn or any other land specially enclosed or the entry on which is prohibited by notice.
8. No bath-chair, perambulator or any children's carriage shall be placed or used so as to be or to be likely to be any obstruction or nuisance and in no case shall such vehicles proceed three or more abreast. Bath chairs and perambulators are not allowed on any paths where they are prohibited by notice.
9. No person shall destroy or injure any tree, shrub or plant, or pluck any flower, bough or leaf or injure or deface any building, structure, seat, railing or other property in the Park or enclosing any part thereof.
10. No unauthorised person shall put up, fix, exhibit or distribute in the Park any advertisement, post-bill or other paper or any printed matter or affix them to any tree, fence, post, railing or gate of or in the Park.
11. No person shall deface any road or footway by writing or other marks.

21. No public address of an unlawful character or for an unlawful purpose shall be delivered in the Park
22. Where a public address is delivered in the Park
  (a) no words, expressions, insinuations or gestures of an obscene, indecent, abusive or insulting nature or of a blasphemous or threatening character shall be used.
  (b) no words shall be used or acts done reasonably calculated to cause a breach of the peace or disorderly conduct of any kind in the Park.
  (c) No words shall be used or information conveyed,
    (1) imparting or purporting to impart information concerning betting, racing or any other wagering or
    (2) advertising that such information can be obtained else-where or
    (3) with the object of advertising that any commodity, facility, service, article or thing can be obtained whether in the Park or elsewhere.
23. No performance or representation, whether spoken or in dumb show or mechanically produced or reproduced, shall be given in the Park without the written authorisation of the Commissioners.
24. No person shall sit, lie, rest or sleep on any seat or in any part of the Park in an indecent posture or behave in any manner reasonably likely to offend against public decency.
25. Brawling, fighting, gambling, betting, playing with cards or dice, begging and telling fortunes are prohibited.
26. No intoxicated person shall enter or remain in the Park.
27. No person in an offensively unclean or verminous condition shall enter or remain in the Park or lie upon or occupy any of the seats.
28. No person shall use indecent or obscene language in the Park.
29. No unauthorised person shall discharge any firearm or make any bonfire and no person shall wantonly throw or discharge any stone or missile to the damage or danger of any person, or throw or set fire to any firework in the Park.
30. No unauthorised person shall wilfully disturb any animal grazing in the Park or take or attempt to take any bird, fish or egg or set any trap or destroy any bird or animal in the Park, and no person shall harry, injure or illtreat any animal, bird or fish.
31. Children's boating is permitted. No boats other than those provided by the Contractor licensed by the Commissioners may be used.
32. No person shall wash clothes or other things in any water in the Park or do any act likely to cause a pollution of the water in any drinking fountain in the Park.
33. Climbing trees, railings or fences or the fastening thereto of ropes or swings is prohibited.
34. Any person found by a Park Keeper or Police Constable committing a breach of these Regulations shall, on demand made by such Park Keeper or Police Constable give his correct name and address.

Dated the 21st day of July, 1932.

Now imagine you are a Park Keeper. You see people doing the following things. Would you let them go on? Put a cross under 'yes' or 'no' according to what you think. If your answer is no, write down next to it the number of the rule which you think has been broken.

		Yes	No →	Rule No.
1	Someone cutting down a tree			
2	A family enjoying a picnic on a bench			
3	Children playing Indians and climbing up trees			
4	Children running along the paths			
5	Someone emptying a bottle of oil into the lake			
6	Someone talking to the public about education in G.B.			
7	Someone sailing in a private boat			
8	Children sailing on a raft they have built			
9	Someone distributing pamphlets for a religious group			
10	Someone collecting money for the blind			
11	Children alone in one of the park's boats			
12	Someone pinning a paper to a tree asking if anybody has seen his dog and offering a reward			
13	Children swimming in the lake			
14	Children playing cards on the lawn			
15	Children playing cards on a bench			

What would you say to those people who are violating one of the rules?

Exercise 2

Specific aim: To help the students to understand the text by asking them to use the information contained in it to make decisions.

Skills involved: Using the information contained in the text. Scanning.

Why? We read many texts hoping to find in them a solution to our problems and it is therefore natural to give the students such problems to solve. The exercise that follows requires on their parts a detailed understanding of the texts as well as the ability to make deductions and comparisons. Although the 'answer' required only consists of the choice of one kind of holiday, it will lead to justifications and discussions between groups.

You've inherited £250 from your great-aunt and decide to spend the money on a holiday some time this year. (You are allowed two weeks off.) If possible, you would like to go abroad, to some outlandish country, as you may not have the opportunity of doing so later.
You would also like
- good food
- a fairly comfortable holiday (you do not want to come back exhausted)
- to practise some sport if possible (swimming? cycling? walking?)
- as friendly an atmosphere as possible (you would like to avoid large international hotels).

So far your friends have suggested these three possibilities. Which would you write to for more information?

1

RATES PER PERSON	1 Week – BP Persons in Room				2 Weeks – BP Persons in Room			
DEPARTURES	3	2	1	Child	3	2	1	Child
Apr 15 - Jun 17	379	399	469	289	479	499	629	319
Jun 24 - Aug 26	389	409	489	289	499	519	669	319
Sep 02 - Oct 28	379	399	469	289	479	499	629	319
Nov 04 - Dec 09	389	409	489	289	499	519	669	319
Tax & Service Charge	12	12	12	6	24	24	24	12

(price in dollars)

ARISTOS IXTAPA

The Aristos Ixtapa is designed and decorated to reflect its active style: tennis, swimming , holes of golf nearby and year round water sports. The nearby Pacific abounds in sailfish, marlin, tuna and red snapper.
The cuisine, both Mexican and international is delicious any time of day. Shoppers will find a boutique specializing in warm weather fashions.

SPECIAL FEATURES

Full Breakfast daily

IXTAPA FRIDAY DEPARTURES VIA AEROMEXICO

YOUR **TREASURE TOURS**
MEXICAN HOLIDAY
INCLUDES:

● Round trip air transportation from Toronto by Aeromexico or Quebecair.

● Complimentary inflight meals and bar service.*

● Transportation between airport and hotel, including baggage handling.

● Meal Plan as indicated.

● Accommodation in air-conditioned room with private bath or shower.

● Treasure Tours ticket wallet and beach bag.

*except on scheduled Aeromexico flights.

IXTAPA
FRIDAY DEPARTURES VIA AEROMEXICO

Another new resort area developed by the Mexican Government — Ixtapa is 125 miles north of Acapulco, nestled between a 24 mile beach and the Sierra Madre mountains.
By day exciting new shops featuring Mexican handicrafts and jewellery beckon to the bargain hunter — skin diving, deep sea fishing and sailing tempt the sports minded while the beautiful beach and relaxed pace sooth the harried.
By evening fine dining and exciting entertainment in Ixtapa or nearby Zihuatanejo will appeal to all.

2

The Canal du Midi crosses a river in Southern France

SOMETHING different for 1978 is the boast of new tour organisation, Wheels, which has come up with an attractive series of trips . . .

They have mixed a camping holiday with nights in comfortable hotels and added an interesting extra — canal cruising.

The number on each trip is limited to 26.

The big interest for me was the idea of tossing in a seven day canal cruise in southern France.

You board a fully equipped and self-contained motorcruiser for a week and decide when to stop, when to go, and where to go.

The week is spent on the Canal du Midi which runs from Bordeaux on the Atlantic Ocean side to the Mediterranean.

Main bases used for the Wheels programme are between Marseilles down from Montpellier, to Castelnaudary, near Toulouse.

It sounds too romantic to be true but the experts say it's so easy all you have to do is try.

There is much commerical traffic on the canal and barges carrying wine, petrol, grain, and other commercial products pass by the holidaymakers.

The skippers are friendly, used to the pleasure craft, and will always slow down if you want to pass or have a chat.

And as you slowly glide through the rich farmlands and vineyards you'll pass through lines of trees on each bank. They were thoughtfully planted by the builder of the waterway so that on the hot days the boatmen and the horses which pulled the barges would have some respite from the heat.

You board your cruiser in groups of six or seven, get detailed maps and canal information, get a lesson in the simple controls and off you go.

In sight of the Pyrenees and in a beautiful climate you just float along. There are bicycles and a dinghy aboard so you can take a short trip inland when you get tired of lazing on the deck.

The travellers use the best campsites available and small local hotels — "people who are expert in the art of true inn-keeping".

3

"The Great Outdoors People"

ARENA

The place you come to get away

HIGH COUNTRY EXPEDITION

13 DAY CAMPING IN ICELAND

Departure Dates:
Sunday mornings,
from Reykjavik:

June 25
July 02, 09, 16, 23, 30
Aug 06, 13, 20

We invite you to enjoy an expedition suitable for all ages. The ultimate in outdoor camping experience, broadening your camping horizons. Criss-crossing the high-country with an ever-varying panorama of vast volcanic plains, swift-flowing rivers, thundering waterfalls, spouting gaysirs, gleaming icecaps and verdant valleys.

Travel **ICELAND**

The travelling is made in comfortable purpose-adapted coaches, accompanied by field-kitchen and equipment truck. Staff members serve breakfast, picnic lunch and dinner, from lunch Day 1 to lunch Day 13. Camping accommodation, tents and air mattresses provided and mobile toilet.

Phone for your copy of our brochure NOW!

Full details from:

TRAILFINDERS
or
ADVENTURE CENTRE
5540 College Avenue, Oakland
California 94618, USA

Breidafjordur
Faxafloi
Reykjavik
Vatnajokull
Myrdals-jokull

Technical Operator:

ARENA TOURS, HVASSALEITI 26, REYKJAVIK

Exercise 3

Specific aim: To ask the students to answer a quiz and rate themselves.

Skills involved: Relating the text to one's own experience.

Why? Besides being usually highly motivating, this kind of text provides its own reading comprehension exercise at the same time, since the fact that one is able to rate oneself for each separate question of the quiz is proof that one has understood the main points of the text.

Do the following quiz to calculate your life expectancy.

Non-linguistic response to the text

DR DIANA WOODRUFF is a psychologist who believes we all have the capacity to live to be 100. In fact, she says, biologists set the top limit for human life even higher—at 120. After years of research on longevity she has drawn up the quiz below which enables most of us to work out how long we will live. Her own view is that contented fun-lovers have the best chance of living to be 100. See how you rate.

Start by looking up your own age in the table at the foot of the next column. Against this, you will find your basic life expectancy, derived from figures produced by insurance actuaries. Then, in answering the questions below, add to or take away from this figure, according to how your life style and personality affect your habits.

Remember one thing; women can expect to live roughly three years longer than men (for whom the table below is designed). Women, therefore, should add three years to start with.

1 Add one year for each of your grandparents who lived to be 80 or more. Add half a year for each one who topped 70.

2 Add four years if your mother lived beyond 80 and two if your father did so.

3 Take off four years if any sister, brother, parent or grandparent died of a heart attack, stroke or arteriosclerosis before 50. Subtract two years for each of these who died between 50 and 60.

4 Take off three years for each sister, brother, parent or grandparent who died of diabetis mellitus or peptic ulcer before 60. If any of these died of stomach cancer before then, take off two years. For any other illnesses which killed them before 60 (except those caused by accidents) subtract one year.

5 Women who cannot have children, or plan none, subtract half a year. Women with over seven children take off one year.

6 If you are a first-born add one year.

7 Add two years if your intelligence is above average.

8 Take off 12 (yes, 12) years if you smoke more than 40 cigarettes a day; 20-40, subtract seven years. Less than 20, take off two years.

9 If you enjoy regular sex, once or twice a week, add two years.

10 If you have an annual check-up (a thorough one) add two years.

11 If you are overweight (or ever have been) take off two years.

12 If you sleep more than 10 hours every night, or less than five, take off two years.

13 Drinking. One or two whiskies, half a litre of wine, four glasses of beer counts as moderate—add three years. Light drinkers—that is, you don't drink every day—add only one and a half years. If you don't drink at all, neither add nor subtract anything. Heavy drinkers and alcoholics—take off eight years.

14 Exercise. Three times a week—jogging, cycling, swimming, brisk walks, dancing or skating—add three years. Weekend walks etc, don't count.

15 Do you prefer simple, plain foods, vegetables and fruit to richer, meatier, fatty, foods ? If you can say yes honestly and always stop eating before you are full, add one year.

16 If you are frequently ill take off five years.

17 Education. If you did postgraduate work at university add three years. For an ordinary bachelor's degree add two. Up to A level add one. O level and below—none.

18 Jobs. If you are a professional person, add one and a half years; technical, managerial, administrative and agricultural workers add one year; proprietors, clerks and sales staff add nothing; semi-skilled workers take off half a year; labourers subtract four years.

19 If, however, you're not a a labourer but your job involves a lot of physical work add two years. If it's a desk job, take off two.

20 If you live in a town or have done for most of your life take off one year. Add a year if most of your time has been spent in the country side.

21 Readers who are married and living with their spouse should add one year. However, if you are a separated man living alone take off nine years, seven if you are a widower living alone. If you live with others take off only half these figures. Women who are separated or divorced take off four years, widows three and a half, unless you live with others in which case take off only two.

22 Unmarried women should subtract one year for each unmarried decade beyond 25 *even if* you are living with someone.

23 If you have changed careers more than once, and have changed houses and spouses, take off two years.

24 If you have one or two close friends in whom you confide everything add a year.

If you are disappointed, don't blame us. You should by now have a clue as to how you can improve things. It probably means second thoughts about that gin and tonic you were just going to pour. . . .

Arnold Legh

The long-life table

To answer the above quiz you need to know your basic life expectancy. This table has been compiled from life insurance statistics applicable to white European males. Women should add three years in each case.

Present Age	Life Expectancy						
15	70.7	32	71.9	49	73.6	66	78.4
16	70.8	33	72.0	50	73.8	67	78.9
17	70.8	34	72.0	51	74.0	68	79.3
18	70.9	35	72.1	52	74.2	69	79.7
19	71.0	36	72.2	53	74.4	70	80.2
20	71.1	37	72.2	54	74.7	71	80.7
21	71.1	38	72.3	55	74.9	72	81.2
22	71.2	39	72.4	56	75.1	73	81.7
23	71.3	40	72.5	57	75.4	74	82.2
24	71.3	41	72.6	58	75.7	75	82.8
25	71.4	42	72.7	59	76.0	76	83.3
26	71.5	43	72.8	60	76.3	77	83.9
27	71.6	44	72.9	61	76.6	78	84.5
28	71.6	45	73.0	62	77.0	79	85.1
29	71.7	46	73.2	63	77.3	80	85.7
30	71.8	47	73.3	64	77.7		
31	71.8	48	73.5	65	78.1		

(*The Sunday Times*)

177

Exercise 4

Specific aim: To train the students to read a text in order to find
                   the solution to a problem.
Skills involved: Using the information contained in the text to solve
                   a problem.
Why?   This is a challenging and motivating kind of
                   activity which requires a detailed comprehension of
                   the text. No further exercise is needed here since the
                   students will constantly have to check the text in
                   order to work out the solution. The fact that they
                   actually find a solution of some kind is proof in
                   itself that the passage has been understood.

You arrive in a strange country where, you are told, two very distinct
groups of people live: one group always tells the truth, the other always
lies. There are many things you want to know about the country, but of
course, first of all, you want to make sure that you can believe the person
who will answer your questions. In other words, you must find someone
who always tells the truth.

Suddenly, you see two persons working in a field. You ask one of them
to come and say to him: 'Go and ask your friend over there if he tells the
truth.' When the man comes back, he says: 'My friend says he always
tells the truth.'

Can you trust the messenger? Or is he one of those who always lie?

Exercise 5

Specific aim: ⎫ Same as for exercise 4 but this time the students
Skills involved: ⎬ are given several questions that will gradually
Why?   ⎭ lead them to the solution. Each question will
                      force them to study the text and think about its
                      implications.

After the cycling competition that had taken place in Winchester, the jury
didn't know what to do. The fog had been so thick that they couldn't
possibly tell who was first. So they decided to ask three of the cyclists,
Alan, Bertie and Cedric what they had seen. Each of them made two
statements but unfortunately one of the three men lied in his statements.
The other two told the truth. Here is what each of them said. Can you help
the jury to find who the first three cyclists were?
Alan said, 'I was first, the last one was Cedric.'
Bertie said, 'Alan wasn't first. The second was Cedric.'
Cedric said, 'I was just before Alan. Bertie wasn't second.'

The following questions should help you solve the problem.
1 Can both Alan and Bertie tell the truth about Cedric?

2 Therefore, can you tell whether Cedric lies or tells the truth?
3 Now that you know whether Cedric tells the truth or not, consider his statement and compare it to what Alan and Bertie said. Who told the truth: Alan or Bertie?
4 Now consider the information in the two statements of the persons who tell the truth.
Who was second? ....
Who was after him? ....
Therefore, who must have been first? ....

Using the information in the text – further hints

- Recipes, instructions to make things – such as origami – or rules for games can also be used in the same way.
- Here is a further example of texts being used in order to make a decision. Give the rules of entry for a competition (the questions asked and the conditions necessary to participate – e.g. age, nationality). The students can then be given a list of five or six persons with information on each of them and the answers they gave and will have – as if they were the judges – to decide who gets the first, second and third prizes and who is eliminated.
- Several texts forming some kind of evidence can also be presented together, the students having to solve a problem by studying or comparing them. They could, for example, be given information about a court case through various types of texts and documents and be asked to find who is guilty or give a verdict.
- Another way of asking the students to use the information of the text is to take the text as a basis for role-play activities.

1.8 Jigsaw reading

Exercise 1

Specific aim:	To help the student to find out how the text is organized and what the relations are between the different parts of a text.
Skills involved:	Predicting and anticipating. Summarizing a passage. Recognizing discourse indicators and relations between parts of a text.
Why?	The students are divided into groups and as each group is given only one passage from the text, they have to pay particular attention to those indicators referring back to something mentioned before or,

conversely, announcing something to come. Groups will have to question each other constantly and check with their passage for significant details giving them a clue to the development of the whole text.

1 Look at the following title and picture.
   What kind of an animal is the unicorn? What are its habits and characteristics? What do you think is the man's attitude towards it?

The Unicorn in the Garden

by James Thurber

2 Now work in groups of two, each group having only *one* of the passages that follow.
   In your group, follow these steps:
   – read the passage carefully
   – sum up what it is about for the other groups
   – try to guess how it is situated in the whole text (e.g. does it come before or after the passage just summed up by one of the other groups? Why? What words, expressions or ideas can help you to justify your opinion?)
   – discuss all this with the other groups until you can reconstitute the whole story, from beginning to end.

GROUP A   As soon as the husband had gone out of the house, the wife got up and dressed as fast as she could. She was very excited and there was a gloat in her eye. She telephoned the police and she telephoned a psychiatrist; she told them to hurry to her house and bring a straight-jacket.

GROUP B   She opened one unfriendly eye and looked at him. 'The unicorn is a mythical beast,' she said, and turned her back on him. The man walked slowly downstairs and out into the garden. The unicorn was still there; he was now browsing among the tulips. 'Here, unicorn,' said the man, and he pulled up a lily and gave it to him. The unicorn ate it gravely.

GROUP C   At a solemn signal from the psychiatrist, the police leaped from their chairs and seized the wife. They had a hard time subduing her, for she put up a terrific struggle, but they finally subdued her. Just as they got her into the straight-jacket, the husband came back into the house.

GROUP D   'Did you tell your wife you saw a unicorn?' asked the police. 'Of course not,' said the husband. 'The unicorn is a mythical beast.' 'That's all I wanted to know,' said the psychiatrist. 'Take her away. I'm sorry, sir, but your wife is as crazy as a jay bird.' So they took her away, cursing and screaming, and shut up her up in an institution. The husband lived happily ever after.

GROUP E   When the police and the psychiatrist arrived, they sat down in chairs and looked at her, with great interest. 'My husband,' she said, 'saw a unicorn this morning.' The police looked at the psychiatrist and the psychiatrist looked at the police. 'He told me it ate a lily,' she said. The psychiatrist looked at the police and the police looked at the psychiatrist. 'He told me it had a golden horn in the middle of its forehead,' she said.

GROUP F   Once upon a sunny morning, a man who sat at his breakfast looked up from his scrambled eggs to see a white unicorn with a gold horn quietly cropping the roses in the garden. The man went up to the bedroom where his wife was still asleep and woke her. 'There's a unicorn in the garden,' he said. 'Eating roses.'

GROUP G   With a high heart, because there was a unicorn in his garden, the man went upstairs and roused his wife again. 'The unicorn,' he said, 'ate a lily.'

His wife sat up in bed and looked at him, coldly. 'You are a booby,' she said, 'and I am going to have you put in the booby-hatch.' The man, who had never liked the words 'booby' and 'booby-hatch', and who liked them even less on a shining morning when there was a unicorn in the garden, thought for a moment. 'We'll see about that,' he said. He walked over to the door. 'He has a golden horn in the middle of his forehead,' he told her. Then he went back to the garden to watch the unicorn; but the unicorn had gone away. The man sat down among the roses and went to sleep.

Exercise 2

Specific aim: To help the students to understand the relations between different parts of a text.
Skills involved: Predicting and anticipating.
Summarizing a passage.
Recognizing discourse indicators and relations between parts of a text.
Why?   Presenting the facts necessary to solve a mystery in such a way will encourage the students to study their passage carefully and to ask questions of the other groups in order to find out relations and links between the various passages.

In this exercise, each group is given a different passage to read. These passages are all part of a short story. The students are not asked to find the order in which the passages appear; they could in fact appear in almost any order. But they have to find out what happened, how a detective problem was solved. No single group has enough information to find out exactly what happened but by summing up their passage and asking the others questions they should be able to work out the solution.

GROUP I   £500 REWARD

'The Evening Messenger,' ever anxious to further the ends of justice, has decided to offer the above reward to any person who shall give information leading to the arrest of the man, William Strickland, alias Bolton, who is wanted by the police in connection with the murder of the late Emma Strickland at 59 Acacia Crescent, Manchester.

DESCRIPTION OF THE WANTED MAN.

The following is the official description of William Strickland: Age 43; height 6ft. 1 or 2 in.; complexion rather dark; hair silver-grey and abundant, may dye same; full grey moustache and beard, may now be clean-shaven; eyes light grey, rather close-set; hawk nose; teeth strong and

white, displays them somewhat prominently when laughing, left upper
eye-tooth stopped with gold; left thumb-nail disfigured by a recent blow.
'Speaks in rather loud voice; quick, decisive manner. Good address.
'May be dressed in a grey or dark blue lounge suit, with stand-up collar
(size 15) and soft felt hat.
'Absconded 5th inst., and may have left, or will endeavour to leave, the
country.'

GROUP 2

Mr. Budd had a younger brother, Richard, whom he had promised his
mother to look after. In happier days Mr. Budd had owned a flourishing
business in their native town of Northampton, and Richard had been a
bank clerk. Richard had got into bad ways (poor Mr. Budd blamed himself
dreadfully for this). There had been a sad affair with a girl, and a horrid
series of affairs with bookmakers, and then Richard had tried to mend bad
with worse by taking money from the bank. You need to be very much
more skilful than Richard to juggle successfully with bank ledgers.

The bank manager was a hard man of the old school: he prosecuted. Mr.
Budd paid the bank and the bookmakers, and saw the girl through her
trouble while Richard was in prison, and paid for their fares to Australia
when he came out, and gave them something to start life on.

But it took all the profits of the hairdressing business, and he couldn't
face all the people in Northampton any more, who had known him all his
life. So he had run to vast London, the refuge of all who shrink from the
eyes of their neighbours, and bought this little shop in Pimlico, which had
done fairly well, until the new fashion which did so much for other
hairdressing businesses killed it for lack of capital.

That is why Mr. Budd's eye was so painfully fascinated by headlines
with money in them.

GROUP 3

Mr Budd, a
hairdresser is
talking to a
new client

'Do you do dyeing?' said the man impatiently.
'Oh!' said Mr. Budd, 'yes, sir, certainly, sir.'
A stroke of luck, this. Dyeing meant quite a big sum – his mind soared
to seven-and-sixpence.
'Good,' said the man, sitting down and allowing Mr. Budd to put an
apron about his neck.
'Fact is,' said the man, 'my young lady doesn't like red hair. She says it's
conspicuous. The other young ladies in her firm make jokes about it. So, as
she's a good bit younger than I am, you see, I like to oblige her, and I was
thinking perhaps it could be changed into something quieter, what? Dark
brown, now – that's the colour she has a fancy to. What do *you* say?'
It occurred to Mr. Budd that the young ladies might consider this abrupt
change of coat even funnier than the original colour, but in the interests of
business he agreed that dark brown would be very becoming and a great
deal less noticeable than red.
'Very well, then,' said the customer, 'go ahead. And I'm afraid the beard
will have to go. My young lady doesn't like beards.'
'A great many young ladies don't, sir,' said Mr. Budd. 'They're not so
fashionable nowadays as they used to be. It's very fortunate that you can
stand a clean shave very well, sir. You have just the chin for it.'

183

'Do you think so?' said the man, examining himself a little anxiously. 'I'm glad to hear it.'

'Will you have the moustache off as well, sir?'

'Well, no – no, I think I'll stick to that as long as I'm allowed to, what?' He laughed loudly, and Mr. Budd approvingly noted well-kept teeth and a gold stopping. The customer was obviously ready to spend money on his personal appearance.

GROUP 4

Mr Budd, a hairdresser is talking to one of his clients about a savage murder that has just taken place

'The police seem to have given it up as a bad job,' said the man.

'Perhaps the reward will liven things up a bit,' said Mr. Budd, the thought being naturally uppermost in his mind.

'Oh, there's a reward, is there? I hadn't seen that.'

'It's in tonight's paper, sir. Maybe you'd like to have a look at it.'

'Thanks, I should.'

Mr. Budd left the drier to blow the fiery bush of hair at its own wild will for a moment, while he fetched the *Evening Messenger*. The stranger read the paragraph carefully and Mr. Budd, watching him in the glass, after the disquieting manner of his craft, saw him suddenly draw back his left hand, which was resting carelessly on the arm of the chair, and thrust it under the apron.

But not before Mr. Budd had seen it. Not before he had taken conscious note of the horny, misshapen thumb-nail. Many people had such an ugly mark. Mr. Budd told himself hurriedly – there was his friend, Bert Webber, who had sliced the top of his thumb right off in a motor-cycle chain – his nail looked very much like that.

The man glanced up, and the eyes of his reflection became fixed on Mr. Budd's face with a penetrating scrutiny – a horrid warning that the real eyes were steadfastly interrogating the reflection of Mr. Budd.

'Not but what,' said Mr. Budd, 'the man is safe out of the country by now, I reckon. They've put it off too late.'

The man laughed.

'I reckon they have,' he said. Mr. Budd wondered whether many men with smashed left thumbs showed a gold left upper eye-tooth. Probably there were hundreds of people like that going about the country. Likewise with silver-grey hair ('may dye same') and aged about forty-three. Undoubtedly.

Mr. Budd folded up the drier and turned off the gas. Mechanically, he took up a comb and drew it through the hair that never, never in the process of Nature had been that fiery red.

GROUP 5

The wireless operator groaned, and switched on his valves.

'Tzee—z—tzee——' a message to the English police.

'Man on board answering to description. Ticket booked name of Watson. Has locked himself in cabin and refuses to come out. Insists on having hairdresser sent out to him. Have communicated Ostend police. Await instructions.'

The Old Man with sharp words and authoritative gestures cleared a way through the excited little knot of people gathered about First Class Cabin No. 36.

Presently came steps overhead. Somebody arrived, with a message. The Old Man nodded. Six pairs of Belgian police boots came tip-toeing down the companion. The Old Man glanced at the official paper held out to him and nodded again.

'Ready?'

'Yes.'

The Old Man knocked at the door of No. 36.

'Who is it?' cried a harsh, sharp voice.

'The barber is here, sir, that you sent for.'

'Ah!!' There was relief in the tone. 'Send him in alone, if you please. I – I have had an accident.'

'Yes, sir.'

At the sound of the bolt being cautiously withdrawn, the Old Man stepped forward. The door opened a chink, and was slammed to again, but the Old Man's boot was firmly wedged against the jamb. The policemen surged forward. There was a yelp and a shot which smashed harmlessly through the window of the first-class saloon, and the passenger was brought out.

'Strike me dead!' shrieked the boy, 'strike me dead if he ain't gone green in the night!'

Green!!

(From 'The Inspiration of Mr Budd' in *In the Teeth of Evidence* by D. Sayers)

Jigsaw reading – further hints

Jigsaw reading exercises can also be done with a series of telegrams that have to be reordered, or an exchange of letters between two persons.

2 Linguistic response to the text

2.1 Reorganizing the information: Reordering events

Exercise

Specific aim: To draw the students' attention to the chronological sequence stated or implied in the passage.

Skills involved: Relating the text to a document (list of events/dates).
Making inferences.

Why? Many texts refer to a sequence of events essential to the understanding of the passage. In this exercise, the students are given a jumbled list of the main events and are asked to reorder them chronologically. This will require constant reference to the text to find out when exactly the various events took place.

See text by Agatha Christie on pages 135–6.

Can you put these events back in their chronological order?
a) Gwenda's father's second marriage.
b) Gwenda lives in India.
c) Gwenda's father leaves the Army.
d) Something unpleasant happens to Gwenda in England.
e) Death of Megan.
f) Marriage of Gwenda's parents.
g) Death of Gwenda's father.
h) Separation of Gwenda's father and stepmother.
i) Gwenda is taken to England by her father.
j) Gwenda goes to New Zealand.

Reordering events – further hints

Many texts refer to a sequence of events but without actually stating them in their chronological order. The reader is expected to reorganize the events mentioned so as to get some coherent sequence which is necessary to understand what happened. In the case of such texts, one can ask the students (a) to find the right chronological order (by reordering a list of events as in the preceding exercise, or by completing a time-table or diary) and (b) to find in which order the events are mentioned in the text (each event can be numbered and numbers can be written in the margin next to the corresponding paragraphs of the text).

Reorganizing the information: Using tables

Exercise 1

Specific aim:	To help the students to understand the main information contained in the text by asking them to fill in a table.
Skills involved:	Selective extraction of relevant points from a text. Note-taking.
Why?	This exercise will lead the students to consider the text globally first, then to reorganize the information it contains. The table will be easier to fill in if the students read the text through first in order to get a general idea and then looks for specific points in different places. It is also an exercise in note-taking that will oblige the students to note down the main points only and leave out unimportant details.

Read this article from *The Sunday Times* and complete the table that follows.

'It's like having a criminal record'

Guest editor Leslie Geddes-Brown

As the new university year gets underway, ELISABETH DUNN meets a man who lost a thousand jobs because he was too well qualified. FRANCIS WHEEN, below, talks to a young hopeful who has just started life as a student and two girls who graduated this summer and are about to launch out into the real world of diplomas and jobs.

MICHAEL GODFREY, you will be relieved to learn, has got a job. It is not much of a job —12 hours a week in a crammer —but with a first in history, an M.Phil. and over 1,000 unsuccessful job applications behind him, Mr Godfrey is in no way complaining about it.

At 25, Michael Godfrey is a casualty of a society where the education and employment systems are at odds with each other. For him, there was a piquancy about Denis Healey's cheery message—"We're winning all the way"—to the Labour Party Conference. He finds that the more educated he becomes, the more he loses.

He left school in 1970 with

three good A levels and a place at the London School of Economics: "I was more ambitious than was warranted by my abilities which is not unusual in 18-year-olds," he says. "But the line they adopted at school was that if you were clever, you should take the subject you were best at and get the best degree you could. It didn't occur to anybody that someone could go through the education system and then stand in the dole queue.

At LSE, Godfrey found the work repetitive and his high-minded intentions of being a conscientious student dissipated: "I didn't read very much and spent most of my time doing things which were not very constructive—drinking and going on silly demonstrations. In my last year, I thought if I pulled myself together I might get a II/I and I started to look around for things to do when I left.

"I'd been to the Warburg Institute and I was extremely impressed, so I applied for a postgraduate place. Then, to my utter astonishment, I got a first, a very good first. I was shattered. I didn't know what to do. I'd got this place at the Warburg and because I had such a good degree, they were very keen to have me."

Bewildered by his unsuspected brilliance, Godfrey spent two further years as a student and wound up with his Master's degree in the summer of 1975. He studied the jobs columns of the educational press and landed a year's lecturing at a college in Canada. Job-hunting, he concluded, was not too arduous a business.

When he came back to England at the end of that year the scales began to fall from his eyes. Succeeding schools, colleges and universities thanked him for his interest but regretted that the post had been filled. So he applied for work in museums and libraries, for retraining courses in television and journalism, for jobs as a postman, a bus conductor, a swimming bath attendant. He calculates that for each job, he was competing with at least 200 other candidates.

"People told me I was too highly qualified. For a postman or a bus conductor, I can understand it because they reckon, quite rightly, that I would leave as soon as I was offered anything better. But as far as academic jobs are concerned, I really don't understand the argument. There seems to be an attitude which says: "You're too highly qualified for us but we're sure someone else will snap you up in no time." Also I think there is an element of jealousy in some cases.

"Around last March I got very depressed. I was going to the public library every day because I couldn't afford to buy the papers; coming home, writing letters, getting up in the mornings and finding a pile of rejections on the doormat. Now I'm much less ambitious. I'm more human, I think. I give more time and thought to relationships."

In practical terms, Mr Godfrey seems to be making the best of difficult circumstances. He rents a small house in a village near Chelmsford. Social Security pays the £10 rent and he gets £11 a week to live on: "Most of it goes on food. Sometimes I go without food if I've had a pint or two. I don't actually scrounge meals from friends but if I am asked out, I arrange to go on a day when I know I'm going to be short of money. The worst thing of all is that at the age of 25, I have to ask my mother for the money to buy a pair of shoes.

"A little while ago I went to see a careers adviser at London University. Do you know, he actually said that with my qualifications, you had to word your applications very carefully so as to turn it to your own advantage. It's like having a criminal record."

When?	Who?	Where?	What?	Why?
1970–3				
1973–5				
1975–6				
end 1976–7				
March 1977				
Now (Oct 1977)				

Exercise 2

Specific aim: ⎫
Skills involved: ⎬ Same as for exercise 1 but the table is more
Why? ⎭ complex and the students are also asked to make a distinction between plain facts and deduced facts.

After reading the short story *Mrs Bixby and the Colonel's Coat* by Roald Dahl, complete the following table.

Here is the completed table.

Mention in *pencil* what you are not told but can guess

	Past eight years	From Baltimore station to her home	On Monday		After she leaves the flat
			Before he brings the neckpiece	After he brings the neckpiece	
What she does/did	sees the Colonel	- is given coat - tries it on - goes to pawnbroker - says she found ticket in taxi	- eager to see the coat - sure it is the coat	pretends to like the neckpiece	'goes out in anger'
What she thinks he does/did	stays at home		goes to pawnbroker and gets coat	thinks he was given the wrong 'article' by the pawnbroker	understands he gave the coat to his secretary
What he thinks she does/did	Spends the two days with her aunt	found the ticket in taxi	impatient to hear what the 'article' will be	Thinks she is pleased	
What he does/did	Spends the two week-end days with his secretary		goes to pawnbroker	took out the coat	gave the coat to his secretary. And gave his secretary's neckpiece to his wife (He had given the neckpiece to his secretary? That's why he knows the price)

Exercise 3

Specific aim: ⎫ Same as for exercise 1 but this time the table is of
Skills involved: ⎬ a different type. It combines the double entries of
Why? ⎭ a table and a diagram with arrows showing the
chronological development of the story.

Read the following short story by James Thurber and complete the table
that follows.

The secret life of Walter Mitty

'We're going through!' The Commander's voice was like thin ice breaking.
He wore his full-dress uniform, with the heavily braided white cap pulled
down rakishly over one cold grey eye. 'We can't make it, sir. It's spoiling
for a hurricane, if you ask me.' 'I'm not asking you, Lieutenant Berg,' said
the Commander. 'Throw on the power lights! Rev her up to 8,500! We're
going through!' The pounding of the cylinders increased: ta-pocketa-
pocketa-pocketa-*pocketa-pocketa*. The Commander stared at the ice forming on the pilot window. He walked over and twisted a row of
complicated dials. 'Switch on No. 8 auxiliary!' he shouted. 'Switch on No.
8 auxiliary!' repeated Lieutenant Berg. The crew, bending to their various
tasks in the huge, hurtling eight-engined Navy Hydroplane, looked at each
other and grinned. 'The Old Man'll get us through,' they said to one
another. 'The Old Man ain't afraid of Hell!' . . .

'Not so fast! You're driving too fast!' said Mrs Mitty. 'What are you
driving so fast for?'

'Humm?' said Walter Mitty. He looked at his wife, in the seat beside
him, with shocked astonishment. She seemed grossly unfamiliar, like a
strange women who had yelled at him in a crowd. 'You were up to
fifty-five,' she said. 'You know I don't like to go more than forty. You
were up to fifty-five!' Walter Mitty drove on toward Waterbury in silence.
'You're tensed up again,' said Mrs Mitty. 'It's one of your days. I wish
you'd let Doctor Renshaw look you over.'

Walter Mitty stopped the car in front of the building where his wife
went to have her hair done. 'Remember to get those overshoes while I'm
having my hair done,' she said. 'I don't need overshoes,' said Mitty. She
put her mirror back into her bag. 'We've been through all that,' she said,
getting out of the car. 'You're not a young man any longer.' He raced the
engine a little. 'Why don't you wear your gloves? Have you lost your
gloves?' Walter Mitty reached in a pocket and brought out the gloves. He
put them on, but after she had turned and gone into the building and he
had driven on to a red light, he took them off again. 'Pick it up, brother!'
snapped a cop as the light changed, and Mitty hastily pulled on his gloves
and lurched ahead. He drove around the streets aimlessly for a time, and
then he drove past the hospital on his way to the parking lot.

 . . . 'It's the millionaire banker, Wellington McMillan,' said the pretty
nurse. 'Yes?' said Walter Mitty, removing his gloves slowly. 'Who has the
case?' 'Dr Renshaw and Dr Benbow, but there are two specialists here, Dr
Remington from New York and Mr Pritchard-Mitford from London. He

flew over.' A door opened down a long, cool corridor and Dr Renshaw came out. He looked distraught and haggard. 'Hello, Mitty,' he said. 'We're having the devil's own time with McMillan, the millionaire banker and close personal friend of Roosevelt. Obstreosis of the ductal tract. Tertiary. Wish you'd take a look at him.' 'Glad to,' said Mitty.

In the operating room there were whispered introductions: 'Dr Remington, Dr Mitty. Mr Pritchard-Mitford, Dr Mitty.' 'I've read your book on streptothricosis,' said Pritchard-Mitford, shaking hands. 'A brilliant performance, sir.' 'Thank you,' said Walter Mitty. 'Didn't know you were in the States, Mitty,' grumbled Remington. 'Coals to Newcastle, bringing Mitford and me up here for a tertiary. 'You are very kind,' said Mitty. A huge, complicated machine, connected to the operating table, with many tubes and wires, began at this moment to go pocketa-pocketa-pocketa. 'The new anaesthetizer is giving way!' shouted an intern. 'There is no one in the East who knows how to fix it!' 'Quiet, man!' said Mitty, in a low, cool voice. He sprang to the machine which was now going pocketa-pocketa-queep-pocketa-queep. He began fingering delicately a row of glistening dials. 'Give me a fountain-pen!' he snapped. Someone handed him a fountain pen. He pulled a faulty piston out of the machine and inserted the pen in its place. 'That will hold for ten minutes,' he said. 'Get on with the operation. A nurse hurried over and whispered to Renshaw, and Mitty saw the man turn pale. 'Coreopsis has set in,' said Renshaw nervously. 'If you would take over, Mitty?' Mitty looked at him and at the craven figure of Benbow who drank, and at the grave, uncertain faces of the two great specialists. 'If you wish,' he said. They slipped a white gown on him; he adjusted a mask and drew on thin gloves; nurses handed him shining . . .

'Back it up, Mac! Look out for that Buick!' Walter Mitty jammed on the brakes. 'Wrong lane, Mac,' said the parking-lot attendant, looking at Mitty closely. 'Gee, Yeh,' muttered Mitty. He began cautiously to back out of the lane marked 'Exit only.' 'Leave her sit there,' said the attendant. 'I'll put her away.' Mitty got out of the car. 'Hey, better leave the key.' 'Oh,' said Mitty, handing the man the ignition key. The attendant vaulted into the car, backed it up with insolent skill, and put it where it belonged.

'They're so damn cocky,' thought Walter Mitty, walking along Main Street; they think they know everything. Once he had tried to take his chains off, outside New Milford and he had got them wound around the axles. A man had to come out in a wrecking car and unwind them, a young grinning garageman. Since then Mrs Mitty always made him drive to a garage to have the chains taken off. The next time he thought, I'll wear my right arm in a sling and they'll see I couldn't possibly take the chains off myself. He kicked at the slush on the side-walk. 'Overshoes,' he said to himself, and he began looking for a shoe store.

When he came out in the street again, with the overshoes in a box under his arm, Walter Mitty began to wonder what the other thing was his wife had told him to get. She had told him twice, before they set out from their house for Waterbury. In a way he hated these weekly trips to town – he was always getting something wrong. Kleenex, he thought, Squibb's razor blades? No. Toothpaste, toothbrush, bicarbonate, carborandum, initiative and referendum? He gave it up. But she would remember it. 'Where's the what's-its-name?' she would ask. 'Don't tell me you forgot the

what's-its-name.' A newsboy went by shouting something about the
Waterbury trial.

'Perhaps this will refresh your memory.' The District Attorney
suddenly thrust a heavy automatic at the quiet figure on the witness stand.
'Have you ever seen this before?' Walter Mitty took the gun and examined
it expertly. 'This is my Webley-Vickers 50.80;' he said calmly. An excited
buzz ran around the courtroom. The judge rapped for order. 'You are a
crack shot with any sort of firearms, I believe?' said the District Attorney,
insinuatingly. 'Objection!' shouted Mitty's attorney. 'We have shown that
he wore his right arm in a sling on the night of the fourteenth of July.'
Walter Mitty raised his hand briefly and the bickering attorneys were
stilled. 'With any known make of gun,' he said evenly, 'I could have killed
Gregory Fitzhurst at three hundred feet *with my left hand.*' Pandemonium
broke loose in the courtroom. A woman's scream rose above the bedlam
and suddenly a lovely, dark-haired girl was in Walter Mitty's arms. The
District Attorney struck at her savagely. Mitty let the man have it on the
point of the chin. 'You miserable cur!' . . .

'Puppy biscuit,' said Walter Mitty. He stopped walking and the
buildings of Waterbury rose up out of the misty courtroom and
surrounded him again. A woman who was passing laughed. 'He said
"Puppy biscuit" to himself,' she said to her companion. 'That man said
"Puppy biscuit".' Walter Mitty hurried on. He went into an A&P, not the
first one he came to but a smaller one farther up the street. 'I want some
biscuit for small, young dogs,' he said to the clerk. 'Any special brand, sir?'
The greatest pistol shot in the world thought a moment. 'It says "Puppies
bark for it" on the box,' said Walter Mitty.

His wife would be through at the hairdresser's in fifteen minutes, Mitty
saw in looking at his watch, unless they had trouble drying it; sometimes
they had trouble drying it. She didn't like to get to the hotel first; she
would want him to be there waiting for her as usual. He found a big leather
chair in the lobby, facing a window, and he put the overshoes and the
puppy biscuits on the floor beside it. He picked up an old copy of *Liberty*
and sank down into the chair. 'Can Germany conquer the World Through
the Air?' Walter Mitty looked at the pictures of bombing planes and of
ruined streets.

. . . 'The cannonading has got the wind up in young Raleigh, sir,' said
the sergeant. Captain Mitty looked up at him through tousled hair. 'Get
him to bed,' he said wearily. 'With the others. I'll fly alone.' 'But you can't,
sir;' said the sergeant anxiously. 'It takes two men to handle that bomber
and the Archies are pounding hell out of the air. Von Richtman's circus is
between here and Saulier.' 'Somebody's got to get that ammunition
dump,' said Mitty. 'I'm going over. Spot of brandy?' He poured a drink
for the sergeant and one for himself. War thundered and whined around
the dugout and battered at the door. There was a rending of wood and
splinters flew through the room. 'A bit of a near thing,' said Captain Mitty
carelessly. 'The box barrage is closing in,' said the sergeant.' 'We only live
once, Sergeant,' said Mitty, with his faint, fleeting smile. 'Or do we?' He
poured another brandy and tossed it off. 'I never see a man could hold his
brandy like you, sir.' Captain Mitty stood up and strapped on his huge
Webley-Vickers automatic. 'It's forty kilometers through hell, sir,' said the
sergeant. Mitty finished one last brandy. 'After all,' he said softly, 'what

isn't?' The pounding of the cannon increased, there was the rat-rat-tatting of machine guns, and from somewhere came the menacing pocketa-pocketa-pocketa of the new flame-throwers. Walter Mitty walked to the door of the dugout humming 'Auprès de ma Blonde.' He turned and waved to the sergeant. 'Cheerio!' he said . . .

Something struck his shoulder. 'I've been looking all over this hotel for you,' said Mrs Mitty. 'Why do you have to hide in this old chair? How did you expect me to find you?' 'Things close in,' said Walter Mitty vaguely. 'What?' Mrs Mitty said. 'Did you get what's-its'-name? The puppy biscuit? What's in that box?' 'Overshoes,' said Mitty. 'Couldn't you have put them on in the store?' 'I was thinking,' said Walter Mitty. 'Does it ever occur to you that I am sometimes thinking?' 'I'm going to take your temperature when I get you home,' she said.

They went out through the revolving doors that made a faintly derisive sound whistling sound when you pushed them. It was two blocks to the parking lot. At the drugstore on the corner she said, 'Wait here for me. I forgot something. I won't be a minute.' She was more than a minute. Walter Mitty lighted a cigarette. It began to rain, rain with sleet in it. He stood up against the wall of the drugstore, smoking . . . He put his shoulders back and his heels together 'To hell with the handkerchief,' said Walter Mitty scornfully. He took one last drag on his cigarette and snapped it away. Then, with that faint, fleeting smile playing about his lips, he faced the firing squad; erect and motionless, proud and disdainful, Walter Mitty, the Undefeated, inscrutable to the last.

(From *My World and Welcome to it* by James Thurber)

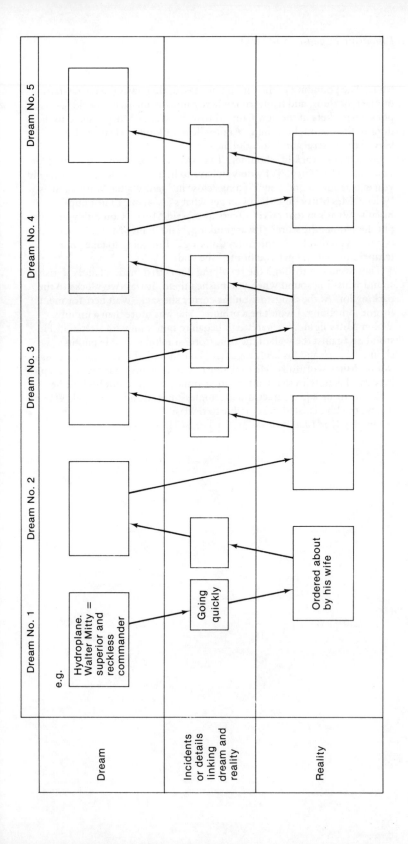

Exercise 4

Specific aim: To help the students to find the main information contained in the text by asking them to find the entries of a table.

Skills involved: Relating the text to a table.

Why? Giving the students a completed table from which some entries are missing is one possible first step in teaching them to take notes and fill in a table, selecting the most important information in the passage. In most cases it will be easier to find the entries than to fill the whole table, but it will nevertheless oblige the students to read the notes carefully, and to find out which parts of the text they refer to and what kind of reorganization of the information the table implies.

The real true purpose

Dr Copeland, a black doctor in a small town in the South of the United States is thinking about his past, his wife Daisy, and his children.

With his eyes wet, so that the edges of things were blurred, Portia was truly like her mother. Years ago Daisy had walked like that around the kitchen, silent and occupied. Daisy was not black as he was – her skin had been like the beautiful colour of dark honey. She was always very quiet and gentle. But beneath that soft gentleness there was something stubborn in her, and no matter how conscientiously he studied it all out, he could not understand the gentle stubbornness in his wife.

He would exhort her and he would tell her all that was in his heart and still she was gentle. And still she would not listen to him but would go on her own way.

Then later there were Hamilton and Karl Marx and William and Portia. And this feeling of real true purpose for them was so strong that he knew exactly how each thing should be with them. Hamilton would be a great scientist and Karl Marx a teacher of the Negro race and William a lawyer to fight against injustice and Portia a doctor for women and children.

And when they were even babies he would tell them of the yoke they must thrust from their shoulders – the yoke of submission and slothfulness. And when they were a little older he would impress upon them that there was no God, but that their lives were holy and for each one of them there was this real true purpose. He would tell it to them over and over, and they would sit together far away from him and look with their big Negro-children eyes at their mother. And Daisy would sit without listening, gentle and stubborn.

Because of the true purpose for Hamilton, Karl Marx, William, and Portia, he knew how every detail should be. In the autumn of each year he took them all into town and bought for them good black shoes and black stockings. For Portia he bought black woollen material for dresses and white linen for collars and cuffs. For the boys there was black wool for trousers and fine white linen for shirts. He did not want them to wear bright-coloured, flimsy clothes. But when they went to school those were the ones they wished to wear, and Daisy said that they were embarrassed and that he was a hard father. He knew how the house should be. There could be no fanciness – no gaudy calendars or lace pillows or knick-knacks – but everything in the house must be plain and dark and indicative of work and the real true purpose.

Then one night he found that Daisy had pierced holes in little Portia's ears for ear-rings. And another time a kewpie doll with feather skirts was on the mantelpiece when he came home, and Daisy was gentle and hard and would not put it away. He knew, too, that Daisy was teaching the children the cult of meekness. She told them about hell and heaven. Also she convinced them of ghosts and of haunted places. Daisy went to church every Sunday and she talked sorrowfully to the preacher of her own husband. And with her stubbornness she always took the children to the church, too, and they listened.

The whole Negro race was sick, and he was busy all day and sometimes half the night. After the long day a great weariness would come in him, but when he opened the front gate of his home the weariness would go away. Yet when he went into the house William would be playing music on a comb wrapped in toilet paper, Hamilton and Karl Marx would be shooting craps for their lunch money, Portia would be laughing with her mother.

He would start all over with them, but in a different way. He would bring out their lessons and talk with them. They would sit close together and look at their mother. He would talk and talk, but none of them wanted to understand.

The feeling that would come on him was a black, terrible Negro feeling. He would try to sit in his office and read and meditate until he could be calm and start again. He would pull down the shades of the room so that there would be only the bright light and the books and the feeling of meditation. But sometimes this calmness would not come. He was young, and the terrible feeling would not go away with study.

Hamilton, Karl Marx, William and Portia would be afraid of him and look at their mother – and sometimes when he realized this the black feeling would conquer him and he knew not what he did.

He could not stop those terrible things, and afterwards he could never understand.

(From *The Heart is a Lonely Hunter* by Carson McCullers)

Complete the following table by finding the headings and completing the boxes that are empty.

	very black skin	
	hard and stubborn passionate	*gentle and stubborn*
	no God – no submission. Each man is holy and should determine his own life	
	very strict. Wants them to become: a scientist a doctor a teacher	*laughing and playing are the most important things*
		fancy, gaudy a lot of jewellery
		knick-knacks every-where: calendars, lace pillows
	fear, embarrassment	
	real – true – strong plain – dark – terrible holy	*quiet-gentle – stubborn bright colored flimsy – fancy – gaudy*

Using tables – further hints

Ask the students to number the boxes in the table according to the order in which the information is mentioned in the text.

2.2 Comparing several texts

Exercise 1

Specific aim: To help the students understand and evaluate the information given in a passage by asking them to compare several passages on the same subject.

Skills involved: Relating the information given in the text to that of other texts.

Note-taking.

Why?   It is natural when reading a passage about a subject which is familiar to us to make mental comparisons between what we already know and the amount of information the new text brings us as well as its possible bias. Therefore, comparing several texts is only a way of systematizing what usually takes place – often unconsciously – in our minds when we read.

This exercise presents three different views of the same event and thereby makes it easier for the students to judge each separate text by emphasizing the differences and contradictions between them.

The three texts that follow all relate to the same incident. Read them carefully and fill in the comparison table.

On the evening of December 1, 1955, a forty-three-year-old Negro seamstress, Mrs Rosa Parks, got on a bus in Montgomery to ride home. She was tired, and took a seat near the front of the bus in the section reserved by custom for whites. When a white man came along, the bus driver ordered her to get up and give him the seat. Mrs. Parks, a leader in her church and in the local chapter of the N.A.A.C.P., refused. She was arrested, jailed briefly, then ordered to trial on December 5th on the charge of violating segregation laws.
(From A. Lewis: *Portrait of a decade* (Bantam, 1965))

Mrs Rosa Parks, a seamstress, might have seemed an odd person to make history, but as Martin Luther King, Jr., said later, she was actually perfect for the role. She was a lady with the courage to defend her human rights – in this case, her right to a seat on the bus.

Many Negro passengers had been insulted by white drivers. It was not unusual for a bus driver to wave a loaded gun and threaten Negroes who got 'out of their place'. If a Negro entered the front door, he was told to get off and board the bus from the rear door. Often, before he could get there, the bus would drive off.

On that first day of December 1955, Mrs Parks was on her way home from work in a Montgomery, Alabama, department store. She had done some shopping after work and she was tired. On the bus home she was seated in the Negro section, behind the white section.

When more white passengers got on, the driver turned around as usual and said, 'Stand up back there so these people can have seats'.

Three Negroes got up at once. Mrs Parks remained seated.

'I'm asking you again to get up back there', the driver said, a little louder.

Mrs Parks did not get up. She acted as if she hadn't heard him at all.

'You won't get up?' he shouted. 'All right, I'm going to fix you.'

He stopped the bus, got off and called the police.

A few minutes later a policeman boarded the bus, with the driver behind him. The driver pointed out Mrs Parks, still sitting quietly in her seat.

Linguistic response to the text

The officer didn't ask Mrs Parks to give up her seat. He just said: 'You are under arrest.'
(From Edward Preston: *Martin Luther King : Freedom Fighter* (Doubleday and Co., 1968))

It began on the fateful December day that this woman – Rosa Parks – left her job at the Fair Department Store near historic Court Square in Montgomery, Alabama. The square, on that day, was festooned with red and green Christmas lights, and there was a big banner over one of the stores, saying 'Peace on Earth, Goodwill to Men.'
Rosa Parks paid no attention to the lights or the banner. She had been working since early morning as a seamstress in the department store, raising and lowering hemlines, mumbling yes ma'am and no ma'am through a mouthful of pins, and she was, she realized suddenly, unutterably weary. There was a little pain across her neck and shoulders, and there were telltale signs of throbbing protests in her aching feet.
It was a little after five on Thursday, December 1, 1955. The Black Revolution was about to begin.
Nobody paid any attention to Rosa Parks, who was a slim woman of 42, tidily and precisely dressed, with every strand of hair in place and rimless glasses perched on her handsome face.
In Montgomery, as in most Southern cities, most of the bus passengers were Black. Despite this fact, or perhaps because of it, the first four seats on all buses were reserved for White people and could not be used, under any circumstances, by Blacks. (It was a common sight in those days to see Black men and women standing in silence and silent fury over the four empty seats reserved for whites.) Behind these four seats was a middle section or no-man's land of two or three seats which Blacks could use if there was no White demand. But 'the rule was,' Rosa Parks remembered later, 'that if the front section filled up and one white person came to sit in the middle section,' *all* Blacks in the middle section 'had to get up and stand in the back.'
There was no need for Rosa Parks to rehearse all this. This was a history engraved in her bones and viscera. In fact, she had been evicted from a bus some twelve years before for refusing to obey the rule that required blacks to pay in the front and enter in the rear. But on this day she wasn't looking for trouble. What she wanted, *what she had to have on this day*, was a comfortable seat. She had had one of those days we all have from time to time, and a person with a keen eye would have seen that this was not the day, this was not the hour, to give this mild-mannered woman a hard time.
None of this was verbalized, none of this reached the stage of consciousness, but it was there, deep in Rosa Parks's mind, as she approached the first Cleveland Avenue bus that came along. At the last moment, she noticed that this bus was crowded, and she let it go by, for she had decided in her mind that 'when I got on the bus I wanted to be as comfortable as I could. . . .' She went across the street to the drug store and got some pills for her aching neck. And when she came back, she noticed 'another bus approaching, and . . . didn't see anybody standing up in the back. But by the time I [got] to the bus door, a number of people had gotten on ahead of me, and when I got on the Negro section in back was

well filled.' There was one vacant seat in the fifth row – the first row in no-man's land – and she sank wearily into the seat next to a Black man, who was sitting by the window. The bus pulled out of Court Square and stopped at the Empire Theater. Several whites got on and took the designated 'White' seats. This left one White man standing, and the driver – J. F. Blake – looked in the rear view mirror and told the four Blacks in the fifth row to get up so the White man could sit down. There must have been something in the air on this day, for at first, nobody moved. Blake noticed this with some surprise and raised his voice:

'Y'all better make it light on yourselves and let me have those seats.'

At that point, the man sitting next to Rosa Parks stood up and she shifted her legs in the seat and let him pass. As she moved to the window, she noticed out of the corner of her eye that the two women across the aisle had also vacated their seats.

Now, as tension rose in the bus, driver Blake approached Rosa Parks and asked if she was going to move. No, she said, she wasn't. Blake said that if she didn't get up, he would have to call the police. 'Go ahead and call them,' Rosa Parks said.

Blake stormed to the front, pulled the ratchet and got off. Several passengers who didn't want to be inconvenienced or who didn't want to get involved followed him. The remaining passengers sat quietly, staring at the woman who was causing all the trouble.

Before too much time passed, the driver returned with two policemen, who asked Rosa Parks if she had understood the driver's request. She said, yes.

'Why didn't you get up?' one of the officers asked.

'I didn't think I should have to,' she replied, and then there came from deep inside her a terrible and unanswerable question.

'Why do you push us around?'

There was no answer, in the police manual, or in any book, to that question, and the officer mumbled: 'I don't know, but the law is the law and you are under arrest.'

There then occurred one of those little vignettes that could have changed the course of history. The officers asked the driver if he wanted to swear out a warrant or if he wanted them to let Rosa Parks go with a warning. The driver said he wanted to swear out a warrant, and this decision and the convergence of a number of historical forces sealed the death warrant of the Jim Crow South.

(From *The Day the Black Revolution Began* by Lerone Bennett, Jr.)

Chronology Write down underneath a detailed chronology of what happened on that day. Put a cross in columns 1, 2 or 3 when the event is mentioned in the text	Text No. 1	Text No. 2	Text No. 3
Which is the most factual dramatic psychologically-oriented objective detailed			
Any contradictions between the texts?			
Difference			
What does the difference reveal?			
Facts about Rosa Parks			
Age			
Physical description			
Character			
Profession			
Social activities			
Her past			
What we learn about segregation laws at that time			

Exercise 2

Specific aim:	Same as for exercise 1 but this time the three
Skills involved:	texts treat the same theme – that of a well-known
Why?	story for children – in three very different ways.

Read these three tales and fill in the table which follows, outlining the differences you can find between the three texts.

Little Red Riding Hood

There was once a sweet little maid, much beloved by everybody, but most of all by her grandmother, who never knew how to make enough of her. Once she sent her a little cap of red velvet, and as it was very becoming to her, and she never wore anything else, people called her Little Red Riding Hood. One day her mother said to her,

'Come, Little Red Riding Hood, here are some cakes and a flask of wine for you to take to grandmother; she is weak and ill, and they will do her good. Make haste and start before it grows hot, and walk properly and nicely, and don't run, or you might fall and break the flask of wine, and there would be none left for grandmother. And when you go into her room, don't forget to say, Good morning, instead of staring about you.'

'I will be sure to take care,' said Little Red Riding Hood to her mother, and gave her hand upon it. Now the grandmother lived away in the wood, half-an-hour's walk from the village; and when Little Red Riding Hood had reached the wood, she met the wolf; but as she did not know what a bad sort of animal he was, she did not feel frightened.

'Good day, Little Red Riding Hood,' said he.

'Thank you kindly, Wolf,' answered she.

'Where are you going so early, Little Red Riding Hood?'

'To my grandmother's.'

'What are you carrying under your apron?'

'Cakes and wine; we baked yesterday; and my grandmother is very weak and ill, so they will do her good, and strengthen her.'

'Where does your grandmother live, Little Red Riding Hood?'

'A quarter of an hour's walk from here; her house stands beneath the three oak trees, and you may know it by the hazel bushes,' said Little Red Riding Hood. The wolf thought to himself,

'That tender young thing would be a delicious morsel, and would taste better than the old one; I must manage somehow to get both of them.'

Then he walked by Little Red Riding Hood a little while, and said,

'Little Red Riding Hood, just look at the pretty flowers that are growing all around you, and I don't think you are listening to the song of the birds; you are posting along just as if you were going to school, and it is so delightful out here in the wood.'

Little Red Riding Hood glanced round her, and when she saw the sunbeams darting here and there through the trees, and lovely flowers everywhere, she thought to herself,

'If I were to take a fresh nosegay to my grandmother she would be very pleased, and it is so early in the day that I shall reach her in plenty of time';

and so she ran about in the wood, looking for flowers. And as she picked one she saw a still prettier one a little farther off, and so she went farther and farther into the wood. But the wolf went straight to the grandmother's house and knocked at the door.

'Who is there?' cried the grandmother.

'Little Red Riding Hood,' he answered, 'and I have brought you some cake and wine. Please open the door.'

'Lift the latch,' cried the grandmother; 'I am too feeble to get up.'

So the wolf lifted the latch, and the door flew open, and he fell on the grandmother and ate her up without saying one word. Then he drew on her clothes, put on her cap, lay down in her bed, and drew the curtains.

Little Red Riding Hood was all this time running about among the flowers, and when she had gathered as many as she could hold, she remembered her grandmother, and set off to go to her. She was surprised to find the door standing open, and when she came inside she felt very strange, and thought to herself,

'Oh dear, how uncomfortable I feel, and I was so glad this morning to go to my grandmother!'

And when she said, 'Good morning,' there was no answer. Then she went up to the bed and drew back the curtains; there lay the grandmother with her cap pulled over her eyes, so that she looked very odd.

'O grandmother, what large ears you have got!'

'The better to hear with.'

'O grandmother, what great eyes you have got!'

'The better to see with.'

'O grandmother, what large hands you have got!'

'The better to take hold of you with.'

'But, grandmother, what a terrible large mouth you have got!'

'The better to devour you!' And no sooner had the wolf said it than he made one bound from the bed, and swallowed up poor Little Red Riding Hood.

Then the wolf, having satisfied his hunger, lay down again in the bed, went to sleep, and began to snore loudly. The huntsman heard him as he was passing by the house, and thought,

'How the old woman snores – I had better see if there is anything the matter with her.'

Then he went into the room, and walked up to the bed, and saw the wolf lying there.

'At last I find you, you old sinner!' said he. 'I have been looking for you a long time.' And he made up his mind that the wolf had swallowed the grandmother whole, and that she might yet be saved. So he did not fire, but took a pair of shears and began to slit up the wolf's body. When he made a few snips Little Red Riding Hood appeared, and after a few more snips she jumped out and cried, 'Oh dear, how frightened I have been! It is so dark inside the wolf.' And then out came the old grandmother, still living and breathing. But Little Red Riding Hood went and quickly fetched some large stones, with which she filled the wolf's body, so that when he waked up, and was going to rush away, the stones were so heavy that he sank down and fell dead.

They were all three very pleased. The huntsman took off the wolf's skin, and carried it home. The grandmother ate the cakes, and drank the

wine, and held up her head again, and Little Red Riding Hood said to herself that she would never more stray about in the wood alone, but would mind what her mother told her.
(From *Grimm's Fairy Tales*)

Some day my prince will crawl

'A group of the women's liberation movement on Merseyside is rewriting fairy tales, in which men and women will be shown to have equal opportunities.'   (*The Guardian*)

. . . so Little Red Riding Hood took off her cloak, but when she climbed up on the bed she was astonished to see how her grandmother looked in her nightgown.

'Grandmother dear!' she exclaimed, 'what big arms you have!'
'All the better to hug you with, my child!'
'Grandmother dear, what big ears you have!'
'All the better to hear you with, my child!'
'Grandmother dear, what big eyes you have!'
'All the better to see you with, my child!'
'Grandmother dear, what big teeth you have!'
'All the better to eat you with, my child!'

With these words, the wicked Wolf leapt upon Little Red Riding Hood, and stopped a short right to the jaw.

'HAI!' cried Little Red Riding Hood, giving a textbook karate jab to the ribs that brought the Wolf to its knees.

'AKACHO!' screamed Little Red Riding Hood, following up with a neck chop, a double finger eye-prod, and a reverse groin kick.

The Wolf coughed, once, and expired on the rug.

At that moment, the door of the little house flew open, and the woodchopper burst in, brandishing his axe.

'Little Red Riding Hood!' he cried, 'are you all right?'

'No thanks to you!' snapped Little Red Riding Hood, snatching the axe from him, breaking it across her knee, and tossing it into the corner. 'And while you're at it, wash the dishes!'

With which she cracked her knuckles and strode out into the forest, slamming the door behind her.
(From Alan Coren: *The Sanity Inspector*; reprinted in *That's Life!* by Alan Duff (CUP, 1979))

The little girl and the wolf

One afternoon a big wolf waited in a dark forest for a little girl to come along carrying a basket of food to her grandmother. Finally a little girl did come along and she was carrying a basket of food. 'Are you carrying that basket to your grandmother?' asked the wolf. The little girl said yes, she was. So the wolf asked her where her grandmother lived and the little girl told him and he disappeared into the wood.

When the little girl opened the door of her grandmother's house she saw that there was somebody in bed with a nightcap and nightgown on. She had approached no nearer than twenty-five feet from the bed when she saw that it was not her grandmother but the wolf, for even in a nightcap a wolf does not look any more like your grandmother than the Metro-Goldwyn lion looks like Calvin Coolidge. So the little girl took an automatic out of her basket and shot the wolf dead.

Moral: It is not so easy to fool little girls nowadays as it used to be.
(From *Fables for our Time* by James Thurber)

	Little Red Riding Hood	*Some day my prince will crawl*	*The little girl and the wolf*
The little girl			
The wolf			
The grandmother			
The huntsman			
The moral			

Exercise 3

Specific aim: *Skills involved:* *Why?*	Same as for exercise 1 but it is no longer the point of view and the attitude of the writer that vary. In this exercise, the students compare two articles about the same event, but written at different dates. It is the information itself which varies this time. The new article partly repeats and summarizes the preceding one, but also brings in some new information.

Read the following articles. The first one appeared in the *Daily Telegraph* on 17 September 1979. The second one appeared in the same paper on the following day.

Families flee to West by balloon

By *MICHAEL FARR in Bonn*

TWO East German families escaped to the West early yesterday by a hot-air balloon made out of curtains and bed sheets.

The balloon, carrying four adults and four children, came down near the Bavarian town of Naila after a 30-minute flight in darkness from Poessneck, East Germany.

But the families were not certain they had reached the West.

While the women and children hid in a barn, the men tried to find out where the balloon had landed.

Eventually they stopped a police car and discovered they were in West Germany. They are the first people to escape from East Germany by balloon.

25-mile flight

The 80ft diameter craft, piloted by a 37-year-old aircraft mechanic, Peter Strelzyk, covered 25 miles.

With him were his wife and two children aged 15 and 11. The other family consisted of a 24-year-old builder, Guenter Wetzel, his wife Petra, and their children aged five and wo.

The sheets and curtains used to make the balloon had been stitched together by the two wives, and the hot air for the craft came from four gas cylinders.

It was the families' second attempt at a balloon escape from East Germany. Bad weather forced them back when they tried to reach the West on July 4.

Searchlight scare

Yesterday the balloon soared about 3,000ft over part of the border fortified by the East Germans with mines and self-firing guns.

The families said they had one unnerving moment when the balloon was caught in a border spotlight. But no shots were fired.

Naila, with 9,300 inhabitants, welcomed the families yesterday. The mayor, Herr Robert Strobel, said flats and jobs would be found for them.

Herr Hans-Peter Strelzyk who built and piloted the balloon, pictured after the escape, and (below) the flight to freedom.

HOMES FOR BALLOON ESCAPERS

By **ROBERT TILLY** in Munich

MONEY was flowing yesterday into four bank accounts set up specially for two penniless East German families who fled to West Germany clinging to a home-made hot-air balloon.

The two married couples and their four children had to leave all their personal belongings behind in the East to lighten the load on the half-hour flight across the heavily-defended border into Northern Bavaria.

Within hours of their landing near the Bavarian town of Naila they had homes, the offer of well-paid jobs in the area and the local fire brigade had collected more than £100 for them.

"It's fantastic what the people of Naila are doing for us," said Herr Peter Stelzyk, an aircraft mechanic. "We really have flown to a new home and a new life."

The East Germans intend to settle in Naila for the time being. They are patching up the damaged balloon and intend to display it in the town.

Idea came from TV

Herr Stelzyk said yesterday that he got the idea for escaping to the West while watching an East German television programme on ballooning about 18 months ago. He added that he studied 18th century hot-air techniques to perfect the plan.

Frau Doris Stelzyk said the two wives sat down at their sewing machines and "in 15 days we had stitched the balloon together with curtains and bed-sheets."

The two couples, with their four boys aged two to 15, had no gondola on the balloon. They had to huddle together on a metal platform 4½ feet square.

They shared the space with four gas containers on the 30-minute, 11-mile flight to a field outside Naila, five miles inside West Germany.

The platform had no sides—there was only a rope from a washline around it.

A West German air force expert said the craft would probably not have shown up on the East German radar system, which was set up to catch fast-flying objects with reflective metal surfaces.

1 In the two articles what information do you learn about:

	Article 1	New information in article 2
The people concerned		
The means of escape		
The escape itself		
The arrival		
Their reception		
The future		

2 Which sentences or paragraphs of article 1 are developed in article 2?
....

3 Which sentences or paragraphs in article 2 repeat information already given in article 1? ....

Exercise 4

Specific aim: ⎫ Same as for exercise 1 but one of the two
Skills involved: ⎬ passages is 'reliable' whereas the second one
Why? ⎭ contains several mistakes which the students
must find and correct.

You are chief editor of a local Newcastle paper. You have just received a short article from one of your new journalists. It is about the interview of a young painter and you are quite sure it will interest your readers. Before sending it to be printed, you have a look at it. You are particularly interested as you happen to have heard a tape of the interview the article is about.
Would you send the article as it is?
If not, what corrections would you make?
1 Text of the interview:

Wall painting is an unusual occupation for a young artist. What made you take it up, rather than a more traditional art form ?
I think mainly the fact that, after two years studying for an M.A. at Newcastle University, I was bored and suspicious of the kind of «art» I was being made to produce. I never left the studio. I began to feel that painters, galleries, and élitist preoccupations with fine art were all very well, but what about the real, dismal, industrial streets of Newcastle outside ? Surely years of training in art must have some kind *of direct relevance* to people other than intellectuals and dilettantes ? I wanted very much to make a contribution to the community.

Was it easy to find a wall to paint ?
Well, finding a wall wasn't too difficult - every bleak, *grimy* wall in Newcastle is crying out for decoration - but getting permission to paint it was a nightmare. It took me a year in all. At first, everybody thought I was mad ! The wall I chose belonged to the town council, and the councillors simply laughed at my suggestion. But, after a lot of persuasion, they agreed to let me bring in some designs. When I brought them, everybody stood around in amazement, until a bloke said he really liked them. Immediately, they all agreed that the designs were great.

So you started painting ?
No. I still had to find the money, which wasn't easy. I started by going around the streets in the area with my designs, asking if people approved. I drank endless cups of sugary, sociable tea, and got a whole lot of ideas : nearly everybody seemed favourable. I documented all this interest and support, and made an application to the Arts Council. In the end, a grant was awarded. Paint, brushes, and *scaffolding* were donated by local firms. At last, I had the green light, and could start work...

Wasn't it tough for a young woman who had never left the studio, to stand on a ladder in the freezing North England weather, doing something 100 times the size of an ordinary canvas ?
Well, it was certainly hard work, especially since I did it all myself. The job took me a couple of months. However, I didn't find it difficult to adjust to the size - the mural measures about 1,000 square feet - as I had always wanted to paint big. As for the area, the locals were fantastic, and gave me lots of encouragement. In fact, with all the offers of tea and cakes, it was difficult to do a good day's work. One old fellow came by every day at 5-30, and made the very *Geordie* comment, «Ee, fellas, it's goin' champion». He even asked me to come and paint some roses on his house - that way, they'd flower all winter !

What was the reaction to the painting ?
Very favourable. It was done in an extremely rough area, and I was expecting immediate vandalism. But it was incredible - the wall remained untouched for 11 months. Just before its first anniversary, someone wrote «Punk Rock» in green on a green leaf. Very considerate-it's hardly visible. In general, the local community seems to be proud of the painting, and the area, which was previously very grim, is now looking up.

Does this lead you to think that all cities should adorn their walls with bright paintings ?
Yes. The more the better ! Most people would agree that big cities are cold, aggressive places, and it's amazing what a little warm colour can do to change them. Slowly, the idea is catching on, particularly in the U.S. I've recently been asked to paint a series of walls in a new hospital, as well as a children's play barn, which was actually designed by an architect with the idea of adding a painting. That's what I call progress : the more cooperation between architects and artists the better.

So, you now have a full-time career as a wall painter ?
Well, I could. The idea has now become popular. But I'm still trying to reserve some time for my intellectual, abstract and elitist canvases ! You see, you can't get rid of your past, after all.

(From an article by Roger Cohen in *Speakeasy*)

2 The article:

Bright future?

Can some of our cities be brightened up by wall-paintings? Patricia Gilman, a young artist from Newcastle, said last week in an interview that more and more cold and dull city walls should be decorated, although the idea is still very unpopular with local inhabitants.

After studying for two years at Newcastle University, Patricia Gilman said she felt the need to relate art to everyday life. She was no longer interested in the more intellectual side of painting and wanted to do something for her community.

Ms Gilman said it was no problem getting money from the Arts Council. Besides, people were very friendly and gave her a lot of ideas. What really took a long time was finding a large and bleak wall that she could paint, as there are not many in Newcastle. But everything went well, she explained, as soon as the painting was started. People in the area were very interested and encouraging and even fed her, which was very pleasant.

The area certainly looks brighter now and Ms Gilman has been asked to paint more walls in the USA. However, she remains very pessimistic about the future.

3 List your corrections (if needed).

Comparing several texts – further hints

This kind of exercise can be done with many different kinds of texts. Here are a few examples:

a) Compare an advertisement and a letter to the editor or a letter to a friend in which somebody recounts what actually happened after he/she bought the product that was advertised.

b) Compare   □ a travel brochure

                    □ an extract from a guide book

                    □ a letter from someone on holiday.

2.3   Completing a document

Exercise 1

Specific aim: To help the students understand a passage by asking them to transfer the information onto a document.

Skills involved: Extracting relevant points from a text.
                 Completing a document.
                 Note-taking.

Why?   It is important to try to relate reading activities to the normal kinds of response one would have in real life. Reading a text may lead to writing a letter to the editor of a newspaper, or to a friend, or to solving a problem.

After reading this text, imagine how Mr Lenitzki filled in the card he was given before leaving the hotel.

Traveller gets $450 award

A MONTREAL man who found bed bugs and mice in his supposedly luxurious Caribbean hotel was awarded $450 in damages yesterday by Provincial Court Judge Roland Robillard.

Lou Lenitzki paid $1,300 to Atlantic Pacific Travel and Tours Inc. in March 1976, for a "luxury" vacation on the island of Martinique.

Travel brochures provided by tour organizer Andre Gingras of Tours Mont Royal promised a luxury hotel, free baggage transport from the airport, free golf course privileges and beaches.

Bed bugs

However, on his arrival, Mr Lenitzki found that there was no one to look after his baggage, the hotel rooms were infested with bed bugs and mice and the golf course had reverted to a pasture.

To make matters worse, the hotel was in bankruptcy and the staff were not carrying out their duties.

Mr Lenitzki sued Mr Gingras for $2,675 – $650 for the plane ticket, $25 to move his luggage to another hotel and $2,000 for aggravating his health.

He told the judge he suffered from nervous tension.

Judge Robillard rejected the $2,000 health claim, but ordered Mr Gingras to pay $450, plus interest, of the remaining total of $675.

No complaints

The judge noted in his judgment that partial restitution had already been made.

In his defence, Mr Gingras said that Mr Lenitzki had made his travel reservations with Atlantic Pacific and consequently he couldn't be held responsible for the problems that arose.

Mr Gingras said he had been organizing trips for several years and he had never received any complaints about the hotel where Mr Lenitzki stayed.

(The Montreal Star)

oceanview

EVALUATION CARD

What prompted you to choose our hotel?

Is it your first visit?   Yes ☐   No ☐

		excellent	good	poor
PLEASE	food quality			
	service			
CHECK	rooms			
WHERE	cleanliness			
APPROPRIATE	grounds			
	transportation			

What did you most appreciate during your visit?

What did you least appreciate?

Comments: ....

....

....

....

Date of visit:

Name:

Address: City:

Exercise 2

Specific aim:
Skills involved: } Same as for exercise 1.
Why?

Janet Horwood talks to Jackie Willis, aged 23, a travel representative at Lloret de Mar, Costa Brava.

A LIFE IN THE DAY OF

JACKIE WILLIS

" My day usually starts at 7.30a.m. when I tumble out of bed, have a shower, put on my uniform, grab a quick glass of orange juice and get a taxi to the hotel.

I've been working at Lloret for three years and this last summer I decided to rent a flat in town instead of living in at the hotel. If you sleep at the hotel you can get woken up if someone's ill or had an accident. I also have a room at the hotel which I use if I've had to go out late to collect clients from the airport and it does mean that I can get up later in the morning.

I wear uniform if I'm on duty. I like the clothes so it doesn't bother me. I have red, white or blue short-sleeved shirts, a navy skirt or trousers, a beige blazer.

I never wear much make-up during the day. If I've got time later in the afternoon I put on some moisturiser, eye shadow, mascara and lipstick. And if I go out to the airport I usually put some lipstick on just as the coach arrives.

I work a six-day week – each day is divided into morning, afternoon and evening shifts. Sometimes I work all three, other times I share with another rep.

The first shift is the busiest because five days a week there's a champagne reception for new arrivals. They just get one glass of champagne – not enough to make anyone drunk even at 10 in the morning. While they're drinking I give a speech with information about the hotel, day trips, local shops and sights.

At the desk in the hotel I make sure the day-trip people go off all right, answer questions and solve any problems. But I do get asked some funny things. One chap sat on his false teeth and I had to glue them together for him. Someone else dropped their camera in the swimming pool and I had to lend him my hairdryer to dry it out.

I often miss breakfast altogether but if things seem quiet I leave a note and dash into the restaurant for a cup of coffee and a roll.

If there's a champagne reception it can go on until after 11. But once or twice a week there's a breather between shifts to go into town or walk round the swimming pool.

The second shift runs from 12-3 but you can still get away for lunch. By then I'm usually starving. The food isn't very exciting – ravioli, chicken and chips, ice cream, or you can have salad or omelette. I always drink just water at lunchtime – wine makes me sleepy.

Sometimes I have a free afternoon and then I often think about putting on a bikini and lying on the beach. That's as far as I get – just the thought – usually going home for a siesta is more appealing.

I don't bother much about trying to get a tan. I come out to Lloret four days before the season starts and that's when I do my sunbathing. I like to get my legs a bit brown because I never wear stockings.

The evening shift's the easiest. After I've had dinner – which is more or less the same menu as lunchtime and I always have a glass of wine with it – I leave a note on the desk and go into the bar to chat with the clients and hear about their day.

There's always plenty of young blokes around ready to buy me a drink. It's quite easy to fend them off if you're not interested because the job takes up quite a bit of time. So if I don't really fancy a bloke I can say to him that I'm busy. If I *do* like someone then I'll sometimes agree to go over the road for a drink.

I've never had a steady boyfriend out in Lloret. It just doesn't work. The job makes me so unreliable and I've not yet met anyone who's happy when he's made a date for 8 o'clock and then finds that I've been delayed for two hours at the airport.

I've never felt relaxed about a boyfriend here. You're watched all the time. I've never taken a boyfriend into the hotel bar, I just wouldn't feel comfortable. Even when you're out of uniform the clients know you and you have to watch your step – not dance too close, not get drunk and so on.

I hardly cook at all during the season. I don't enjoy it much – except for frying bacon! But I do manage to eat quite a lot – all my meals seem to come at the end of the day. Quite often, when I'm off duty after 10 o'clock I'll go out and have another full meal – a proper Spanish one with squid, which I love, or lobster. And there are some English foods that I really crave after I'd been in Lloret for a while. Bacon, cheese and, most of all, Marks and Spencer cakes.

I'm usually pretty tired by the end of the day. If the weather's fine it's easier of course – people are happy – but if it's pouring with rain and they haven't got much to do that's when you get all the complaints and I have to grit my teeth and keep my patience.

My day off is very precious. If I've had a really late night before then I'll sleep until mid-day but then I feel guilty. So usually I try to get up about 9.30, have a leisurely breakfast and then go off to another resort for the day.

When I go to bed I sometimes read for a bit. It's a treat if a client has just come over and passed on an up-to-date copy of *Cosmopolitan* or *Woman*. If there are no magazines to read then I switch the light out straight away and I'm asleep within minutes.

(*The Sunday Times*)

Below you will find a list of some of the things Jackie Willis does in one of her typical days of work but they are out of order. Can you reorder them by filling in the diary?

dress well and put on make-up

have breakfast

have a drink with boyfriend

get up

check at reception if everyone is all right

have champagne with people arriving

dinner

lunch

give speech to inform clients about their holiday

drink orange juice

read some new magazines

afternoon shift

discuss the day with clients

It is also possible simply to ask the students to fill the diary without the assistance of a list of points.

Time	Monday January **31**
7	
8	
9	
10	
11	
12	
13	
14	
15	
16	
17	
18	
19	
20	
21	
Notes	

Linguistic response to the text

Exercise 3

Specific aim:	To help the students understand the text by asking them to use its information to complete another text.
Skills involved:	Predicting.
	Extracting relevant points from a text.
	Relating the information given in the text to that of another text.
	Completing a text.
Why?	The best way of checking that one has understood a letter is through the answer one writes to that letter. In the following exercise, the students are asked to complete the answer to a letter which they are given. It corresponds to a natural activity and will lead the students to a close scrutiny of the two texts.

Read the following letter carefully and complete the reply.

Saturday, July 29, 1978
Cambridge, Mass.

Dear Françoise,

Thanks for your letter; It came just as I was wondering what I should do. I'm not surprised at your decision, I must admit. I couldn't imagine your not taking on such interesting and challenging work. I only hope you've dropped an appropriate number of other commitments. I am sorry you're not coming — I would have liked very much to show you around. But there's no need to worry that I'll be depressed this summer. Somehow my life in Sèvres seems to have rubbed off on me, and I'm busier than I can handle.

At my ballroom dance class, I met two men who really like to dance. So I've been going out more than is good for my thesis. Add to that work, which takes a lot of time. And I spend evening after evening fiddling with my apartment. The bed finally made its appearance, but I have yet to look for a table.

In August I'm going to North Carolina to visit my grandmother before she moves into a rest home. Besides that, I have great hopes of visiting a friend of mine near Washington DC, in September. Last weekend I spent two very hot days in Maine – on the beach, in the woods, at the discotheque. Upon demand (though slight) I showed some of my slides from la belle France, including that of my good friend, Françoise. The people I work with are clambering to see them.

I'd appreciate it if you could send my tape recorder when you feel like doing

213

nothing else (ha, as if that ever happened). I shouldn't have left it with you when you told me about the job offer. But there's no rush about it. Right now I have more than enough to do without having the possibility of transcribing and editing tapes. The only other thing I can think of at the moment (and this, also, is of little importance) is the Pléiade edition of Pascal. If you go to FNAC for books could you get it for me if it is no longer abîmé — or is it épuisé? Please let me know how much all this costs; I still have my account in Sèvres. And what may I do for you? I am sure there are things you were counting on getting here. Anything I can help with?

How was England? What did you do? How many afternoons in the B.M. Reading Room? I still wish we could have taken that trip through Devon we considered. I'm saving money each week in the hope that I can indeed spend next Summer in Sèvres. And see some of Scotland.

My love,
Marva

Dear Marva,

.... for your letter which I received yesterday. I'm pleased to see you're so busy. I didn't really think you would.......... .... but you did say it might be a little hard to settle back in .... I wish I could have been with you when you ....: I might not have accompanied you to the discotheque, but .... certainly do appeal to me right now. But I shouldn't complain as I had .... in ...., taking pictures most of the time and visiting friends. But you're quite right and I spent most .... working in .... I read a few books by Charlotte Smith that are not available anywhere else. I also regret .... but why not do it next year if you come over?

It must really be fun trying to .... now that you have a place of your own. I wish I had enough room - and money - to do the same thing here!

Don't worry about your ....: I've just come back from the post office and I hope you'll .... it next month. As for the .... I'll look for it next time I go to Paris. I'm sure I'll manage to find a .... And thanks for your offer to .... I can't think of anything right now, but I'll let you know when I need something.

I'm going to stay here for the rest of .... working on this new .... I hope I can cope with it. When I get tired or bored, I'll think of next summer: please do try to .... as you suggest. That would really be great!

Well, have a good time in .... and .... I'll write soon and will let you know how I'm doing. Take care of yourself.

Love,

Rex.

Completing a document – further hints

- With texts giving detailed information about someone, the students can be asked to fill the identity card that the person might have completed (e.g. a disembarkation card) or that someone else might complete about him (e.g. a card which belongs to police records). It is important, however, that it should come as a *natural* follow-up activity after reading the text.
- Ask the students to complete instructions after reading a text describing the steps of an operation of some kind.
- Ask the students to complete a one-sided telephone conversation after reading a letter that refers to it or the notes taken by the person who answered the phone.
- See also exercise 4, question 1 on page 162.

2.4 Question-types

Besides the above-mentioned activities, many types of comprehension questions can be used. The following list is certainly not exhaustive but aims at giving an idea of the most commonly used kinds of exercises.

For easier reference, the same text (*The Unicorn in the Garden*) has been chosen as a starting point for most of these exercises. Before giving the list of question-types, a possible way of dealing with the text has been suggested as a kind of summary of the various kinds of activities mentioned in parts 1, 2 and 3.

The unicorn in the garden

Once upon a sunny morning, a man who sat at his breakfast looked up from his scrambled eggs to see a white unicorn with a gold horn quietly cropping the roses in the garden. The man went up to the bedroom where his wife was still asleep and woke her. 'There's a unicorn in the garden,' he said. 'Eating roses.' She opened one unfriendly eye and looked at him. 'The unicorn is a mythical beast,' she said, and turned her back on him. The man walked slowly downstairs and out into the garden. The unicorn was still there; he was now browsing among the tulips. 'Here, unicorn,' said the man, and he pulled up a lily and gave it to him. The unicorn ate it gravely. With a high heart, because there was a unicorn in his garden, the man went upstairs and roused his wife again. 'The unicorn,' he said, 'ate a lily.' His wife sat up in bed and looked at him, coldly. 'You are a booby,' she said, 'and I am going to have you put in the booby-hatch.' The man, who had never liked the words 'booby' and 'booby-hatch', and who liked them even less on a shining morning when there was a unicorn in the garden, thought for a moment. 'We'll see about that,' he said. He walked over to the door. 'He has a golden horn in the middle of his forehead,' he told her. Then he went back to the garden to watch the unicorn; but the unicorn had gone away. The man sat down among the roses and went to sleep.

As soon as the husband had gone out of the house, the wife got up and dressed as fast as she could. She was very excited and there was a gloat in her eye. She telephoned the police and she telephoned a psychiatrist; she told them to hurry to her house and bring a straight-jacket. When the police and the psychiatrist arrived, they sat down in chairs and looked at her, with great interest. 'My husband,' she said. 'saw a unicorn this morning.' The police looked at the psychiatrist and the psychiatrist looked at the police. 'He told me it ate a lily,' she said. The psychiatrist looked at the police and the police looked at the psychiatrist. 'He told me it had a golden horn in the middle of its forehead,' she said. At a solemn signal from the psychiatrist, the police leaped from their chairs and seized the wife. They had a hard time subduing her, for she put up a terrific struggle, but they finally subdued her. Just as they got her into the straight-jacket, the husband came back into the house.

'Did you tell your wife you saw a unicorn?' asked the police. 'Of course not,' said the husband. 'The unicorn is a mythical beast.' 'That's all I wanted to know,' said the psychiatrist. 'Take her away. I'm sorry, sir, but your wife is as crazy as a jay bird.' So they took her away, cursing and screaming, and shut her up in an institution. The husband lived happily ever after.

Moral: Don't count your boobies until they are hatched.

(From *The Thurber Carnival* by James Thurber)

A Using some of the exercises mentioned in parts 1, 2 and 3, here is a possible way of dealing with the text.

1 *Anticipation*
Look at the title and at the drawing that accompanies the story. What can you infer from the two? What is a unicorn? What do you think the story is about?

2 *Organization*
Is the text organized in a ☐ logical   way?
                                   ☐ argumentative
                                   ☐ chronological
What link-words or expressions reflect this organization?

3 There is obviously a great difference between the behaviour of the husband and that of his wife in the story. Read it again, paying particular attention to the various ways this difference is revealed, then complete the following table:

	Husband	Wife
How they react to the unicorn		
Pronoun used to refer to the unicorn		
Attitude towards their wife/husband		
Their surroundings		
How does the vocabulary/style reflect the differences in their rhythm of life?		
How *you* interpret their behaviour		

4 Find another *title* for the story:
....

5 Find another *moral*:
....

6 In what 'literary genre' would you classify the story?
   ☐ short story
   ☐ fairy tale
   ☐ legend
   ☐ tale

7 Here is a drawing by the same author, James Thurber.

'All Right, Have It Your Way – You Heard a Seal Bark'

Try to find as many common points as you can between the story
and the drawing.
Can you think of any differences?

B Here is a list of the main question-types that can be used.
  1 *Multiple-choice questions*
     Under a similar appearance, multiple-choice exercises can
     cover very different types of activities and involve very
     different skills.
     a) The *aim* of the multiple-choice question may differ.
         It may be used:
         i) To *test* the students' comprehension of the text.
         ii) To *help* the students *understand* what would otherwise
             be too difficult to understand. It may, for instance,
             give a clue to the students who would not have been
             able to infer the meaning of a word.
             e.g.
             In the sentence 'You are a booby', the word 'booby' means:
             ☐ an animal
             ☐ a person who is ill
             ☐ a person who is mad
             In this case, two possibilities out of three can easily be
             eliminated and the student is therefore given a clue as
             to the meaning of the word 'booby'.
         iii) To *help* the students *think* about a word and infer its
             meaning, or think about the text, their attention being
             drawn to an idea – expressed or implied – which they
             might not have noticed otherwise.
             (Even when the students understand every single word
             in the text, it may be interesting to make them discover
             the particular connotation of a word in a given context.
             Most words potentially have dozens of slightly
             different 'meanings' and take on one or two of these
             aspects in a given context.) A multiple-choice question
             may then be useful to draw the students' attention to
             the real value of the word in the sentence.
                In the introduction to his book *Read and Think*, John
             Munby advocates a different kind of multiple-choice
             question from the ones commonly used. He thinks that if
             two answers are possible, or at least correspond to two
             different ways of reading the text, then the exercise will
             require the students to think about (and mentally 'discuss')
             the possibilities. In that way, reading becomes a much
             more active process. In addition, correcting the exercise in
             the class may give rise to discussions and justifications.

e.g.
The husband said he had never seen a unicorn because:
- [ ] he didn't like psychiatrists and did not want to tell them the truth
- [ ] he was hoping to get rid of his wife that way
- [ ] he didn't remember what had happened to him in the morning
- [ ] he had never seen a unicorn and had told his wife a lie, knowing she would call the psychiatrist and be shut up in an institution

b) The *function* of the multiple-choice question can also vary.
  i) In a multiple-choice question such as the following the student is asked to understand what was actually said in the text. He may have to think in order to understand the structure of the sentence or try to infer the meaning of unfamiliar words, but he is basically asked to retrieve some information from the text.
  At the end of the text:
  - [ ] the husband succeeds in getting rid of his wife
  - [ ] the wife succeeds in obliging her husband to admit he'd never seen a unicorn
  - [ ] both husband and wife gain something

  ii) Consider now the following multiple-choice question:
  The police and the psychiatrist looked at the wife with great interest because:
  - [ ] they were interested in knowing more about the husband
  - [ ] they were already quite sure *she* was crazy
  - [ ] it was part of their job always to seem interested in what people told them

  Here, the answer is not actually given in the text. However, if one reads the beginning of the second paragraph again, one will see that the wife's excitement, the 'gloat in her eye', must have led the police and the psychiatrist to suspect her from the very beginning, so that the second answer must be the correct one. This second type of multiple-choice question may be a little more difficult but is essential to help the student to read 'between the lines'.

  iii) It is possible to go one step further and ask questions the answers of which have to be deduced from the text. For instance, this is the case when we ask the student to generalize, i.e. to extend the meaning of the passage and draw some kind of rule from it.
  e.g.
  The railway clerk demanded a 10p lost-property fee from secretary Sandra Heselden before he would return her lost handbag. Trouble was, all Sandra's money was in the bag.

The clerk was adamant: no money, no bag. 'It's the rules,'
he said.
  So Sandra borrowed 10p from a porter, retrieved her bag,
and repaid the porter.
The passage suggests that:
☐ one should never go out without one's purse
☐ some administrative rules are stupid
☐ most railway clerks are very helpful
☐ you can get into trouble if you lose your property

Some other multiple-choice questions may lead the
student to judge and evaluate what he has read. This
type of question often admits of more than one correct
answer, which leads to discussions of interpretation.

c) Finally, the multiple-choice question can be *focused on*
    i)   just one word of the text
    ii) an expression, a clause or a sentence
    iii) one or several paragraphs
    iv) the whole text
         e.g.
         See text by Agatha Christie on pages 135–6.
         Choose the possibility which best describes the main idea of
         each paragraph:
         1 ☐ Miss Danby's worries
           ☐ Miss Danby's bad memory
           ☐ Miss Danby's apology and explanation
         2 ☐ Megan's death
           ☐ How Megan's death affected her husband and
             daughter
           ☐ Gwenda's life in India
         3 ☐ Consequences of Major Halliday's second marriage
           ☐ Gwenda's life in England
           ☐ Major Halliday's death
         4 ☐ Why Miss Danby didn't like Major Halliday's second
             wife
           ☐ Where Gwenda lived in England
           ☐ What Miss Danby knows about Gwenda's life in
             England and her stepmother

Whatever the type of multiple-choice questions used, it is
essential that the students do not consider them as a guessing
game and to encourage the class to justify their choice of one
answer and their rejection of the others. It is important because it
will be an incentive to a more careful consideration of the text (it
may even, in many cases, lead to a change of opinion!) and it will
also be a link with oral production. When dealing with
multiple-choice questions in the class, it may be a good idea,
after the students have worked on their own, to ask them to
discuss their answers in pairs or in groups. Each pair or group

The multiple-choice question can be about:	Function of multiple-choice question	Aim of multiple-choice question	Type of multiple-choice question
a word	to help understand:	to *test* the comprehension	
a sentence	a *fact*, or piece of information in the text	to *explain* or help understand a difficult word or passage	varying the number of possible answers
a paragraph	an *implied* fact	to lead the student to go back to the text and *scan* it carefully	only one answer is correct
the whole text	some meaning or interpretation that must be *deduced* from the text	to help the student *think* about the text and mentally discuss several interpretations of possibilities	possibility of no correct answer
	or to help the student *evaluate* the text himself		N.B. Whatever the type of multiple-choice question chosen, it must be clearly explained to the students

will then *explain* (not only tell) to the rest of the class the solution they have agreed on.

2 *Right or wrong?* (True or false?)
   In this kind of exercise, the student is given a list of statements about the text and must decide whether they are true or false. There are several possibilities.
   a) All the statements given are either right or wrong. The answers can be found in the text and the students must write R or W next to each sentence:
      The man found it hard to believe there could be a unicorn in his garden.
      The wife didn't believe in unicorns.
      The wife told her husband he was stupid.
      The wife was worried when she called the police and the psychiatrist.
   b) An extension of the preceding exercise consists of asking the students to justify their answers underneath. They can do so by quoting a few words from the text when it is possible, or by briefly giving their reasons, in their own words. This is a process the students have to go through anyway in exercise

(a) but the mere fact of having to justify what one thinks clearly and concisely will lead the students to a closer scrutiny of the text.

c) One may also ask the students to *rewrite* and *correct* the statements that are false.

e.g.

The wife was worried when she called the police and the psychiatrist: W

The wife was happy to call the police and the psychiatrist.

In all these cases the more interesting statements will obviously be those that are wrong since they will necessitate a justification. (The students can just copy a sentence from the text when the statement is correct.)

d) It is also possible to include statements that are neither right nor wrong but which we cannot check because we are not given enough information in the passage. In that case, the students are asked to write D (don't know) or ? next to the sentence. In the case of *The Unicorn in the Garden*, the following statements would enter that category.

- The unicorn is in fact a neighbour who disguised himself.
- The police and the psychiatrist knew before arriving that it was the wife – not the husband – who was mad.

This additional possibility usually permits more general statements which will oblige the student to *think* about the passage.

e) A variation of this exercise consists of giving statements that are all 'right' but that cannot be justified easily by referring to one word or one small section of the text. Instead, the student will have to find his justification in different parts of the text or in a passage where the idea is expressed in quite a different way.

e.g.

The wife is definitely more materialistic than her husband.

   (Because she only believes what she sees, and he doesn't question the existence of the unicorn; because she 'belongs' in the modern American society of her environment: the telephone, the police, the psychiatrist.)

f) H. Widdowson in *Teaching Language as Communication* suggests inserting the statements in the reading passage itself so that the reader may check his interpretation of the passage as he is reading. He further suggests accompanying the statements by solutions that the students must work out (by completing statements).

3 *Can you tell?*
This type of exercise is somewhat related to 2(d). The student is given a list of points to look for in the text. The answers to some of the questions will be fairly obvious; in other cases the information will be more difficult to find. But it will not always be possible to find an answer as there may not be enough evidence in the text.
e.g.
Can you tell
– whether the unicorn is real?
– what the wife told the police and the psychiatrist on the telephone?
– why the unicorn went away?
– whether the husband was sincere when he said: 'The unicorn is a mythical beast'?
– what happened to the wife after the police took her away?

4 *Find the reason*
a) In this kind of exercise, the students are provided with a list of sentences or phrases from the text, describing an action, an event, or quoting a character. What they must do is briefly explain *why* things happened that way. The interest of the exercise lies in the fact that the answer is not often given in the text and must be inferred from the rest of the information given.
e.g.
How would you explain the following statements (particularly the underlined expressions):
– The man walked *slowly* downstairs (para. 1)
– The wife got up and dressed *as fast as she could* (para. 2)
– They sat down in chairs and looked at her *with great interest* (para. 2)
b) A variation of the exercise is to give a list of adjectives and ask the class to find out who/what they refer to and to find out on what occasion and why they were applied to that person/event/action, etc.
e.g.

Adjective	Who?	When?	Why?
cold			
excited			
happy			
solemn			
quiet			

The same thing can be done with some of the words spoken

by the various characters, instead of adjectives.
e.g.

	Who?	When?	Why?
'You are a booby'			
'The unicorn is a mythical beast'			
'We'll see about that.'			

5 *Expanding statements*
e.g.
Find as many details as you can to expand the following statements:
– 'The man had never liked the words "booby" and "booby-hatch".'
– 'I'm going to have you put in the booby-hatch.'
This exercise may be useful to show how different parts of a text may contribute to convey the same idea since the students will find supporting details all through the passage.

6 *Find the link-word*
The students are asked to supply the missing link-words in a series of sentences. Several are structurally and semantically possible but only some (and their equivalents) are in keeping with the meaning of the text.
e.g.
Supply the missing link-words so that the sentences reflect the meaning of the text:
– The wife telephoned the police .... her husband was asleep in the garden.
– .... the wife looked excited, the police and the psychiatrist thought she was crazy.
– .... she wanted the police to arrest her husband, she was arrested herself.

7 *Complete the summary*
The students are given a summary of the text in which certain words, expressions or sentences have been left blank. The exercise will be more interesting if it requires a global understanding of the text and if the summary has to be completed in the students' own words. Besides encouraging them to draw out the main information in the text, the exercise will help the weaker students by giving them an outline and focusing their attention on what is eesential in the passage.
e.g.
This is the story of a man who, one day, ... in his garden.

His first reaction is .... but she .... When he
goes back to the garden the man .... and he is so happy
and excited that he goes back .... However, she threatens
to .... When he wants to see the unicorn again,
....

8 *Complete the sentences*
Instead of asking the students to complete a summary one can
ask them to complete a number of sentences that some of the
characters in the text might have said.

This may be a difficult exercise, involving a good
understanding of the characters.

There are a number of variations of the last two exercises.
a) Instead of completing a summary, the students can complete
a one-sided conversation.
e.g. A friend of the husband phones him and asks him a lot of
questions about what happened to him, some of them very
general (e.g. What happened to your wife?), others more
detailed (e.g. What did you say the unicorn was like?). The
students can only hear what the friend says and his questions.
They must supply the husband's answers.
b) A choice of words or expressions can also be given instead of
leaving the students free to fill the blanks as they wish. One
can, for instance, give them a choice of verbs which would be
grammatically and semantically acceptable in the sentence,
although only one allows them to form a sentence in keeping
with the meaning of the text.
e.g.
At the beginning of the story the husband .... quite
mad.
☐ is
☐ becomes
☐ is considered as
☐ pretends to be
At the end of the story the wife .... as crazy as a
jay-bird.
☐ becomes
☐ is believed to be
☐ believes she is
☐ calls her husband
(In the first example, both (c) and (d) are possible according to
the interpretation one gives to the text.)

9 *Find the errors*
For this exercise, the students are given a summary of the text in
which a certain number of errors have been inserted. It is a

variant of the 'Right or Wrong' exercise but may appear more
difficult as the summary thus created may seem perfectly
coherent.

e.g. (para. 2)

When the husband went out, the wife left the house as quickly as she
could and called the police and the psychiatrist. When they arrived she
told them there was a unicorn in the garden and they realized she was
mad. They finally jumped on her and had no difficulty putting her into
the straight-jacket.

The students must rewrite and correct the summary.

10 *Sentence-building*
   a) The students are given all the elements (words or
      expressions) of a sentence but they have been jumbled and
      must be reordered.

      e.g.
      – more / husband / the / poetic / wife / is / the / than
      – crazy / psychiatrist / never / was / believed / that the / the /
        husband
      – life / in / enjoyed / the / an / live / had / his / husband / wife / his /
        after / to / institution / gone

   b) Another possibility is to give only the key-words of the
      sentences which have to be formed.

      e.g.
      – wife / want / husband / asylum
      – man / not / question / unicorn / garden

   c) One can also ask the students to match elements from
      different columns in order to build sentences.

      e.g. see text by Agatha Christie, pages 135–6.

      Match elements from columns 1 and 2 so as to get sentences
      corresponding to the meaning of the text:

1 Megan married Gwenda's father	a had offered to bring up Gwenda
2 Gwenda	b died in England
3 Gwenda's mother	c while he was in England
4 Megan	d died in India
5 Gwenda's father married his second wife	e didn't like Gwenda's step-mother very much
6 Miss Danby's family	f was from New Zealand
7 Gwenda's father	g couldn't remember her life in England very well
8 Miss Danby	h while she was in India

   d) The same exercise can be done with more than two
      columns. Another way of rendering it more complex is to
      associate it with a reordering exercise. After matching the
      elements and finding the sentences, the students have to
      reorder them.

      e.g. Read the following text.

No Entry to Midwich

One of the luckiest accidents in my wife's life is that she happened to marry a man who was born on the 26th of September. But for that, we should both of us undoubtedly have been at home in Midwich on the night of the 26th–27th, with consequences which, I have never ceased to be thankful, she was spared.

Because it was my birthday, however, and also to some extent because I had the day before received and signed a contract with an American publisher, we set off on the morning of the 26th for London, and a mild celebration. Very pleasant, too. A few satisfactory calls, lobster and Chablis at Wheeler's, Ustinov's latest extravaganza, a little supper, and so back to the hotel where Janet enjoyed the bathroom with that fascination which other people's plumbing always arouses in her.

Next morning, a leisurely departure on the way back to Midwich. A pause in Trayne, which is our nearest shopping town, for a few groceries; then on along the main road, through the village of Stouch, then the right-hand turn on to the secondary road for – But, no. Half the road is blocked by a pole from which dangles a notice 'ROAD CLOSED', and in the gap beside it stands a policeman who holds up his hand. . . .

So I stop. The policeman advances to the offside of the car, I recognize him as a man from Trayne.

'Sorry, sir, but the road is closed.'

'You mean I'll have to go round by the Oppley Road?'

''Fraid that's closed, too, sir.'

'But –'

There is the sound of a horn behind.

''F you wouldn't mind backing off a bit to the left, sir.'

Rather bewildered, I do as he asks, and past us and past him goes an army three-ton lorry with khaki-clad youths leaning over the sides.

'Revolution in Midwich?' I inquire.

'Manoeuvres,' he tells me. 'The road's impassable.'

'Not *both* roads surely? We live in Midwich, you know, Constable.'

'I know, sir. But there's no way there just now. 'F I was you, sir, I'd go back to Trayne till we get it clear. Can't have parking here, 'cause of getting things through.'

Janet opens the door on her side and picks up her shopping-bag.

'I'll walk on, and you come along when the road's clear,' she tells me.

The constable hesitates. Then he lowers his voice.

'Seein' as you live there, ma'am, I'll tell you – but it's confidential like. 'T isn't no use tryin', ma'am. Nobody can't get into Midwich, an' that's a fact.'

We stare at him.

'But why on earth not?' says Janet.

'That's just what they're tryin' to find out, ma'am.'

(From John Wyndham: *The Midwich Cuckoos* (Penguin, 1960))

After reading the above text, combine elements from columns 1, 2, 3 and 4 so as to get meaningful sentences corresponding to what is said in the text. All elements should be used.

(a) The author	kept	the hotel	near their home
(b) Even	went	to Midwich	in London
(c) A policeman	liked	people	was forbidden
(d) They	signed	the author and his wife	where they were staying in London
(e) The author's wife	had	a contract	for a book
(f) The constable	wanted	supper	to wait in Trayne
(g) The author and his wife	walking	shopping	from taking the road to Midwich

Write out the complete sentences.
a e.g. The author signed a contract for a book.
b
c
d
e
f
g
Now can you put these events back in the order in which they happened?

11 *Inferring what happened before*
In this kind of exercise, the students are asked to use the
information in the text to make deductions about facts and
events that are not actually mentioned.
e.g. see text by Agatha Christie, pages 135–6

Miss Danby writes: 'I am sending this off hurriedly in answer to your wire.'
Which of the following points do you think Gwenda mentioned in her
wire?
Gwenda probably
☐ asked why her stay in England had been so short when she was
young
☐ asked who her father was
☐ said that something unpleasant had just happened to her
☐ asked if she had ever been to England before
☐ wanted to know where exactly she had lived in England
☐ asked when and how her mother died
☐ wanted to know whether Dillmouth was the name of the place where
she used to live in England
☐ asked what her stepmother's name was

12 *Could they have said it?*
Another way of encouraging students to deduce meaning is to
give them several opinions (some derived from ideas in the text,
others quite different) and to ask them to decide whether one or
several characters in the text would agree or disagree with these

opinions. In some cases, the students may decide that they cannot possibly tell.

13 *Open questions*

Questions can obviously be more or less open. They can be interesting as a straightforward way of drawing the students' attention to one particular sentence or fact. But open questions which otherwise aim only at a repetition of the information given in the text tend to be of less use since they do not really help the students *think* about the text and ask themselves questions.

It is often more fruitful to ask questions to which there is not *one obvious answer*. They will oblige the students to return to the text constantly and to scrutinize it for details to support their opinion.

e.g.

less and less 'obvious' answers

- What does the wife think of unicorns?
- What happens when the husband goes back to the garden the second time?
- What made the psychiatrist and the police suspect the wife?
- Why did the husband say he hadn't seen a unicorn?

One of the possible disadvantages of such questions, however, is that the activity required of the students is one of production as much as comprehension, and it may be difficult for the teacher to decide whether wrong answers are due to a failure to understand the text, or the students' inability to express themselves properly.

14 *Drawing up a list*

The students can be asked to draw up a list of nouns, verbs, words, sentences, ideas, characters, arguments for and against, etc., in the text or in a passage from the text.

e.g.

In the second part of the text, list the words that show the wife's excitement.

Find three words or expressions showing how violent the wife becomes at the end of the text.

This can also be done by asking the students to underline, box or ring words or expressions in the text.

15 *Classifying*

Students can be given a list of words, expressions, names, etc. drawn from the text and asked to classify them according to various criteria.

e.g.
- classifying words under two or three main ideas
- classifying expressions according to their degree of
  politeness, strength, formality, etc.
- classifying characters according to their reactions

16 *Selecting words or expressions from a list*
The list can be a list of people, events, actions, etc. from which
the students have to make a choice.
e.g.
The following verbs all appear in the text. Which one of them implies
most hatred?
scream   tell   curse   say
A variation of this type of exercise is to ask the students to
underline the odd man out
e.g.
Underline the odd man out.
scream   tell   subdue   curse

17 *Find the equivalent sentence*
e.g.
Find the sentences or clauses equivalent to the following (from paras.
2 and 3).
- It was difficult to calm her.

....
- Unicorns do not exist.

....
- Your wife is completely mad.

....
- They put her in an asylum.

....

18 *Find the equivalent*
e.g.
Read the first paragraph carefully and find words or expressions
which mean the same thing as:
- eating: ....
- to wake somebody up: ....
- happily: ....
- a madman: ....
- imaginary: ....

19 *Find the right word*
This exercise is very similar to the preceding one but instead of
being given an equivalent, the students are given a definition of
the word they have to find.
e.g.
Find the words which mean: (from para. 1)
- a lunatic asylum: ....

Linguistic response to the text

— to wake somebody up: ....

This exercise can also take the form of a matching exercise, the words being given in one column, the definitions, or equivalents, out of order, in another.

20 *Find the opposite*
e.g.
Read para. 2 carefully and find the words or expressions which mean the opposite of:
— to excite: ....
— to let someone go free: ....
— it was easy for them to: ....
— she did not resist: ....

21 *Choose the right adverb*
The aim of this exercise is to make the students ask themselves questions about the degree or intensity of certain feelings, ideas, etc., in the passage. Several possibilities will often be correct and this may lead to interesting discussions in the class or between groups when comparing answers. It is also extremely useful to familiarize the students with a number of commonly used adverbs.
e.g.
The wife is □ almost   happy at the idea of sending her husband to
                         a 'booby-hatch'.
□ rather
□ very
□ extremely
When the husband told his wife he'd seen a unicorn, she regarded
him □ sadly
□ angrily
□ excitedly
□ strangely

22 *Matching* (see also pages 135ff)
This exercise can take several forms. For instance: matching words and definitions; characters and adjectives; events, actions and characteristics; characters and attributes.
e.g.
Below, you will find a list of adjectives: in front of each of them, write the name(s) of the person(s) you think they best characterize (the husband? the wife? the police and psychiatrist?) Some adjectives may not apply to anybody at all!
— poetic: ....
— interested: ....
— kind: ....
— cold: ....
— matter-of-fact: ....

- hypocritical: ....
- cunning: ....
- enthusiastic: ....

23 *Find the reference* (see also pages 45–7)
e.g.
Explain what the underlined word refers to in the following sentence:
'We'll see about *that*'
The exercise will gain interest if the reference is not
immediately apparent (e.g. reference to a single word
mentioned just before).

24 *Using semic tables*
When a text contains a number of words belonging to the same
semantic field, it may be useful to draw the students' attention
to the differences between the various elements of the set (i.e. to
the connotations of words that all refer to a certain feeling,
object or action). One way of doing this is to draw a semic table
in which the words appearing in the text are entered on one side
and the possible connotations or semantic constituent features
on the other. Such an exercise will lead the students to think
about words which they may have considered as mere
synonyms before. It may also lead them to refer back to the
context in which the words appear in order to find out which
features the words have. It is for that reason that the exercise is a
real help to an in-depth understanding of language rather than
merely a means of enriching one's vocabulary.
e.g.
To look, to watch and to gloat all belong to the same semantic field.
Put crosses in the boxes corresponding to the features that
differentiate each of them:

	perceive with one's eyes	following something that moves	idea of selfish delight
watch			
look			
gloat			

25 *Exercises on word formation and derivation*
See part 1.

2.5   Study skills: Summarizing

1 Writing a good summary is a difficult exercise which is rarely
done satisfactorily, even by advanced students. The best way of
training the students to write summaries is to prepare them
through practice in underlining important words or sentences, in
finding the topic sentence and main ideas and in perceiving the
structure of the text.

2 Besides these preparatory exercises, one should insist on
conciseness and accuracy when asking for summaries. One way
of doing this is to set a certain length to the summary (e.g. thirty
words). The students will then have to condense the information
to just this number of words (plus or minus one or two). This
will force them to select only what is important and often, when
they find their summaries are still too long, to reject some further
adjectives or adverbial phrases that they consider less important.
e.g.
  a) Read the article that appears on pages 208–9 and write a
      twenty-word summary of it.
  b) Read the passage on pages 208–9 and write a fifty-word summary
      of it.
  Can you now write a thirty-word summary of the same passage?

3 An exercise such as the following can also be given as a
preparation to make the students conscious of what constitutes a
good summary.

Exercise

Specific aim: To train the students to identify the main ideas of a
                  text.
Skills involved: Extracting salient points to summarize the text.
Why?   A comparison of several summaries of the same
                  passage will allow students to become conscious of
                  the most common mistakes made when
                  summarizing.

Read the following article and the summaries written by four students.
Then decide which of the summaries is the best.

The secret few people guess

(*Jenny Stevens writes about Brenda, one of two million adults with a secret life.*)

Brenda Linson never goes anywhere without an empty spectacles case. It is
as vital to her as her purse. Yet, she doesn't wear glasses. The reason she
can't do without it is because she can't read and she can't write. If ever she

gets into any situation where she might be expected to do either of these things, she fishes around in her bag for the specs case, finds it's empty, and asks the person concerned to do the reading for her. Brenda is now in her late thirties. She's capable and articulate and until a few months ago hardly anybody knew she was illiterate. Her husband didn't know and her children didn't know. The children still don't.

She had any number of tactics for concealing her difficulty – for example, never lingering near a phone at work, in case she had to answer it and might be required to write something down. But, in fact, it is easier for illiterates to conceal the truth than the rest of us might imagine. Literacy is so much taken for granted that people simply don't spot the giveaway signs. . . .

It has never occurred to the children that their mother cannot read. She doesn't read them stories, but then their father doesn't either, so they find nothing surprising in the fact. Similarly they just accept that Dad is the one who writes the sick notes and reads the school reports. Now that the elder boy Tom is quite a proficient reader, Brenda can skilfully get him to read any notes brought home from school simply by asking, 'What's that all about, then?'

Brenda's husband never guessed the truth in 10 years of marriage. For one thing he insists on handling all domestic correspondence and bills himself. An importer of Persian carpets, he travels a great deal and so is not around so much to spot the truth. While he's away Brenda copes with any situations by explaining that she can't do anything until she's discussed it with her husband.

Brenda was very successful in her job until recently. For the last five years she had worked as waitress at an exclusive private club, and had eventually been promoted to head waitress. She kept the thing a secret there too, and got over the practical difficulties somehow.
(From *The Observer*)

Summary 1

> This article descri bes the case of an adult woman who has never been able to learn how to read and write. For a long time, her husband and chil dren never discovered the truth but they now know about her problem.

Summary 2

This article is about Brenda, who always carries an empty spectacle case because it may provide her with an excuse as she cannot read nor write. Her children don't know she is illiterate. Her husband didn't know for a long time. She had a lot of ideas to hide her problem (for instance she was afraid of having to take notes if someone telephoned at work — she was a waitress — and never stayed near a telephone, she let her husband do all the domestic writing, she asked her elder son to read things for her ...) but in fact it is easier than one may think to hide this deficiency as people never think of it. Her husband wasn't often at home and as for her children, they found it normal to ask their father for everything.

Summary 3

The story of Brenda's secret life.

Summary 4

An article describing
the case of Brenda, a
married woman in her
late thirties who cannot
read. By using a number
of tactics, she has so far
managed to hide this
deficiency from the people
she works with and
even from her family.

Summary 5

An article showing how
lonely people who can't
read are.

The best summary is Summary ....
Now consider the summaries you have rejected and decide why they are
not good. Is it because
a) They are too short and the main idea is not expressed.
b) They are too long.
c) There are too many details and the key-ideas do not stand out.
d) The wrong key-ideas have been selected.
e) The information they contain is wrong.
Summary .... : ....   Summary .... : ....
Summary .... : ....   Summary .... : ....
(More than one reason may be true for a given summary.)

Study skills: Note-taking

Exercise

Specific aim: To train the students to grasp the overall
                   organization of the passage and its main ideas.
Skills involved: Recognizing the structure of the text.
                   Extracting the main ideas from the text.
Why?   A comparison of several notes on the same text will
                   allow students to become conscious of the most
                   common mistakes made when taking notes.

Read the article on pages 101–2 ('Just call him 181213 3 1234 5') and the
notes taken by three students below. Which of these notes is the best,
according to you?

Linguistic response to the text

①

1975 : Each German citizen may have a number. Will keep it all his life + 30 years after death.

I Reasons for

- to help computarization
- to avoid confusion

II Reasons against

- too much bureaucratization already.

(31% of the pop. against)

②

Plan to give each citizen a number in Germany. Will disappear only thirty years after his death. Done to be like other countries and that way there will be less confusion between names. (cf the great number of people called Müller.) Most people think it will simplify the system. (Now, for instance when moving to another town, you have pages of forms to fill). 31% want to keep their names.

③

The project : giving each German citizen a number.

I gvt's explanation
  3 reasons :
  - computers now used in registration
  - will reduce the possibility of confusion between names
  - already done in other count.

II Reactions in W. Germany.
  - For : won't make much difference
  - Against : 31% of the pop.

237

Now consider the ones you rejected and decide why you don't think them as good.

no clear plan visible		
too long		
not enough use of abbreviations		
wrong structure given		
too dense – no clear presentation		

Note-taking – further hints

- Give a text and notes taken from it. These notes are incomplete or unsatisfactory and the students must correct them.
- One should also encourage the students to practise note-making, that is to say, writing down their reactions to the text.

IV · ASSESSING THE TEXT

1 Fact versus opinion

Exercise 1

Specific aim: To train the students to discriminate between facts and opinions.
Skills involved: Understanding the function of sentences.
Why? Being able to dissociate facts from opinions is an essential first step in acquiring a critical reading ability. Exercises of the following type are useful to help the students discriminate between the simple reporting of something that actually happened and the more or less straightforward expression of approval or disapproval.

Read the following statements and decide whether they are *facts* or *opinions.*
1 Edgar Allan Poe is the greatest writer of horror stories in the world.
....
2 Poe had to leave the University of Virginia because he couldn't pay his debts. ....
3 Edgar Allan Poe should not have drunk so much. ....
4 Lovecraft has often been compared to Edgar Allan Poe.
....
5 When Lovecraft died, he was practically unknown. ....
6 Lovecraft died in conditions of shameful neglect. ....
7 Lovecraft's stories are far more horrible than those of Edgar Allan Poe. ....
8 Edgar Allan Poe's stories reflect his powerful imagination and his love for analysis. ....
9 Baudelaire wrote that Edgar Allan Poe 'pursued imagination and subjected it to the most stringent analysis'. ....
10 It is because of Baudelaire that Edgar Allan Poe became famous in France. ....

Exercise 2

Specific aim:
Skills involved: } Same as for exercise 1
Why?

In the following passage a journalist explains why people join the Peoples Temple. Read the passage through, then consider the underlined statements – sentences or phrases – and decide whether they are facts or opinions. Whenever you think they are opinions, write down in the second column which words mostly influenced your decision.

Why People Join	Fact or opinion?	Words turning the statement into an opinion

Why People Join

(He has) no more pressing need than the one to find somebody to whom he can surrender, as quickly as possible, that gift of freedom which he, the unfortunate creature, was born with   (Dostoyevsky. The Brothers Karamazov)

THE LANDSCAPE of their minds was as grotesque as the corpse-littered village they left behind. They had started as seekers after meaning, direction, comfort and love. The Peoples Temple, which provided a number of social services to the poor, had filled their lives with purpose. But in the jungle of Guyana, it had all turned into fear and hatred.

Why did they join an organization like the Peoples Temple? And why did they stay in it? Few if any of the thousands of cult groups in the U.S. are as violent as the Guyana group was in its last days, but many of them share a number of unusual characteristics. Social scientists who have studied these groups agree that most cult members are in some sort of emotional trouble before they join. . .

Once recruits start going to meetings, they are frequently subjected to various drills and disciplines that weary them both physically and emotionally, producing a sort of trance.

Cut off from family and friends, the new member gets repeated infusions of the cult's doctrines. The lonely, depressed, frightened and disoriented recruit often experiences what amounts to a religious conversion. Former members of such cults frequently say that something in them "snaps", report Flo Conway and Jim Siegelman, authors of *Snapping,* a new book on what they call "America's epidemic of sudden personality change."

At this point, the cultist's life is no longer his own. Personalities change from the lively and complex patterns of normality to those of an automaton reciting what he has been taught. The usual problems of living have been replaced by a nearly childish existence in which the cult and its leaders supply all rules and all answers. Erich Fromm, in his classic treatise on the rise of Nazism, called this process the "escape from freedom.". . .

JUST AS the cult members give themselves up to the group, the leader too takes his entire identity from his followers.

Both leader and followers thus see an overwhelming necessity to keep the group alive and intact. Dissenters are often punished severely. Loyalty is intensified by claims that the outside world is evil and threatening. Return to normal life becomes more and more difficult, even terrifying.

240

"The gravest threat imaginable to such a group is for someone to try to take members out of the 'family,' " says U.C.L.A. Psychologist David Wellisch. Leo Ryan's mission to Guyana may have been just such a threat, the spark that triggered the tragedy.

With Jones' own behaviour growing more paranoid and the sudden presence of the Congressman and the press, some experts believe there was almost a psychological inevitability to the disaster. "Following that type of fragmentation, there was only one thing left," says Dr. Stanley Cath, a Boston psychiatrist. "They could return to the world of reality, but they would have had to face their own inadequacies, the world they had already discarded, the families they had already discarded. So for them, death was preferable because death had already been proclaimed rebirth."

(*Time*)

2 Writer's intention

Exercise 1

Specific aim: To train the students to judge the communicative value of a text.

Skills involved: Understanding the function of the text.

Why? A first step towards evaluating a passage may be to give a variety of texts of different types (an advertisement, an excerpt from a novel, a warning notice, a passage from a textbook, etc.) and to ask the class to answer the following questionnaire for each of the texts.

Students can do this on their own at first, then discuss what they have written with a friend. During the discussion, problems such as the author's intention, the quality of the information given or the use of devices such as irony will naturally come up.

Students will then be ready to study these points in more detail.

Title of the passage:
Who wrote this text? (author's name, occupation)
What is the aim of the message? (informing, teaching, entertaining)
Who was it written for? (specialists, consumers, children)
Do you think it fulfils its aim? (i.e. is it successful?)

Many of the exercises in this section can admit of more than one answer. It is therefore a good idea to ask the students to discuss their answers in pairs before 'correcting' the exercises with the whole group.

Exercise 2

Specific aim: To help the students to understand the writer's intention and attitude.

Skills involved: Understanding the communicative value of the text and of the sentences.
Interpreting the text.

Why?   If one fails to recognize the writer's intention and attitude, one can easily misunderstand the whole passage, even though all the sentences have been understood. It is therefore important to train the students to ask themselves questions such as the ones in this exercise before dealing with a more detailed comprehension of the passage.

Dublin
Nov. 1967

Dear Reader!

Human beings will become so used to being crushed together that when they are on their own, they will suffer withdrawal symptoms. 'Doctor – I've got to get into a crowded train soon or I'll go mad.' So, special N.H.S. assimilated rush hour trains will be run every other Sunday for patients. At 9 o'clock on that morning, thousands of victims will crowd platforms throughout England, where great electrically powered Crowd Compressors will crush hundreds of writhing humans into trains, until their eyes stand out under the strain, then, even more wretches are forced in by smearing them with vaseline and sliding them in sideways between legs of standing passengers. The doors close – any bits of clothing, ears or fingers are snipped off. To add to the sufferers' relief great clouds of stale cigarette smoke are pumped into the carriages. The patients start to cough, laugh and talk. They're feeling better already. But more happiness is on its way. The train reaches 80 m.p.h.; at the next station the driver slams the brakes on shooting all the victims up to one end of the carriages. Immediately the doors open, and great compressed air tubes loaded with up to 100 passengers are fired into the empty spaces, this goes on until the rubber roofs of the carriages give upwards, and the lumps you see are yet a second layer of grateful patients. Off goes the train, and one sees the relief on the travellers' faces. Who wants LSD when you can get this? Ah! you say, the train can't possibly take any more. Wrong! At the next stop the train is sprayed with a powerful adhesive glue, and fresh passengers stuck to the outside and so, crushed to pulp, pop-eyed and coughing blood, the train carries out its work of mercy. Those who are worried about their children's future in the 20th century need not fear. We are prepared.

(From Spike Milligan: *The Bedside Milligan* (Star, 1979))

1 *Recognizing type of texts*
After reading this passage, can you tell whether it is
☐ a letter to the editor
☐ a passage from a novel
☐ a passage from a science-fiction story
☐ a passage from a textbook on sociology
☐ a satire on modern society
☐ a passage from a horror story

2 *The author's intention*
What is the author's intention in this passage? (There may be more than one answer.)
☐ to amuse the reader
☐ to predict what the future will be like
☐ to shock the reader
☐ to reassure the reader about the future
☐ to criticize society
☐ to teach us something about life in the future

3 *The author's attitude*
In this passage you can feel that the author's attitude towards the human beings he describes is one of
☐ indifference
☐ sympathy
☐ pity
☐ admiration
☐ anxiety
☐ detachment hiding concern
☐ criticism

4 *Tone*
Write a, b or c in front of the following sentences according to what you think the tone of the sentence is.
a) matter of fact
b) humorous
c) ironic
'Human beings will become so used to being crushed together that when they are on their own, they will suffer withdrawal symptoms.'
'The patients start to cough, laugh and talk.'
'They're feeling better already.'
'Ah! you say, the train can't possibly take any more.'
'We are prepared.'

Exercise 3

Specific aim: ⎫ Same as for exercise 2 but with a series of critical
Skills involved: ⎬ judgements implying either approval or
Why? ⎭ disapproval.

Here are different sentences all taken from critical articles. Decide which ones imply disapproval and which ones, on the contrary, carry praise.
a) Of all the so-called *How To* books in existence . . . , Mr Hollingsworth's *How To Drive a Steam Locomotive* is surely the most discouraging.

b) There is so much wrong with this *Richard* that we had better start with what's right.

c) Another Flaxborough novel, and one of the best, possibly because it is much solider and more plausible than earlier, flimsier items in the series.

d) Mr Bingham has done better than this . . . and we must hope that he will have regained his customary high form in the next [book].

e) I cannot praise this book too highly.

f) A review cannot do justice to the wealth of topics, the rich store of ideas with which Lorenz presents us.

Exercise 4

Specific aim:	To train the students to recognize prejudice and bias.
Skills involved:	Understanding the communicative value of the text.
	Interpreting the text.
Why?	Most writers are prejudiced in some way and try to influence their readers to look at things in a certain way. It is therefore important that the students should be able to recognize 'slanted writing'.

Read the following headlines, sentences, or paragraphs and decide
– which one is the most biased (write a or b in column 1)
– if the bias is for or against (write F or A in column 2)
– what the bias is for or against (column 3)
– what clues (words or expressions) led you to discover the bias

	most biased sentence	for or against	for or against what?	clues
a) **Secret London hearings on Muldergate**				
b) **Scandal that's rocking South Africa**				
a) Richard Beckinsale, who appeared as Godber in the BBC comedy series "Porridge" and "Going Straight," was found dead at his home in Sunningdale, Berks, yesterday. He was 31.				
b) **ACTOR Richard Beckinsale, the boyish star of TV's "Porridge" and "Rising Damp" died yesterday at 31.**				

	most biased sentence	for or against	for or against what?	clues
a) **Another savage racial attack** b) **Pupils attack black teacher**				
a) *TONY BODLEY urged England to appoint Davis last month... now it's happened. We get things right!* **Mighty Mike is new leader** Mike Davis—a man feared even by the mighty Colin Meads—has been given the job of picking English rugby off the floor. b) **New coach Davis aims to make England arrogant** The Rugby Union announced yesterday that they had accepted the recommendation of their coaching sub-committee and appointed Mike Davis, the England Schools coach, to replace Peter Colston as the England team coach.				
a) ANY MOVIE written by Neil Simon is a bonus in this critic's year. When one of his wry, bitter-sweet comedies is chosen to be the official Royal Performance Film I can only congratulate the selectors on their discriminating good sense. b) THE CHOICE of a Neil Simon film for the Royal performance at the Odeon, Leicester Square, last night indicated good judgement, at least on past form.				

Exercise 5

Specific aim:
Skills involved: } Same as for exercise 4.
Why?

Below, you will find the beginning of two articles on Mrs Thatcher that appeared in two newspapers on the same day (before she became Prime Minister).
a) Read each article carefully and underline the words or expressions that, according to you, bias the opinions of the readers.

On behalf of Mrs Thatcher, the reply to a plea for HELP!

COUNCIL tenant Evelyn Collingwood was stunned by the letter she received from the office of Tory leader Margaret Thatcher.

Mrs. Collingwood had dropped a chatty note "to let Mrs. Thatcher know what ordinary people are thinking."

The reply she got, sent in the Tory leader's name, came as a bombshell.

Mrs. Collingwood described it last night as "grossly insulting."

She said: "This letter makes out that all council house tenants are scroungers. Mrs. Thatcher must think we are all blooming peasants."

Mrs. Thatcher was upset, too. She said she hadn't known about Mrs. Collingwood's letter OR the reply.

And she sent a messenger with a hand-written apology to 53-year-old Mrs. Collingwood's home at Erith, Kent.

(Daily Mirror)

You're on your way, Mrs T.

AFTER Wednesday night's triumph Mrs Thatcher did not get to sleep until after 2.30 a.m. But by 7 a.m. she was awake and reading the morning papers' accounts of her victory.

Then it was a large cooked breakfast, and soon after Mrs Thatcher emerged from her home in Flood Street, Chelsea.

Wearing a floral-patterned silken headscarf and a camel coat she beamed at waiting newspapermen and said : 'My troops are ready and we are looking forward to the election campaign.

'We have been ready since October and we are confident of victory. We will just keep working hard. We are organising our election strategy. There are great issues to be decided.'

With that she was driven away flanked by three police outriders for what she termed 'a pretty busy day.'

She went straight to her office at the Commons where already messages of congratulations and goodwill were pouring in. A team of secretaries answered endless phone calls and opened letters delivered by hand to beat the postmen's go-slow.

In mid-morning she presided over a Shadow Cabinet meeting in their oak-panelled room hung with oil paintings

By WILLIAM LANGLEY
and
GARETH WOODGATES

of Winston Churchill and Nelson.

(Daily Mail)

b) Which article favours Mrs Thatcher?
c) Considering those two articles, would you rely on the information given by one newspaper rather than the other?
   Justify your answer.
d) Beside the choice of the words or expressions you have underlined other devices are used to bias the readers' opinion.
   For instance
   – whose words are most often quoted in the first article?
   ....
   – Whose words are most often quoted in the second article?
   ....
e) Which article will most appeal to
   – people who admire activity
   – people who want to defend justice
   – people who think one should fight for one's rights
   – people who admire organization
   – people who think the way a Prime Minister looks and behaves in public is important.

Exercise 6

Specific aim:
Skills involved: } Same as for exercise 4.
Why?

1 Look at the advertisement for TIMEX. In each of the sentences that
   follow, decide whether the information is presented in an objective or
   slanted way. Write O or S in front of each sentence.
   a) Over the last decade, some of man's most notable achievements
      were made possible by the development of quartz timekeeping
      technology.
   b) But none has been able to manufacture a quartz watch that's within
      the buying power of the general public.
   c) They've managed to bring the prices of Quartz watches right down
      to earth.
   d) At this moment, there are three watches in the Timex quartz range.
   e) Incredibly, that is well under half the price of what is, to the best of
      our knowledge, the cheapest alternative available in this country.
   f) These days £30 is quite a normal price to pay for a watch.
   g) From the point of view of accuracy, it would be difficult for anyone to
      go one better.
   h) In fact, the inside of a Timex Quartz is a micro-computer.
   i) Never before has a watch offered so much for so little.
   Discuss your answers with a friend.
2 The sentences that follow tend to 'deceive' us in some way. Decide
   which explanation best describes the technique used to bias our
   opinion. In some cases, more than one technique may be used.
   a) Incredibly, that is well under half the price of what is to the best of
      our knowledge, the cheapest alternative available in this country.
      ☐ the watches are presented as 'cheap' compared to others. But
         £28 is still a lot of money.
      ☐ 'to the best of our knowledge' is very vague. So there is no real
         guarantee that Timex is the cheapest watch.
      ☐ there is nothing 'incredible' about this statement.
      ☐ 'in this country' may lead us to think that there may be cheaper
         and better such watches in other countries.
   b) In other words, it has a precision and sophistication which makes
      the ordinary watch movement seem as primitive as the wheel.
      ☐ there is nothing primitive about the wheel. It is just as essential
         nowadays as it used to be.
      ☐ the word 'ordinary' is too vague to describe all the watches that
         now exist.
      ☐ the word 'sophistication' may sound good, but it doesn't mean
         very much.
      ☐ one cannot check the truth of this statement.
3 Find two more instances of what you consider as 'slanted writing'.
   Show them to a friend and ask him to find out why.
4 Does this advertisement appeal mainly to the reader's
      ☐ emotions

☐ intelligence
☐ admiration for technology
☐ desire to get his money's worth

5 Does the advertisement make you want to buy a Timex watch?
Justify your answer.

QUARTZ TIMEKEEPING TOOK MAN TO THE MOON. NOW TIMEX BRING IT BACK TO EARTH

Over the last decade, some of man's most notable achievements were made possible by the development of quartz timekeeping technology. For instance, the quartz principle was crucial to the breathtaking precision of the Apollo moon missions.

For several years, many manufacturers have struggled to bring the phenomenal sophistication and accuracy of the quartz watch within reach of every technologically-minded man. But none has been able to manufacture a quartz watch that's within the buying power of the general public.

Until Timex took a hand. They've

managed to bring the prices of Quartz watches right down to earth.

INCREDIBLE £28 PRICE TAG.
At this moment, there are three watches in the Timex quartz range. The most expensive is £31. Incredibly, that is well under half the price of what is, to the best of our knowledge, the cheapest alternative available in this country.

GUARANTEED ACCURACY.
These days, £30 is quite a normal price to pay for a watch. So it's worth reflecting just how much value you're getting if you invest that sum in a Timex Quartz.

From the point of view of accuracy, it would be difficult for anyone to go one better. The Timex Quartz has been so finely engineered that it is guaranteed not to vary from true time by more than 15 seconds a month. In other words, it has a precision and sophistication which makes the ordinary watch movement seem as primitive as the wheel.

THE MIRACLE OF QUARTZ.
The key to the incredible accuracy of these watches lies in a very small crystal of pre-historic rock known as quartz. The value of a quartz crystal in a watch or clock is that when it is stimulated with an electric current it will always vibrate at an exact and known number of times, according to the way it has been cut. The more frequent the vibrations, the greater is the accuracy of a watch or clock. The frequency of vibration in a Timex Quartz is 49,152 Hz (cycles per second).

When you know that the frequency of vibration which controls the movement of an ordinary watch is only 2½ Hz, you'll understand why a Timex Quartz is so many times more accurate.

BUILT-IN COMPUTER.
Naturally the problem when dealing with something as small as a watch is how to convert 49,152 electronic pulses per second into the precise movement of second, minute and hour hands. This is done by a micro-dimensional transistorised circuit which reduces the frequency, without loss of accuracy, to a mere 6 Hz.

INTEGRATED CIRCUIT

QUARTZ CRYSTAL

In fact, the inside of a Timex Quartz is a micro-computer. The system contains over 300 transistors and is able to continually sense and correct any timekeeping variation in the watch. In this way, a Timex Quartz watch is tuned to you and the way you wear it.

LOOK FOR THE Q.
You'll find the new range of Timex Quartz watches at your jeweller's now. You'll recognise them by the Q on their faces. Never before has a watch offered so much for so little.

TIMEX Q

248

Exercise 7

Specific aim:
Skills involved: } Same as for exercise 4.
Why?

At the top of each of the columns in the following table, you will find a common technique used in advertisements to convince the reader. Decide which technique(s) is/are used in each of the slogans or sentences listed below. Write the words which helped you make your decision in the corresponding boxes.

	statement you cannot check	complex scientific evidence	use of words that sound good but are vague	comparison with other products	claim to be unique	other
Only Shell Super Multigrade has the unique 'muscle – molecule' with the stubborn strength to resist the daily grinding your engine deals out.						
A limited number of one of the world's most advanced colour television sets, in superb cabinets to match your period furniture.						
Benédictine's rarity is in its unique way of blending the warm scents of summer with the hospitality of Christmas.						
You won't find a finer Gin.						
It's like falling in love all over again.						
See how the unique water-clearing Aquajet system pumps						

slippery water away so the tyre can get safely to grips with the road.						
Q.E.2 World Cruise. What other ship would send a chauffeur to pick you up?						

Select bibliography

I have found these books and articles useful for my work on reading.

Byrne D. and Holden S., *Outlook, A reading practice book at intermediate level* (Longman, 1977)
Cooper J., *Think and Link, An advanced course in reading and writing skills* (Arnold, 1979)
Cooper M., Heah C., Kailasapathy M. and Howatt A., *Reading for Meaning* (University of Malaya, 1977)
Davies E. and Whitney N., *Reasons for Reading* (Heinemann Educational Books, 1979)
Enkvist, Nils Erik, 'Some aspects of applications of text linguistics', in *Text Linguistics, Cognitive Learning and Language Teaching*, edited by V. Kohonen and N. E. Enkvist (Text Linguistics Research Group, 1978)
Frank C., Rinvolucri M. and Berer M., *Challenge to Think* (Pilgrim English Language Course)
Halliday M. and Hasan R., *Cohesion in English* (Longman, 1976)
Mackay R. and Mountford R., 'Pedagogic Alternatives to "Explication de texte" ', in *Bulletin Pédagogique des I. U. T.* (no. 44, Oct. 1976)
Munby J., *Read and Think* (Longman, 1968)
Munby J., *Communicative Syllabus Design* (CUP, 1978)
Smith F., *Reading* (CUP, 1978)
White R., *Functional English*, vol. 1 Consolidation, vol. 2 Exploitation, (Nelson, 1979)
Widdowson, H., *Teaching Language as Communication* (OUP, 1978)
Widdowson, H., *Explorations in Applied Linguistics* (OUP, 1979)
Widdowson, H. (ed.), *Reading and Thinking in English*, vol. 2 Exploring Functions, vol. 3 Discovering Discourse (OUP, 1979)
Wiener H. and Bazeralan C., *Reading Skills Handbook* (Houghton Mifflin Company, 1978)

Acknowledgements

The author and publishers are grateful to the authors, publishers and others who have given permission for the use of copyright material identified in the text. It has not been possible to identify sources of all the material used and in such cases the publishers would welcome information from copyright owners.

Penguin Books for extracts from *Britain in the Modern World* © E. N. Nash and A. M. Newth on pp. 32, 33 and 34; Chatto & Windus Ltd for extracts from *The Rise of the Novel* by Ian Watt on p. 61; Hamish Hamilton Ltd for the extract from *Two for the River and other Stories* © 1973 the Executors of the Estate of L. P. Hartley on pp. 79–81; *The Sunday Times* for articles from *The Sunday Times* and *The Sunday Times Magazine* on pp. 83–4, 119–20, 141–2, 177, 187–8 and 211–12; the *Radio Times* for permission to reproduce the programme on p. 86; Oxford University Press for the extract from *The Oxford Advanced Learner's Dictionary* by A. S. Hornby on p.88; *Time Magazine* for the articles on pp. 101–2 and 240–1 © *Time* Inc. 1979; United Feature Syndicate for the cartoon from *Nobody's Perfect Charlie Brown* by Charles Schulz on p. 104; Biological Sciences Curriculum Study for the extract from *Biological Science: An Inquiry into Life* on pp. 109–11; Mary Glasgow Publications Ltd for the article on p. 117; *The Observer Magazine* for the article on pp. 118–19; Doubleday and Co. Inc. for the extract on pp. 123–5 from *The Beginning and the End* by Isaac Asimov © 1974 Triangle Publications Inc.; Hughes Massie Ltd (London) and Dodd, Mead and Co. Inc. (New York) for the extract from *Sleeping Murder* by Agatha Christie on pp. 135–6 © Agatha Christie, Ltd 1976; Orbis Publishing Limited for the extract from *The Mississippi* ed. A. Miller on pp. 137–9; Jonathan Cape Ltd for the extract from *Manwatching* (published in U.S. by Harry N. Abrams Pub. Inc.) by Desmond Morris on pp. 143–6 and Elsevier Publishing Projects (UK) Ltd for the accompanying illustrations; New Directions Publishing Corporation for the reproduction of 'Landscape with the Fall of Icarus' from *Pictures from Brueghel and Other Poems* by William Carlos Williams on p. 152 © 1960 William Carlos Williams; Faber and Faber Ltd (London) and Random House Inc. (New York) for the reproduction of 'Musée des Beaux Arts' by W. H. Auden from *Collected Poems* (ed.) E. Mendelson © 1940 renewed 1968 by W. H. Auden on p. 152; The *Daily Express* for the article on pp. 160–3; David Higham Associates Ltd (London) for an extract from *In the Teeth of the Evidence* by Dorothy L. Sayers on pp. 182–5; Mrs James Thurber (U.S.) and Hamish Hamilton Ltd (London) for permission to reproduce the stories and illustrations by James Thurber on pp. 190–3, 215–16 and 217 from *Vintage Thurber* the collection copyright © 1963; Laurence Pollinger Ltd (London) and Houghton Mifflin Company (New York) for an extract from *The Heart is a Lonely Hunter* by Carson McCullers on pp. 195–6; Ebony Magazine for the extract from *The Day the Black Revolution Began* by Lerone Bennett, Jr © 1977 Johnson Publishing Company, Inc. on pp. 199–200; The *Daily Telegraph* for the articles on p. 206; Nathan for the article by Roger Cohen on pp. 207–8; *Timex* Corporation for the advertisement on p. 248.